A GAPING WOUND
MOURNING IN ITALIAN POETRY

LEGENDA

LEGENDA is the Modern Humanities Research Association's book imprint for new research in the Humanities. Founded in 1995 by Malcolm Bowie and others within the University of Oxford, Legenda has always been a collaborative publishing enterprise, directly governed by scholars. The Modern Humanities Research Association (MHRA) joined this collaboration in 1998, became half-owner in 2004, in partnership with Maney Publishing and then Routledge, and has since 2016 been sole owner. Titles range from medieval texts to contemporary cinema and form a widely comparative view of the modern humanities, including works on Arabic, Catalan, English, French, German, Greek, Italian, Portuguese, Russian, Spanish, and Yiddish literature. Editorial boards and committees of more than 60 leading academic specialists work in collaboration with bodies such as the Society for French Studies, the British Comparative Literature Association and the Association of Hispanists of Great Britain & Ireland.

The MHRA encourages and promotes advanced study and research in the field of the modern humanities, especially modern European languages and literature, including English, and also cinema. It aims to break down the barriers between scholars working in different disciplines and to maintain the unity of humanistic scholarship. The Association fulfils this purpose through the publication of journals, bibliographies, monographs, critical editions, and the MHRA Style Guide, and by making grants in support of research. Membership is open to all who work in the Humanities, whether independent or in a University post, and the participation of younger colleagues entering the field is especially welcomed.

ALSO PUBLISHED BY THE ASSOCIATION

Critical Texts
Tudor and Stuart Translations • *New Translations* • *European Translations*
MHRA Library of Medieval Welsh Literature

MHRA Bibliographies
Publications of the Modern Humanities Research Association

The Annual Bibliography of English Language & Literature
Austrian Studies
Modern Language Review
Portuguese Studies
The Slavonic and East European Review
Working Papers in the Humanities
The Yearbook of English Studies

www.mhra.org.uk
www.legendabooks.com

ITALIAN PERSPECTIVES

Editorial Committee
Professor Simon Gilson, University of Oxford (General Editor)
Dr Francesca Billiani, University of Manchester
Professor Manuele Gragnolati, Université Paris-Sorbonne
Dr Catherine Keen, University College London
Professor Martin McLaughlin, Magdalen College, Oxford

Founding Editors
Professor Zygmunt Barański and Professor Anna Laura Lepschy

In the light of growing academic interest in Italy and the reorganization of many university courses in Italian along interdisciplinary lines, this book series, founded by Maney Publishing under the imprint of the Northern Universities Press and now continuing under the Legenda imprint, aims to bring together different scholarly perspectives on Italy and its culture. *Italian Perspectives* publishes books and collections of essays on any period of Italian literature, language, history, culture, politics, art, and media, as well as studies which take an interdisciplinary approach and are methodologically innovative.

Managing Editor
Dr Graham Nelson, 41 Wellington Square, Oxford OX1 2JF, UK
www.legendabooks.com

A Gaping Wound

Mourning in Italian Poetry

❖

EDITED BY ADELE BARDAZZI, FRANCESCO GIUSTI,
AND EMANUELA TANDELLO

l

LEGENDA

Italian Perspectives 54
Modern Humanities Research Association
2022

Published by Legenda
an imprint of the Modern Humanities Research Association
Salisbury House, Station Road, Cambridge CB1 2LA

ISBN 978-1-83954-049-3 (HB)
ISBN 978-1-83954-050-9 (PB)

First published 2022

Copy-Editor: Dr Anna J. Davies

CONTENTS

❖

ACKNOWLEDGEMENTS

❖

We gratefully acknowledge having received permission to reproduce the following copyrighted material:

ANTONELLA ANEDDA, *Dal balcone del corpo* (Milan: Mondadori, 2007, © Arnoldo Mondadori Editore S.p.A.)
—— *Salva con nome* (Milan: Mondadori, 2012, © Arnoldo Mondadori Editore S.p.A.)
—— *Historiae* (Turin: Einaudi, 2018, © Giulio Einaudi editore S.p.A.)
GIORGIO CAPRONI, *L'opera in versi*, ed. by Luca Zuliani (Milan: Mondadori, 1998, © 1998 Arnoldo Mondadori Editore S.p.A., Milano; © 2015 Mondadori Libri S.p.A., Milano)
AMELIA ROSSELLI, *Le poesie*, ed. by Emmanuela Tandello (Milan: Garzanti, 1997, © Garzanti Editore S.p.A., 1997).
—— *War Variations*, trans. by Lucia Re and Paul Vangelisti (Los Angeles: Otis Books/ Seismicity Editions, 2016, © Otis Books/Seismicity Editions)

We are grateful to Paola Bassani for granting permission to reproduce Bassani's poems in Chapter 4. Vivian Lamarque's poems are reproduced with kind permission by Mondadori (© 2016 Mondadori Libri S.p.A.).

Every effort has been made to trace copyright holders and to obtain their permission for the use of copyright material. The editors apologise for any errors or omissions in the above list and would be grateful for notification of any corrections that should be incorporated in future reprints or editions of this book.

INTRODUCTION:
WHY MOURNING IN POETRY?

❖

Adele Bardazzi, Francesco Giusti, and Emanuela Tandello

1. Mourning and the Lyric

It is almost a commonplace in the contemporary literary and cultural criticism that engages with mourning to react against the far too linear and teleological account of *working through* a personal loss that Sigmund Freud sketches in *Mourning and Melancholia* (1917).[1] Although the father of psychoanalysis himself reconsidered his earlier attempt to describe this enigmatic process in his later *The Ego and the Id* (1923),[2] many scholars attempting to theorise mourning in recent decades have returned to *Mourning and Melancholia* in order to position themselves in opposition to that authoritative, though admittedly tentative, description. The essays collected in this volume share, to a certain extent, this general tendency to revise the linearity of 'successful' or 'healthy' *mourning*, and to sympathise instead with its originally negative counterpart — the allegedly 'pathological' *melancholia* — or to present a non-linear oscillation between the two conditions, in order to explore the potentialities of such an unresolved state and its resonances with lyric discourse. In light of the blurring of this rigid dichotomy, therefore, the image of a gaping wound that gives the volume its title refers less to the 'open wound' that Freud associates with 'the complex of melancholia'[3] in his 1917 essay than to the *blessure du deuil* [wound of mourning] that Roland Barthes mentions in his *Journal de deuil: 26 octobre 1977–15 septembre 1979* [Mourning Diary, 26 October–15 September 1979], written after the death of his mother and published posthumously in 2009.[4] The former is an injury that should heal but does not, and thus impoverishes the ego; the latter is a wound that keeps bleeding, perhaps not uninterruptedly, but with no prospect of healing.[5] To our eyes, the intense plasticity of Alberto Burri's *Rosso Plastica L.A. 1966* on the book cover powerfully captures how a 'gaping wound' calls for a reshaping rather than a restoration of the subject in mourning.

The scope of this volume, however, is much broader and somewhat more ambitious. It seeks to bring Italian poetry and theory into the lively international debate about mourning in literature that has been going on in the Anglophone world at least since the publication of Jahan Ramazani's seminal study *Poetry of Mourning: The Modern Elegy from Hardy to Heaney* (1994).[6] Yet the theoretical frame of the scholarly debate is much broader and dates back at least to Melanie Klein's and Jacques Lacan's influential rethinking of Freud's account.[7] The Italian poetic tradition, after all, famously 'begins' with two collections of poems devoted to mourning for the beloved: Dante's *Vita nuova* and Petrarch's *Rerum Vulgarium Fragmenta*. Twentieth-century Italian scholarship and theory, furthermore, have delved into conceptions and practices of mourning, from Ernesto De Martino's anthropology,[8] through Giovanni Nencioni's poetic anthropology,[9] and Salvatore Natoli's philosophy,[10] up to the recent reflections on the impact of social media on mourning by the philosopher Davide Sisto in his successful *La morte si fa social.*[11]

The defining idea of this volume is that all contributors shared a set of theoretical texts with which they could explicitly or implicitly engage in their chapters. Jonathan Culler's *Theory of the Lyric* (2015), which offers a transhistorical account of the 'ritualistic' aspects of the lyric and defines the lyric as an 'event' that happens in the present, rather than the representation of a previous event, was a point of departure for the reflections pursued here and it emerged as a main reference point in the discussion of the relationship between mourning and the lyric.[12] Although less present in the final contributions, Ramazani's *Poetry of Mourning* provided a crucial frame of reference for investigating the ways in which modern elegy challenges both the sublimatory dynamics of traditional elegy and the normative methods of mourning imposed by society. As will be further elaborated later in this introduction, according to Ramazani, modern elegy does so by actively engaging with the disruptive dimension of bereavement and mourning. Nencioni's work was also significant in the conception and development of the project, albeit in different ways. Stressing how lyric poetry recalls important anthropological structures, such as the funeral eulogy, Nencioni's approach led to an 'anthropological' theory of the lyric, which is one of the possibilities explored in this volume. The references to Ernesto de Martino's studies in some of the contributions seem to move in a similar direction. Although, in the Italian context, the question of mourning has been explored in individual authors or in specific literary works, it seemed to us that a broader reflection on the potential connections between poetry — more specifically lyric poetry — and mourning with reference to Italian case studies was still lacking. It is the intention of this volume, therefore, to bring the Italian poetic tradition into the recent international debates on mourning and the lyric, briefly sketched in the following pages, as well as to offer a contribution to this research field. The double perspective at the centre of this volume allows it to explore, on the one hand, how lyric poetry deals and perhaps cooperates with mourning and, on the other hand, the extent to which mourning can be considered a crucial dimension of lyric discourse.

In his *Western Attitudes toward Death* (1974), Philippe Ariès famously claimed that death, once so discursively omnipresent in the social life of European communities, has been increasingly marginalised in modern culture. Not only has it been gradually effaced as a subject matter; it has also become shameful and forbidden, to the point of becoming unutterable. In short, the modern attitude towards death involves its absolute interdiction from everyday practices and discourses in order to shelter us from any intimations of our mortality that would impinge on the pursuit of happiness. This makes mourning an even more difficult and painful experience. It is no longer perceived as a necessary period encouraged by society, but rather as a 'morbid state which must be treated, shortened, erased'.[13] As a result, for Ariès, modern subjects seem to lack the emotional ability to record and process their losses. If this depiction of a historical condition holds true, an initial question arises and animates our enquiry: what are the functions of mournful or elegiac poetry in a social context in which mourning seems to have become unutterable? Poetry, as a social and cultural practice, appears to provide the public space that is otherwise lacking in society and to assume three fundamental functions that will be explored in this volume: firstly, by displaying private grief publicly, it reaffirms the centrality of human emotions relating to loss; secondly, it acquires the responsibility for passing on traumatic experience by framing it and allowing it to be recorded; and finally, it brings to the fore a less self-contained subjectivity that opens itself up to the dead other.

The psychoanalytic and philosophical reaction against Freud's early account of mourning as a process that, when successfully accomplished, frees the subject from emotional attachments to the deceased and restores to the subject the capacity to direct investments of libido (*cathexis*) towards someone else corresponds to Ramazani's account of elegy. According to Ramazani, in fact, twentieth-century poets tend to react against the traditional idea of elegy as sublimation and consolation. This enduring idea involves the usually male poet sublimating loss and grief into forms of poetry and 'his' temporarily scattered self into a poetic voice. This is the kind of treatment that so many dead beloveds have received in the long Western elegiac tradition. In recent scholarship, indeed, the pre-modern love elegy has often been reproached for constructing an image of the beloved, mostly a woman, that the male elegist exploits as a means to his own ends and, above all, for the sake of poetry. Petrarch's treatment of his beloved Laura may be considered emblematic of the dynamic whereby, as Juliana Schiesari argues, the discourse of the melancholic male poet appropriates an absent but desired woman and recasts her in the position of lack itself, so that this lack in turn can become the source of his own poetic creativity.[14] The real person, if she ever existed, is thus obscured, internalised, and somehow consumed by the speaker in order for the speaker to gain a new, and perhaps stronger, voice. In broad terms, this is the hideous crime against Eurydice with which the mythological poet Orpheus has often been charged. While this may be historically true in plenty of cases in the elegiac tradition, including for instance John Milton's much-discussed 'Lycidas' (1637), a more complex and complicated process can sometimes also be detected in pre-modern poetry, beginning with the ambiguities of the myth of Orpheus itself, which, as Charles Segal writes, 'oscillates between the power of form to master intense passion and the power of intense passion to engulf form'.[15]

This volume is informed by three different but closely related international debates that have animated the second half of the twentieth century and the first two decades of the twenty-first century: (1) The ethics of mourning: Freud's historical *loss* against Jacques Lacan's ontological *lack*; Vladimir Jankélévitch's reflections on the singularity of *you are dying* and the impersonal *everybody dies*; Jacques Derrida's insistence on the unaccountable singularity of the deceased other;

and all the revisions of and discussions on *mourning* by Julia Kristeva, Dominick LaCapra, Slavoj Žižek, Judith Butler, and many others. (2) The ethics and poetics of elegy: from the already mentioned Ramazani's *Poetry of Mourning: The Modern Elegy from Hardy to Heaney* to Diana Fuss's *Dying Modern: A Meditation on Elegy.*[16] (3) The ancient and long-lasting psycho-aesthetic ideas of *compensation, reparation,* and *redemption* (a work of literature or art should repair the damages of life and re-establish order out of chaos), and contemporary reconsiderations of them, according to which texts enact desire rather than sublimate it, beginning with Leo Bersani's pioneering book *The Culture of Redemption.*[17] Against this backdrop, and by looking closely at cases taken from Italian poetry, this volume aims to offer new historical observations and theoretical reflections, with a particular focus on the relationship between the dynamics of mourning and specific features ascribable to lyric discourse, from acts of apostrophic address to its long intertextual memory and non-narrative temporalities, starting with Giacomo Leopardi's radical and revealing challenging of a certain notion of lyric poetry, explored by Emanuela Tandello.

Though focusing primarily on twentieth-century poetry, the essays collected here sometimes refer to earlier poetic works not only to highlight cultural connections within the longer tradition, but also because the poems themselves invite readers and critics to do so. Poems, in fact, establish their own intertextual connections and place themselves in a certain tradition, or trace their own tradition of poetry of mourning. This is a characteristic that, though not exclusive to this kind of poetry, is a notable feature of it. As shown by Giorgio Caproni's 'Versi livornesi' [Livorno verses], discussed here by Francesco Giusti, while often striving to attest the singularity of its own loss, mournful poetry seems to need to take part in a tradition, and to make that tradition somehow explicit. This kind of poetry displays a significant degree of awareness that it is not entirely 'original', as it were: almost every poem of grief contains traces of other poems that deal with a similar existential and linguistic condition. Each bereaved lyric speaker seems to know that plenty of other speakers have already mourned their beloved in verse. This phenomenon and the self-awareness shown in the poems undoubtedly adds to the ritualistic character — the element of *performance* — that Jonathan Culler aptly emphasises as a main feature of the lyric as a transhistorical literary genre.[18]

The embeddedness of each individual poem within longer and broader traditions plays a significant role not only in establishing transhistorical connections, but also in foregrounding transnational ones, as Ramazani claims in his *A Transnational Poetics*. As Ramazani writes, 'If you study a work generically, as an instance of ode or pantoum or epic, you transnationalise it. Even with the benefit of a "historical poetics," you cannot dispense altogether with interculturality or cross-historicity in approaching genre. [...] Indeed, if you analyse a text without reference to its cross-border generic cousins, as well as antecedents and successors, you preclude, ironically, an understanding of its specificity.'[19] Ramazani opens the chapter specifically devoted to the opposed nationalistic and trans-nationalistic tendencies of elegy by claiming that 'we recognise the elegy's ever-mutating affective universe across boundaries of place and culture: grief, love, and anger; the search for, and thwarting of, consolation; commemorative and anticommemorative impulses'.[20] And, referring to Judith Butler's 'differential allocation of grievability', which 'operates to produce and maintain certain exclusionary conceptions of who is normatively human',[21] Ramazani concludes his investigation of the various phenomena that transnationalise the poetry of mourning with these words:

> While nations erect hierarchies of grievability, transnational elegy's cross-cultural influences, solidarities, and migrations, its border-crossing influences, forms, and ontologies, suggest other ways of mourning death than within physical barriers and conceptual lines patrolled by militaries and enforced by violence.[22]

Significantly, though apparently focused on a national poetic tradition, the contributions collected here have to face, implicitly or explicitly, these aspects of mourning. While situating itself on the unknowable threshold between life and death, poetry of mourning crosses a variety of other borders, even within what is alleged to be a single literary or linguistic tradition: the divide between high lyric and vernacular forms, the personal and the political, the local and the national, the individual and the collective, one's own story and public history, personal experience and the common condition, individual expression and shared language — to mention just a few. If observed on these unstable thresholds, and from transhistorical and transnational perspectives, 'Italian', in the title of this volume, points more to a varied and complex field of tensions than to a unified and self-contained tradition.

An extraordinary transnational and transhistorical phenomenon marks the history of Italian and European lyric poetry: Petrarch's *Rerum Vulgarium Fragmenta* provided, for many poets of the sixteenth century, a shareable poetic language with which they could voice not only a certain way of loving, but also a peculiar triangulation of love, death, and mourning — a triangulation to be explored in a particular form. Vittoria Colonna, Berardino Rota, and Francesca Turini Bufalini are just a few representatives of a much larger group. Additionally, while the existence of Petrarch's Laura may be called into question, this later poetry certainly mourns the death of real, individuated beloveds. The extraordinary case of Petrarchist poetry also suggests that poetry concerned with mourning often goes beyond the boundaries of a single poem and articulates its discourse in a macrotext that ranges from a short sequence, through a book section, to an entire book. This is the form that Giusti has dubbed *canzoniere in morte*, which has survived and flourished well into the twenty-first century.[23] This kind of collection of poems is a complex organism made of recollected and selected fragments of speech and memory between which a problematic interaction develops, thus allowing the speaking subject to undergo its non-linear, non-narrative, and not necessarily 'successful' (in Freudian terms) mourning process. Poetry sequences, indeed, allow for gaps, silences, detours, repetitions, and shortcomings.

If Renaissance poets could at least rely on recognisable paradigms in terms of form and diction, modern poetry of mourning further exposes the problematic attempt to give a *form* to the formless materials of (traumatic) experience. Therefore, it foregrounds the effort to create a structured *archive* of memories out of the random accumulation of memory fragments. For centuries, art has been thought of as a device (among many other such devices) that can bestow sense upon the world of experience, but a fundamental question arises: is it really possible to create a definitive *form* and a compensative narrative that could bring the mourning process to an end and relieve the subject of any emotional or existential involvement with the deceased? Or, rather, is a different subject produced in the process of mourning and in the very attempt to construct a new *form*? The reparative effect that poetry is supposed to have is contrasted with the effect the verses actually have. They do not heal the wounded old subject, but seem to create a (partially) new one in the process. Reconsidering Freud's idea of mourning as *work*, Giusti suggests that mourning becomes a new modality of speech and subjectivity that the grieving 'I' performs after having experienced death in the beloved's singularity. In this performance, the speaking I is compelled to recognise the provisional and permeable nature of their own subjectivity, which opens up to the otherness of the deceased, just as their allegedly individual language opens up to host the language of the other. Poetry of mourning, indeed, presents an interesting case of poetic *hospitality*.

Different but not unrelated are the poetic treatments of 'public' mourning either in elegies composed in response to the death of public figures, collective ideas or ideals, and historical catastrophes; or in poems about a personal loss that, owing to external circumstances, exceeds the boundaries of the individual and is brought into the arena of public discourse. A famous instance of the second category, in twentieth-century poetry in English, is *Birthday Letters* (1998) — the collection of poems written by Ted Hughes for his wife Sylvia Plath, who committed suicide in 1963 — which has been as acclaimed internationally as it has been harshly criticised. Twentieth-century Italian poetry offers two excellent examples that are situated in between the two possibilities outlined above, two problematic negotiations between the private and the public. On the one hand, Marzia D'Amico's contribution discusses the issue of mourning in Amelia Rosselli's poetry, which deals with her grief for her father and uncle, well-known Italian public intellectuals murdered by the Fascist regime whose violent deaths are forcibly inserted into the political history of the country. On the other hand, Martina Piperno investigates negotiations between private experience and public history in Giorgio Bassani's poems about Nazi–Fascist racial persecution, written by one of the persecuted who, however, never experienced concentration camps.

Is the language of lyric poetry particularly appropriate for articulating trauma and, above all, speaking from a 'traumatised' perspective? The 'language of literature', according to Cathy Caruth, fails to achieve a full comprehension of its own language and, in the repetition of the traumatic event, the voice of the *other* can be heard, though it can never be completely understood.[24] This book asks whether there may be anything in the 'lyric' as a discursive mode that makes it particularly suitable for mourning or, conversely, whether there may be something in mourning that makes it particularly 'lyric'. For instance, apostrophe, which Culler considers a typically lyric device,[25] is a quintessentially mournful gesture in that it is an act of addressing an absent human being or non-human entity that invokes a presence while also creating a distance between the speaker and the apostrophised. As Vilma De Gasperin's contribution shows, the act of apostrophic address discloses temporal as well as spatial complications underlying the attempted relationship with the absent other, which, in the case of Vivian Lamarque's poetry, are further complicated by the act of looking at a portrait of her mother. The use of apostrophe, as Giusti suggests, also seems to highlight the hetero-foundation of subjective discourse and, as far as the lyric is concerned, of subjectivity itself.[26] By bringing the addressee directly into the speech and by excluding the listeners/readers from the scene, while implicitly presupposing their presence as a silent audience (a rhetorical strategy that Culler dubs *triangulated address*),[27] the apostrophe signals that the object is not just a subject matter, but also the external motivation of the utterance.[28]

Mourning in poetry also involves questions of repetition and symbolisation. It demonstrates an attempt, by the speaker, to organise an archive of memories and regain some agency in their life and in their story after having been painfully deprived of power by an event that cannot be controlled. However, the real objects involved in the mourning process seem to resist a forced symbolisation: the effort to include them in a system of meaning and thus make sense of the singular loss. They maintain a degree of unassimilable reality that seems to be essential to the mourning process itself. These objects are material traces left behind by the lost person and are relevant because they were touched, used, and chosen by that person.[29] Even explicit symbols and metaphors are often declared to have been born in the real world, rather than directly in poetry; this, in turn, invites us to reflect even more carefully on the problematic and indeterminate relation between the poet as a real person and the speaker of the poem.[30] Mourning poems are marked by a continuous effort to reduce their own *fictionality* as much as possible and to attest to the *reality* of what enters the textual space. They are perfectly aware of the literariness of the operation (as is made clear by intertextuality, metapoetic reflections and awareness of the elegiac tradition), but at the same time they appear to reject any 'untruth'. The material concreteness of certain selected objects is often relevant to the mourning performed in the poems. Interestingly, Guido Gozzano's poems, investigated by Fabio Camilletti, seem to challenge this assertion of *reality* and contribute to the discussion in crucial ways.

An ethics of mourning appears to be linked to a poetics of mourning, and the lyric seems to constitute a literary genre and a discursive mode that is particularly apt for such a problematic negotiation. As Giusti points out, it is never possible for the lyric speaker to create a complete image of the departed in order to repair the self and compensate for their bereavement. The speaker is urged to go beyond any still images they create for themselves and to keep looking for a missing singularity that, in this way, may be recognised as different from the I and their projections.[31] Moreover, the speaking subject is deeply tied to the lost corporeal presence of the beloved person; their actual absence also involves a physical loss that must be taken into consideration. Death reveals itself to be not only an event in human life and a topic for poetic discourse, but also a new point of view on reality that may require a different language. By experiencing death so close to the self, the speaker realises their own mortality and experiences a partial loss of their self and a weakening of their power. As a result, the perception of the surrounding world can change radically. Therefore, death is not simply an object of (impossible) knowledge, but can become a practice of life, a new modality for the interaction between the subject and the world.[32]

However, the lyric seems to reject a full *ontologisation* of mourning like that which many scholars have observed (and criticised) in Lacanian theory, because it would cut off the singularity of each incarnated body. For Lacan, according to critics such as Dominick LaCapra, the self is doomed *a priori* to an inner division and the Freudian historical *loss* becomes a metaphysical *lack*.[33] Many ethical questions arise from such an approach. If the lack is ontological, 'I' might not be directly responsible to and for any individual loss. Lyric poetry, instead, shows how grief can become a shareable condition of being human without being fully subsumed into an impersonal 'universal' condition. One can recognise a common situation and share at least part of it because each individual experiences their own losses in their own body. As Roland Barthes suggests in his *Mourning Diary*, singular human mortality resists its own inclusion in an impersonal *everybody dies* that might eventually relieve singular subjects of painful responsibility.[34] Yet, a shareable position based on the reciprocal recognition of our individual mortality can still be found and could eventually lead to us taking care of others. This is the specific meaning that Maurizio Bettini and Umberto Curi identify in Orpheus's *looking back* (*respicere*) at Eurydice: it is a desire to open up a channel of *communication* with the beloved person, which also involves a willingness to *take care* of the dead other.[35] Poetry of mourning exhibits this constitutive double nature, whereby it is both one's own language and the language of many others, and it is both about the loss of one singular individual and death as a condition of being alive, one's own personal devastating experience and a shareable existential space. By looking at Antonella Anedda's *Attittos* [Dirges], Adele Bardazzi's contribution to this volume offers an excellent reflection on how these poems are situated in between an (original) individual voice and a (traditional) communal ritualistic practice, inasmuch as they are in between two languages, Italian and the Sardinian dialect Logudorese.

This intersection between the singular and the collective may be a reason why mourning performed in poetry is considered an 'anthropological' gesture. This gesture is 'anthropological' not so much because it was part of the practices of archaic or primeval societies (i.e. in funeral eulogies) and was then translated into poetic forms, as Nencioni seems to imply,[36] but because it offers a shareable 'form' in which each singularity can inscribe their own individual performance without wholly making it their own. They can do so by selecting and re-enacting a certain gesture in their own specific situation and bringing to it their own contextual meanings. In this way, the poetic tradition(s) can be considered a transhistorical repertoire of gestures available for re-enactment by readers across time and space.[37] Anedda and Caproni are good examples of these dynamics. Looking at lyric discourse as a selection of gestures may add a further layer to Ramazani's account of the transnational character of elegy.[38]

Diana Fuss suggests that, in poetry that deals with the trauma of death, it is ethical to grant a voice to the dead, as in the so-called *corpse poems* in which the speaker is a cadaver.[39] However, such a stance seems quite problematic in cases of real losses. Claiming to know what the dead would have said could constitute an abuse of the singular otherness of the dead. Those who are alive have no right to speak for the dead. Furthermore, doing so would involve a degree of fictionality that mourning poems seem to strive to avoid. They cannot give life or a voice back to the dead, but they can keep desire alive; this desire is directed towards the empty place previously occupied by the other person and keeps pointing to it, just as the language of mourning points to the empty space previously occupied by its referents. This is evident in Caproni's poems for his dead mother Annina. Mourning poems often let the other into their discourse, as if in an intertextual exchange, by changing form and style, speaking the other's words, ventriloquising the sounds of the other's voice, expressing the interpretations of the other. In short, the speaking subject has to make themselves other, at least partially. The imaginary identity of the *me* has to be broken down in order to acknowledge the heterogeneity of the practices of the *I*.

In the poetry of mourning, the other does not return as a *phantom*, as Nicolas Abraham and Maria Torok suggest,[40] that is to say, as a secret that one will eventually come to know, but rather as Derrida's *spectre*, something that cannot (yet) be articulated in language, a not-knowing that underlies what we think we know and can undermine it.[41] By examining a case of poetic mourning for a woman whom the speaker never actually met, Fabio Camilletti's contribution explores, in its psychanalytic dimensions, the attempted phantasmatic evocation, in the present, of Carlotta and the lost epoch she represents in Gozzano's poetry. Reconsidering Freud's basic idea of mourning as *work*, as something to be done, one could conclude that mourning is a practice in which the lost other intervenes, with the survivor being called to receive the haunting presence of the other. Orpheus's act of looking back at Eurydice — a *respicere* that is also a *regarder* in the double sense of Derrida's use of the French word[42] — embodies this necessary act of paying attention to, and taking care of, the one who has been lost. The subject is compelled to look back at, and regard, the one who regards them. According to Derrida, the acknowledgement of the other as a secret is not the implementation of some objective knowledge, but is, rather, a practical freedom that escapes knowledge. The grieving subject who speaks in a lyric voice admits this secret and, though they cannot explicitly voice it, they perform their practice, taking on, even if only partially, the responsibility of the other's singularity. Mourning, therefore, may not be a task to be accomplished, but a new, more porous self to be practised.

2. Contributions

Proceeding in chronological order, which does not prevent individual contributions from moving across the centuries of the Italian poetic tradition following the trajectories that poetry traces for itself, the volume begins with two inquiries into two poets, Giacomo Leopardi and Guido Gozzano, whose work is a constant negotiation with the past and its survival into the present and is therefore crucial for an exploration of mourning in Italian poetry. In her chapter 'The Loss of Poetry: Leopardi's "Coro di morti"', Emanuela Tandello considers the unique — and highly fluid — status that the 'Coro di morti', from the *operetta morale* 'Dialogo di Federico Ruysch e delle sue Mummie' [Dialogue of Frederick Ruysch and his Mummies] (written in August 1824), enjoys in Leopardi's poetry. Generally considered one of his best lyric 'poems', it is difficult (and potentially misleading?) to treat it as a *canto*; the fictional, dialogic text that frames it, and the searing irony that pervades it, almost undermine its powerfully elegiac form *and* tone, forcing it into a dramatic performativity that teeters more towards *vaudeville* than classical tragedy. On the other hand, an undeniable undercurrent — as lexical as it is metaphysical — binds it to the 'Canto notturno' [Nightsong] and to the later 'A se stesso' [To himself]. Of course, this is a text about mourning: about performing it, and about enduring it; about the repeatability — the ritual — of mourning, and about its *never-to-be-worked-through* essence. It is also a text that transcends, if not positively rejects, subjectivity in favour of a voice that declares a sustained, passionate anti-modernity. Tandello explores this seismic instability, this anti-heroic resistance, and seeks to articulate a reading of this text's transformative influence on the very lyric discourse that it both embraces and rejects.

In the following chapter, 'Carlotta's Ghost', Fabio Camilletti analyses the multifaceted presence of the 'phantasm' in Guido Gozzano's poetry, particularly *L'amica di nonna Speranza* [Grandmother Speranza's Friend] (first published in 1907) and *L'esperimento* [The Experiment] (1909), two poems devoted to the conjuring of a long–dead girl, Carlotta, in the domestic space of the parlour. In speaking of 'phantasm', Camilletti is not referring uniquely to Carlotta as a revenant or a ghost, but rather, following Nicolas Abraham and Maria Torok, as the emblem of a secret 'encrypted' in the unconscious, which only the poetic word can make manifest. Moreover, in its lamentation of the loss of someone whom the poetic 'I' never met because of the historical distance between them, Gozzano's poetry exhibits a process of poetic mourning that, on the one hand, intersects the Troubadour tradition of *amor de lonh* and, on the other, invests the loss of the Other (in all the Lacanian nuances of this expression). The 'shadow of nineteenth–century Turin', the 'nostalgic psychogeography of Risorgimento', the 'tactile experience of objects', the role of photographs and images, as well as the process whereby the past is beheld 'through the self-consciousness of the present', are all features of Gozzano's poetry to which Camilletti pays attention, thus introducing a set of elements that will recur and be further explored in the other chapters.

Decades later, in an attempt to narrate a prelapsarian age threatened but as yet untouched by History (and war), Giorgio Caproni collects delicate poems devoted to his dead mother Anna Picchi in the section of his 1959 book *Il seme del piangere* [The seed of weeping] entitled 'Versi livornesi'. In these fragile verses, he portrays a lively and sensual young woman of whom he can imaginatively be the son and lover at the same time. In the third chapter, 'Mourning Over Her Image: The Re-enactment of Lyric Gestures in Giorgio Caproni's "Versi livornesi"', Caproni's combination of a personal loss and the retrieval of Cavalcantian poetics allows Francesco Giusti to address crucial issues for the theory of the lyric both in its historical-contextual and trans-historical dimensions. Through the creation of memory-bearing images that do not belong to the poet's own experiential memory, Caproni presents both mourning and poetry as an attempt to go back in time towards a place (and a language) where his mother could have been. This attempt does not acquire significance in relation to the intertextual game pursued in the text (as Michael Riffaterre would have it),[43] but does so rather in relation to the verbal gestures it re-enacts and the desire for contact that it embodies. Mourning exposes the open referentiality of lyric deixis, which makes the poem both personal and shareable at the same time. The iterativity encapsulated in the single poem (which can be re-enacted in the 'now' of each reading, as Culler maintains)[44] and the lack of direct referents break the very fictionality of the consoling image that the poem attempts to construct. To understand the inner workings and the singularity of the lyric, one should thus look at the frame of enunciation — the gesture performed by the utterance — rather than the narrative fragments sometimes included in the text. In disclosing these features, Giusti finds a helpful guide in Roland Barthes's meditations on the death of his mother Henriette collected in *Journal de deuil: 26 octobre 1977–15 septembre 1979* (2009). Finally, taking inspiration from Jean Laplanche's notion of 'translation' of the 'enigmatic message' that comes from the other, Giusti suggests that the poetic re-translation one finds in Caproni's poems for his mother requires the retrieval of a certain degree of impersonality 'through the adoption of another language, or a language of the other'.

Moving from Caproni's pre-First World War Livorno to Giorgio Bassani's Ferrara during the Second World War, the fourth chapter, 'Giorgio Bassani, the Poet-Ghost, and the Memorial Duty of the Survivor', opens up the exploration pursued in the volume to poetry mourning a collective historical catastrophe, the racial persecution and deaths in Nazi work camps during the Second World War, and to Bassani's relationship with a place, the town of Ferrara, marked by the trauma he suffered in his youth. In this chapter, Martina Piperno suggests that Bassani claimed for himself the role of survivor and witness of the largest historical trauma of the twentieth century. As the author remarks, the recurrence of the theme of death in Bassani's novels has already been noted by scholarship. These novels 'are dominated by a need to remember the dead' and '[t]his desire is rooted in Bassani's *ethos* of remembrance and recollection, perhaps enhanced by survivor guilt'. Elucidating the differences between the narrative and the poetic project in Bassani's oeuvre with respect to the preservation of memory, Piperno proposes that his collections *Epitaffio* [Epitaph], published in 1974, and *In gran segreto* [Secretly], published in 1978, both included in the section 'Senza [rima]' [Without [rhyme]] in Bassani's 1982 volume of collected poems *In rima e senza* [With and without rhymes], can be read as the 'in morte' section of Bassani's lifetime poetry book, following the traditional subdivision established in Dante's *Vita nuova* and Petrarch's *Rerum vulgarium fragmenta*. In his deployment of the form of the epitaph, moreover, Bassani seems, on the one hand, to retrieve something of the epitaphial features that some scholars have recognised as crucial for poetry (for instance, the 'animation' that the words inscribed on a tombstone require from their reader);[45] on the other hand, he presents a model of mournful poetry that is distinct from the elegiac mode that has been dominant in poetic mourning. Piperno also detects, in Bassani's 'metaphorical death' and visit to hell, an incorporation of Dante's model, which contributes to the construction of his role as a witness and survivor who comes back 'from hell with a powerful story to tell the living', but who is now forced 'to live a half-life, the life of a living dead, at least until he has completed his memorial duty'.

The complications arising from history and politics in the work of mourning return in the fifth chapter, 'The Space of Mourning: Electra's *mise en abyme*', in which Marzia D'Amico explores the intersection of the personal and the political and the construction of a female voice in Amelia Rosselli's grief for the traumatic loss of her father Carlo Rosselli, who was murdered by the Fascist regime. Indeed, as D'Amico writes, 'Rosselli's grieving is mediated by the consciousness of what is symbolically expected from her as a woman, the request of being functional to the community in mourning her father — a martyr, a hero. She nonetheless plays with this role, exploring what she is willing to perform as an author'. The space of mourning in Rosselli's writing thus becomes a device for defining female agency in and outside of poetry. In *The Mourning Voice: An Essay on Greek Tragedy*,[46] Nicole Loraux highlights that the grief was usually symbolised and exorcised through drama and, in particular, the use of female characters as representatives of the whole community. The ritual of crying and lamenting was associated with and circumscribed to female identities, both in the city and in theatre. A clear case of distorted feminine identity that merges completely with the established role is the case of Electra, whose only reason for existence is figurative. Referring to Loraux, D'Amico examines the space accorded to mourning, the tension between the private and public experience of mourning, and where the biographical experience yields to the attempt to represent a universal experience. Rosselli's detachment from the *persona* represented in her *opera* results in an independent Subject that cannot be entirely assimilated with the author's personal self. The public experience of mourning in the rewriting of Electra (in *Variazioni Belliche* [War Variations]) positions Rosselli's work in strict relation to a chronological interest in a pantheon of female characters in the literary tradition. As suggested by Rosi Braidotti, the evolution of one's subjectivity is always in tension with creation and restriction because of the social power dynamic underlying any relation.[47] In the case of women's subjectivity, the re-contextualisation of female models is a powerful device for constituting a renewed shared memory. The re-writing of the female myth is a necessary stage in the construction of female subjectivity and the definition of its autonomous agency as distinct from the 'universal masculine'.[48]

The last two chapters focus on very recent cases of poetic mourning in the work of Antonella Anedda and Vivian Lamarque, which offer further opportunities to explore the issue of translation and the opening up of one's language to the language of the other(s) in the context of mourning, as well as the entanglement of the individual and the collective, the singular and the universal, in the experience of loss and grief. In 'Mourning in Translation: The Sardinian Poetry of Antonella Anedda', Adele Bardazzi focuses on a series of eight 'attittos' [dirges] included in the section 'Limba' in Anedda's collection *Il balcone del corpo* [From the Body's Balcony] (2007). *Attittos* are archaic Sardinian verse laments traditionally performed at the graveside by a group of women only, which Anedda — born in Rome, but with Sardinian parentage that goes back generations — transposes to the written space of the page. These poems are written in Logudorese, a language spoken in the centre of Sardinia that is considered one of the purest: the 'limba de oro', a golden language. These texts highlight Anedda's engagement with the ritualistic, oral dimension of Sardinian culture and collective mourning practices. This is related to her attempt to de-personalise the lost object of love and envision mourning as a collective, rather than individual, experience and practice. In fact, concentration and contraction emerge as two key notions for understanding the nature of the poetic subject and mourning in Anedda's work. Her 'art of losing' consists in a movement towards the concentration and contraction of the poetic subject: a 'scavamento' [digging/ self-emptying], a withdrawal. Until 2007, Anedda had written only in Italian, but an experience of loss, which coincided with a profound feeling that Italian did not have the words she needed, led her to start writing in Logudorese. This engagement with her Sardinian identity deeply influenced her poetic practice, and in particular her exploration of mourning. Furthermore, through the process of self-translation, Anedda has been able to renew her poetry by engaging with the fundamentally oral tradition of this dialect, which is very different to the traditionally written space of Italian poetry. Anedda creates relations between the texts in Italian and those in Logudorese, which are presented side by side, and, as Bardazzi argues, the poetic interplay between the two printed texts generates a 'third text' that is a space of cohabitation from which new images and suggestions arise. Thus, Anedda's process of self-translation emerges as a particularly interesting practice that allows her to explore the ways in which self-translation creates a multilingual, non-linear poetic space that echoes the non-linear process of mourning.

In the last chapter, 'Mourning and Lyric Address in Vivian Lamarque's *Madre d'inverno*', Vilma De Gasperin focuses on the first three sections of Lamarque's collection *Madre d'inverno* [Mother in Winter] (2016), which constitute a tripartite depiction of the experience of mourning the death of the (poet's) mother. In this work of mourning, the lyric subject positions itself at different angles and temporal perspectives with respect to the lost one. The first section, entitled 'Poesie ospedaliere' [Hospital poems], recalls the mother during her terminal illness in hospital: it depicts the memories of a still living mother, it is dominated by past tenses, and it addresses an irretrievable past that is at once acutely painful and infinitely precious. The second section, 'Ritratto con neve' [Portrait with snow], is a series of twelve poems in which the poet's voice addresses the painted image of her mother as a younger woman. The poet and the mother are placed in a spatial relationship with one another in an attempt to negotiate absence: the poet is on one side, on the sofa, looking at and addressing the silent painting of the mother, whose eyes irretrievably gaze beyond her own living presence, without allowing for an encounter. The poems in the third section, 'Compro oro' [We buy gold], focus on the aftermath of death, as well as harking back to childhood memories. De Gasperin explores the ways in which poems in the first three sections of *La madre* create a lyric address between the speaking voice and the silent *you* and thereby appear to transfigure mourning through 'a ritualistic invocation'.[49] Thus, apostrophe emerges as 'a rhetorical figure of loss'. The metamorphosis of the 'tu' [you], the role of objects in recalling the lost one, the (denied) hypothesis of an afterlife, and the play of gazes and mirrors acquire a significant function in these poems. The personal experience of grief, once again, does not prevent the speaker from reaching out to an ideal community of co-sufferers, on the basis of shared experience and hence understanding. De Gasperin quotes the philosopher Salvatore Natoli on this double dimension of mourning, an experience that is both radically singular and necessarily universal: 'grief is at once a personal and a cosmic event [...]. It is only its universal reverberation — inherent in each individual experience of grief — that enables the sufferers to communicate their grief and enables the onlookers to feel it and recognise it'.[50]

Gordon Braden and Elizabeth Fowler's entry on 'elegy' in the fourth edition of *The Princeton Encyclopedia of Poetry and Poetics* (2012) begins with a concise definition: 'In mod. usage, an *elegy* is a poem of loss and mourning.' After illustrating first that the elegy was a metrical form used for various subjects in antiquity and then the relevance of pastoral models for the later developments of elegy, they acknowledge that poems about death and loss '(which may or may not call themselves elegies) show an immense diversity, within which filiations can be complex'.[51] We have deliberately used the word 'elegy' in all its broadness in this introduction, because the set of questions we had in mind while working on this volume related less to any attempt to provide a definition of a literary genre called 'elegy' than to something Braden and Fowler wonder about in their discussion of criticism on the elegy: 'Other puzzles invite attention. Why, if elegy is "a process of mourning," are so many elegies lyrics with little narrative or processional content? Standard definitions of *elegy* can strain against the temporality of lyric. Elegy's recourse to emotion seems incompletely explained by psychological or social models of grief or even by a notion of the poem as expressive.'[52] Elegy as a poem of loss and mourning often presents itself as lyric, which, as the two authors observe, calls for an investigation of the connections between mourning and lyric, as well as a revision of both the 'processuality' of mourning and expressivist notions of lyric. Leopardi's 'Coro di morti', with which this volume begins, questions, as early as 1824, the conception of the lyric as the expression of an individuated subject and thus immediately gives rise to a reconsideration of a 'romantic' notion of lyric. We have pursued this reconsideration in dialogue with Culler's recent theorisation, without always being in agreement with it. Through the works of four male and three female Italian poets, the volume addresses a variety of interrelated issues that, though observed from different perspectives, recur throughout the chapters and are crucial to rethinking the lyric in the context of its longer history, including questions of temporality and repetition, as well as rethinking it in relation to the function of images (photographs, portraits, and imaginary scenes); rituality and shareability; the lowering of style and tone to emulate more popular forms; the retrieval of archaic laments voiced by women and medieval poetic forms; and attempts to restore a choral and collective dimension to lyric poetry.

This edited volume originates from the research project on Mourning in Italian Poetry led by Adele Bardazzi, Francesco Giusti, and Emanuela Tandello. Several scholars from different institutions gathered at Christ Church, Oxford, for a first conference in March 2017 (co-organised with Jennifer Rushworth) and a subsequent conference in April 2018. The project was generously funded by the Faculty of Medieval and Modern Languages of the University of Oxford, Christ Church, St John's College, the Society for Italian Studies (SIS), and Oxford Medieval Studies at The Oxford Research Centre in the Humanities (TORCH). The contributions to the volume are the result of the exchange of ideas and discussion initiated through these conferences centred on the relationship between mourning, death, and the lyric.

Bibliography

ABRAHAM, NICOLAS, and MARIA TOROK, *The Shell and the Kernel: Renewals of Psychoanalysis*, with an Introduction by Nicholas T. Rand (Chicago: Chicago University Press, 1994)

—— *The Wolf Man's Magic Word: A Cryptonymy*, trans. by Nicholas T. Rand, foreword by Jacques Derrida (Minneapolis: Minnesota University Press, 2005)

ARIÈS, PHILIPPE, *Western Attitudes toward Death: From the Middle Ages to the Present*, trans. by Patricia M. Ranum (Baltimore: Johns Hopkins University Press, 1974)

BARTHES, ROLAND, *Mourning Diary*, ed. by Nathalie Léger, trans. by Richard Howard (London: Notting Hill Editions, 2011)

BERSANI, LEO, *The Culture of Redemption* (Cambridge, MA: Harvard University Press, 1990)

BETTINI, MAURIZIO, *Antropologia e cultura romana* (Florence: La Nuova Italia, 1986)

BRADEN, GORDON, and ELIZABETH FOWLER, 'Elegy', *The Princeton Encyclopedia of Poetry and Poetics*, 4th edn, ed. by Roland Greene and Stephen Cushman (Princeton: Princeton University Press, 2012), pp. 397–99

BRAIDOTTI, ROSI, *Nomadic Subjects: Embodiment and Sexual Difference in Contemporary Feminist Theory* (New York: Columbia University Press, 1994)

BUTLER, JUDITH, *Precarious Life: The Powers of Mourning and Violence* (London: Verso, 2004)

CARUTH, CATHY, *Unclaimed Experience: Trauma, Narrative, and History* (Baltimore: Johns Hopkins University Press, 1996)

CAVARERO, ADRIANA, *In Spite of Plato: A Feminist Rewriting of Ancient Philosophy* (London: Routledge, 1995)

—— *Tu che mi guardi, tu che mi racconti*, 6th edn (Milan: Feltrinelli 2005)

CULLER, JONATHAN, 'Apostrophe', in *The Pursuit of Signs: Semiotics, Literature, Deconstruction*, 2nd edn (London: Routledge, 2001), pp. 149–71

—— *Theory of the Lyric* (Cambridge, MA: Harvard University Press, 2015)

CURI, UMBERTO, *La cognizione dell'amore* (Milan: Feltrinelli, 1997)

DE MAN, PAUL, 'Lyrical Voice in Contemporary Theory', in *Lyric Poetry: Beyond New Criticism*, ed. by Chaviva Hošek and Patricia Parker (Ithaca, NY: Cornell University Press, 1985), pp. 55–72

DE MARTINO, ERNESTO, *Morte e pianto rituale: Dal lamento funebre antico al pianto di Maria*, 2nd edn (Turin: Bollati Boringhieri, 2000)

DERRIDA, JACQUES, *The Gift of Death* (Chicago: University of Chicago Press, 1995)

—— *Specters of Marx: The State of the Debt, the Work of Mourning and the New International*, trans. by Peggy Kamuf (New York: Routledge, 1994, 2006)

—— 'To Speculate — On "Freud"', in *The Post Card: From Socrates to Freud and Beyond*, trans. by Alan Bass (Chicago: University of Chicago Press, 1987), pp. 257–337

ENG, DAVID, and DAVID KAZANJIAN (eds), *Loss: The Politics of Mourning* (Berkeley: University of California Press, 2003)

FREUD, SIGMUND, *The Ego and the Id*, The Standard Edition of the Complete Psychological Works of Sigmund Freud (1923–1925), XIX: *The Ego and the Id and Other Works* (London: The Hogarth Press and the Institute of Psychoanalysis, 1961), pp. 1–66

—— 'Mourning and Melancholia', in *The Standard Edition of the Complete Psychological Works of Sigmund Freud*, trans. by James Strachey in collaboration with Anna Freud, assisted by Alix Strachey and Alan Tyson (1914–1916), XIV: *On the History of the Psycho-Analytic Movement, Papers on Metapsychology and Other Works* (London: The Hogarth Press and the Institute of Psycho-analysis, 1957), pp. 237–58

FUSS, DIANA, *Dying Modern: A Meditation on Elegy* (Durham, NC: Duke University Press, 2013)

GILBERT, SANDRA M., *Death's Door: Modern Dying and the Ways We Grieve* (New York: W. W. Norton, 2006)

GIUSTI, FRANCESCO, *Canzonieri in morte: Per un'etica poetica del lutto* (L'Aquila: Textus Edizioni, 2015)

—— 'Transcontextual Gestures: A Lyric Approach to the World of Literature', in *The Work of World Literature*, ed. by Francesco Giusti and Benjamin Lewis Robinson (Berlin: ICI Berlin Press, 2021), pp. 75–103

HAMBURGER, KÄTE, *The Logic of Literature*, 2nd edn (Bloomington: Indiana University Press, 1993)

LACAPRA, DOMINICK, *Reflections on Trauma, Absence, and Loss*, in *Whose Freud? The Place of Psychoanalysis in Contemporary Culture*, ed. by Peter Brooks and Alex Woloch (New Haven, CT: Yale University Press, 2000), pp. 178–204

LORAUX, NICOLE, *The Mourning Voice: An Essay on Greek Tragedy* (Ithaca, NY: Cornell University Press, 2002)

MILLS-COURTS, KAREN, *Poetry as Epitaph: A Study of Representation and Poetic Language* (Baton Rouge: Louisiana State University Press, 1990)

NATOLI, SALVATORE, *L'esperienza del dolore: Le forme del patire nella cultura occidentale* (Milan: Feltrinelli, 2002)

NENCIONI, GIOVANNI, 'Antrolopologia poetica?', *Strumenti critici*, 19 (1972), 243–58; now in *Tra grammatica e retorica* (Turin: Einaudi, 1983), 161–75

RAE, PATRICIA (ed.), *Modernism and Mourning* (Lewisburg: Bucknell University Press, 2007)

RAMAZANI, JAHAN, *Poetry of Mourning: The Modern Elegy from Hardy to Heaney* (Chicago: Chicago University Press, 1994)

—— *A Transnational Poetics* (Chicago: University of Chicago Press, 2009)

RICCIARDI, ALESSIA, *The Ends of Mourning. Psychoanalysis, Literature, Film* (Stanford, CA: Stanford University Press, 2003)

RIFFATERRE, MICHAEL, *Semiotics of Poetry* (Bloomington: Indiana University Press, 1978)

RUSHWORTH, JENNIFER, *Discourses of Mourning in Dante, Petrarch, and Proust* (Oxford: Oxford University Press, 2016)

SACKS, PETER M., *The English Elegy: Studies in the Genre from Spencer to Yeats* (Baltimore: Johns Hopkins University Press, 1985)

SCARRY, ELAINE, *The Body in Pain: The Making and Unmaking of the World* (Oxford: Oxford University Press, 1985)

SCHIESARI, GIULIANA, *The Gendering of Melancholia: Feminism, Psychoanalysis, and the Symbolics of Loss in Renaissance Literature* (Ithaca, NY: Cornell University Press, 1992)

SEGAL, CHARLES, *Orpheus: The Myth of the Poet* (Baltimore: Johns Hopkins University Press, 1989)

SISTO, DAVIDE, *La morte si fa social: Immortalità, memoria e lutto nell'epoca della cultura digitale* (Turin: Bollati Boringhieri, 2018); English translation, *Online Afterlives: Immortality, Memory, and Grief in Digital Culture* (Cambridge, MA: MIT Press, 2020)

SMITH, ERICH, *By Mourning Tongues: Studies in English Elegy* (Ipswich: Boydell Press, 1977)

SPARGO, R. CLIFTON, *The Ethics of Mourning: Grief and Responsibility in Elegiac Literature* (Baltimore: Johns Hopkins University Press, 2004)

STATEN, HENRY, *Eros in Mourning: Homer to Lacan* (Baltimore: Johns Hopkins University Press, 1995)

SVENBRO, JESPER, 'Phrasikleia: from Silence to Sound', in *Phrasikleia: An Anthropology of Reading in Ancient Greece*, trans. by Janet Lloyd (Ithaca, NY: Cornell University Press, 1993), pp. 8–25

TANNER, LAURA E., *Lost Bodies: Inhabiting the Borders of Life and Death* (Ithaca, NY: Cornell University Press, 2006)

VICKERY, JOHN B., *The Modern Elegiac Temper* (Baton Rouge: Louisiana State University Press, 2006)

WATERS, WILLIAM, *Poetry's Touch: On Lyric Address* (Ithaca, NY: Cornell University Press, 2003)

WATKIN, WILLIAM, *On Mourning: Theories of Loss in Modern Literature* (Edinburgh: Edinburgh University Press, 2004)

ZEIGER, MELISSA F., *Beyond Consolation: Death, Sexuality and the Changing Shapes of Elegy* (Ithaca, NY: Cornell University Press, 1997)

Notes to the Introduction

1. Sigmund Freud, 'Mourning and Melancholia', in *The Standard Edition of the Complete Psychological Works of Sigmund Freud*, trans. by James Strachey in collaboration with Anna Freud, assisted by Alix Strachey and Alan Tyson, (1914–1916), XIV: *On the History of the Psycho-Analytic Movement, Papers on Metapsychology and Other Works* (London: The Hogarth Press and the Institute of Psycho-analysis, 1957), pp. 237–58.

2. Sigmund Freud, *The Ego and the Id*, *The Standard Edition of the Complete Psychological Works of Sigmund Freud* (1923–1925), XIX: *The Ego and the Id and Other Works* (London: The Hogarth Press and the Institute of Psychoanalysis, 1961), pp. 1–66.

3. Freud, 'Mourning and Melancholia', p. 253.

4. Roland Barthes, *Journal de deuil: 26 octobre 1977–15 septembre 1979*, ed. by Nathalie Léger (Paris: Seuil, 2009); *Mourning Diary*, ed. by Nathalie Léger, trans. by Richard Howard (London: Notting Hill Editions, 2011), p. 95 (18 February 1978).

5. See Jennifer Rushworth, *Discourses of Mourning in Dante, Petrarch, and Proust* (Oxford: Oxford University Press, 2016), pp. 96–102.

6. Jahan Ramazani, *Poetry of Mourning: The Modern Elegy from Hardy to Heaney* (Chicago: Chicago University Press, 1994).

7. To provide just a synthetic overview of the broader scholarly interest in mourning: Henry Staten, *Eros in Mourning: Homer to Lacan* (Baltimore: Johns Hopkins University Press, 1995); Alessia Ricciardi, *The Ends of Mourning: Psychoanalysis, Literature, Film* (Stanford: Stanford University Press, 2003); *Loss: The Politics of Mourning*, ed. by David Eng and David Kazanjian (Berkeley–Los Angeles, CA: University of California Press, 2003); Sandra M. Gilbert, *Death's*

Door: Modern Dying and the Ways We Grieve (New York: W. W. Norton, 2006); *Modernism and Mourning*, ed. by Patricia Rae (Lewisburg: Bucknell University Press, 2007); and many others.

8. Ernesto de Martino, *Morte e pianto rituale: Dal lamento funebre antico al pianto di Maria*, 2nd edn (Turin: Bollati Boringhieri, 2000).

9. Giovanni Nencioni, 'Antrolopologia poetica?', *Strumenti critici*, 19 (1972), 243–58; now in *Tra grammatica e retorica* (Turin: Einaudi, 1983), pp. 161–75 (pp. 170–71).

10. Salvatore Natoli, *L'esperienza del dolore: Le forme del patire nella cultura occidentale* (Milan: Feltrinelli, 2002).

11. Davide Sisto, *La morte si fa social: Immortalità, memoria e lutto nell'epoca della cultura digitale* (Turin: Bollati Boringhieri, 2018); English translation, *Online Afterlives: Immortality, Memory, and Grief in Digital Culture* (Cambridge, MA: MIT Press, 2020).

12. Jonathan Culler, *Theory of the Lyric* (Cambridge, MA: Harvard University Press, 2015).

13. Philippe Ariès, *Western Attitudes toward Death: From the Middle Ages to the Present*, trans. by Patricia M. Ranum (Baltimore: Johns Hopkins University Press, 1974), p. 100.

14. Juliana Schiesari, *The Gendering of Melancholia: Feminism, Psychoanalysis, and the Symbolics of Loss in Renaissance Literature* (Ithaca, NY: Cornell University Press, 1992).

15. Charles Segal, *Orpheus: The Myth of the Poet* (Baltimore: Johns Hopkins University Press, 1989), p. 8. The use of the Orpheus myth in Milton's 'Lycidas' and in the Orphean tradition serves as a starting point in Melissa F. Zeiger, *Beyond Consolation: Death, Sexuality and the Changing Shapes of Elegy* (Ithaca, NY: Cornell University Press, 1997).

16. Among previous studies on elegy, one should mention at least Erich Smith, *By Mourning Tongues: Studies in English Elegy* (Ipswich: Boydell Press, 1977) and Peter M. Sacks, *The English Elegy: Studies in the Genre from Spencer to Yeats* (Baltimore: Johns Hopkins University Press, 1985). After Ramazani's book, many other studies appeared, including Melissa F. Zeiger, *Beyond Consolation: Death, Sexuality and the Changing Shapes of Elegy* (Ithaca, NY: Cornell University Press, 1997); William Watkin, *On Mourning: Theories of Loss in Modern Literature* (Edinburgh: Edinburgh University Press, 2004); R. Clifton Spargo, *The Ethics of Mourning: Grief and Responsibility in Elegiac Literature* (Baltimore: Johns Hopkins University Press, 2004); John B. Vickery, *The Modern Elegiac Temper* (Baton Rouge: Louisiana State University Press, 2006); and Diana Fuss, *Dying Modern: A Meditation on Elegy* (Durham, NC: Duke University Press, 2013).

17. Leo Bersani, *The Culture of Redemption* (Cambridge, MA: Harvard University Press, 1990).

18. Culler, *Theory of the Lyric*.

19. Jahan Ramazani, *A Transnational Poetics* (Chicago: University of Chicago Press, 2009), p. 71.

20. Ramazani, *A Transnational Poetics*, p. 72.

21. Judith Butler, *Precarious Life: The Powers of Mourning and Violence* (London: Verso, 2004), pp. xi–xv.

22. Ramazani, *A Transnational Poetics*, p. 93.

23. Francesco Giusti, *Canzonieri in morte: Per un'etica poetica del lutto* (L'Aquila: Textus Edizioni, 2015).

24. Cathy Caruth, *Unclaimed Experience: Trauma, Narrative, and History* (Baltimore: Johns Hopkins University Press, 1996), p. 3.

25. Culler, *Theory of the Lyric*, pp. 211–43, and Jonathan Culler, 'Apostrophe', in *The Pursuit of Signs: Semiotics, Literature, Deconstruction*, 2nd edn (London: Routledge, 2001), pp. 149–71. See also Paul de Man, 'Lyrical Voice in Contemporary Theory', in *Lyric Poetry: Beyond New Criticism*, ed. by Chaviva Hošek and Patricia Parker (Ithaca, NY: Cornell University Press, 1985), pp. 55–72; William Waters, *Poetry's Touch: On Lyric Address* (Ithaca, NY: Cornell University Press, 2003).

26. Giusti, *Canzonieri in morte*, pp. 317–25.

27. Culler, *Theory of the Lyric*, pp. 186–211.

28. Giusti, *Canzonieri in morte*, p. 323.

29. Laura E. Tanner, *Lost Bodies: Inhabiting the Borders of Life and Death* (Ithaca, NY: Cornell University Press, 2006). See also Elaine Scarry, *The Body in Pain: The Making and Unmaking of the World* (Oxford: Oxford University Press, 1985).

30. Culler, *Theory of the Lyric*, pp. 105–07, where Culler discusses Käte Hamburger's reflections on the lyric I in *The Logic of Literature*, 2nd edn (Bloomington: Indiana University Press, 1993), pp. 276–77, 285.

31. Giusti, *Canzonieri in morte*, pp. 447–60.

32. Giusti, *Canzonieri in morte*, pp. 377–92.

33. Dominick LaCapra, *Reflections on Trauma, Absence, and Loss*, in *Whose Freud? The Place of Psychoanalysis in Contemporary Culture*, ed. by Peter Brooks and Alex Woloch (New Haven: Yale University Press, 2000), pp. 178–204. See also Ricciardi, *The Ends of Mourning: Psychoanalysis, Literature, Film*.

34. Roland Barthes, *Mourning Diary*, p. 15.

35. Maurizio Bettini, *Antropologia e cultura romana* (Florence: La Nuova Italia, 1986), p. 135; Umberto Curi, *La cognizione dell'amore* (Milan: Feltrinelli, 1997), p. 129. For Adriana Cavarero, Orpheus sings about Eurydice but not to her, in Adriana Cavarero, *Tu che mi guardi, tu che mi racconti*, 6th edn (Milan: Feltrinelli 2005), p. 131.

36. Giovanni Nencioni, 'Antropologia poetica?', pp. 168, 173.

37. Francesco Giusti, 'Transcontextual Gestures: A Lyric Approach to the World of Literature', in *The Work of World Literature*, ed. by Francesco Giusti and Benjamin Lewis Robinson (Berlin: ICI Berlin Press, 2021), pp. 75–103.

38. Ramazani, *A Transnational Poetics*, pp. 71–93.

39. Fuss, *Dying Modern: A Meditation on Elegy*, pp. 67–73.

40. Nicolas Abraham and Maria Torok, *The Shell and the Kernel: Renewals of Psychoanalysis*, with an Introduction by Nicholas T. Rand (Chicago: Chicago University Press, 1994), and Nicolas Abraham and Maria Torok, *The Wolf Man's Magic Word: A Cryptonymy*, trans. by Nicholas Rand, foreword by Jacques Derrida (Minneapolis: Minnesota University Press, 2005).

41. Jacques Derrida, *Specters of Marx: The State of the Debt, the Work of Mourning and the New International*, trans. by Peggy Kamuf (New York: Routledge, 1994, 2006). See also Derrida's notion of *demi-deuil*, whereby the impossibility of 'successful' mourning opens up a space for the return of *revenants*, in Jacques Derrida, 'To Speculate — On "Freud"', in *The Post Card: From Socrates to Freud and Beyond*, trans. by Alan Bass (Chicago: University of Chicago Press, 1987), pp. 257–337. For relevant reflections on Derrida's *demi-deuil* in literature, see Rushworth, *Discourses of Mourning in Dante, Petrarch, and Proust*.

42. Jacques Derrida, *The Gift of Death* (Chicago: University of Chicago Press, 1995), p. 91.

43. Michael Riffaterre, *Semiotics of Poetry* (Bloomington: Indiana University Press, 1978).

44. Culler, *Theory of the Lyric*, p. 226.

45. Jesper Svenbro's studies on Hellenistic funeral tombstones are an interesting reference for this kind of 'animation'. See Jesper Svenbro, 'Phrasikleia: from Silence to Sound', in *Phrasikleia: An Anthropology of Reading in Ancient Greece*, trans. by Janet Lloyd (Ithaca, NY: Cornell University Press, 1993), pp. 8–25. See also Karen Mills-Courts, *Poetry as Epitaph: A Study of Representation and Poetic Language* (Baton Rouge: Louisiana State University Press, 1990).

46. Nicole Loraux, *The Mourning Voice: An Essay on Greek Tragedy* (Ithaca, NY: Cornell University Press, 2002).

47. Rosi Braidotti, *Nomadic Subjects: Embodiment and Sexual Difference in Contemporary Feminist Theory* (New York: Columbia University Press, 1994).

48. Adriana Cavarero, *In Spite of Plato: A Feminist Rewriting of Ancient Philosophy* (London: Routledge, 1995).

49. Culler, *Theory of the Lyric*, p. 188.

50. Natoli, *L'esperienza del dolore*, pp. 8–9.

51. Gordon Braden and Elizabeth Fowler, 'Elegy', in *The Princeton Encyclopedia of Poetry and Poetics*, 4th edn, ed. by Roland Greene and Stephen Cushman (Princeton: Princeton University Press, 2012), pp. 397–99 (p. 397).

52. Braden and Fowler, 'Elegy', p. 398.

CHAPTER 1

❖

The Loss of Poetry:
Leopardi's 'Coro di morti'

Emanuela Tandello

Between 1823, the year of 'Alla sua donna' [To His Lady],[1] and 1828, the year of the miraculous *risorgimento* of the *canti pisano-recanatesi*[2] Leopardi's poetry fell almost completely silent. The perception of the definitive end of *illusioni*, and the consequent onset of what he was to call in the verse epistle 'Al Conte Carlo Pepoli' [To Count Carlo Pepoli] 'l'acerbo vero' [the bitter truth] (l. 140), led to a temporary, painfully born inhibition towards poetry, and a determined turn towards the prose of the *Operette morali*. Among the very few exceptions — 'Al Conte Carlo Pepoli' being one — is the poetic text that introduces the operetta 'Dialogo di Federico Ruysch e delle sue mummie' [Dialogue between Frederick Ruysch and his Mummies].[3] The 'Coro di morti'[4] [Chorus of Mummies] has been celebrated as one of the highest expressions of Leopardi's poetry. Intimately bound to — and the culmination of — what Gilberto Lonardi calls a 'linea mortifera'[5] [deathly lineage of poetry] that includes the *canti* 'Ad Angelo Mai' [To Angelo Mai], the 'Pepoli', and 'Ultimo canto di Saffo' [Sappho's Last Song], and that will further continue with 'A se stesso' [To Himself] and 'Il tramonto della luna' [The Setting of the Moon], the 'Coro' is widely considered as a crossroads[6] between the early *canzoni*, and the *canti pisano-recanatesi*, an elective 'place'[7] where we are given to observe the fundamental transformations that would affect the lyric self of the *Canti*. The movement from the *canzone* to the *canzone libera leopardiana*, of which 'A Silvia' [To Silvia] is the first exemplary embodiment, goes through a complex process of re-positioning of the poetic self that in its most extreme form — the 'Coro' indeed — leads to a total self-identification; indeed, a self-annihilation of the 'io' with(in) the voice(s) of the Dead. This chapter will argue how the genre contamination that occurs in this text — a *stanza di canzone* that adopts the mode of the chorus, both in its tragic, and comic configuration (Sophocles, Homer, vis-à-vis Aristophanes; and the chorus of late Renaissance Guarinian provenance)[8] — and the essentially parodic context of the macrotext it belongs to (that of the *operetta* it introduces) places the lyric mode, and the lyric self, under huge strain. At a time when the poet is experiencing a personal, philosophical and aesthetic crisis of formidable magnitude, the 'constatazione del decesso dell'io' [acknowledgement of the death of the self][9] informs a discourse on loss that works on two, parallel levels: the loss of lyric poetry as viable discourse about a self-as-dead (thus the choral voice), and, paradoxically, poetry's own loss/defeat as it ultimately fails to go beyond a perfect, but lifeless, still, stone-like, indeed mummified formal balance, beyond which there is no future, nor any possibility for redress.

In order to argue for this double-faced dimension of loss in the 'Coro', I will be drawing on different theoretical, and poetic positions, in particular Denise Riley's *Time Lived, Without its Flow;*[10] Jonathan Culler, and Paul De Man on *prosopopoeia*; Diana Fuss's *Dying Modern: A Meditation on Elegy;*[11] and last, but not least, Franco D'Intino's reflection on Leopardi's view of 'equilibrio' [balance] in poetry, explored in his important book *La caduta e il ritorno.*[12]

My concluding argument will be that in the *Coro* we witness the questioning of the lyric genre itself, and a declaration of its own loss in the face of the non-lyrical. I will argue that the 'Coro' is thus not only a special tassel in the discourse of mourning that is Leopardi's poetry, universally acknowledged as a 'poetry of loss', but a lapidary statement on the loss of poetry at this juncture in Leopardi's life. It is also poetry's own losing discourse, in dire need of a way out, a *risorgimento*, something which would indeed come with the *canti pisano-recanatesi*.

1. The body-sepulchre

Between December 1819 and August 1820, Leopardi's letters to his friend and mentor Pietro Giordani return obsessively on the same images of dejection and despair. In his letter of 17 December 1819, he claims that despite the affection for 'questo bel cuore' (Giordani's), which would point to life being worth living ('Bisogna ben che il mondo sia qualche cosa, e ch'io non sia del tutto morto, poiché mi sento infervorato d'affetto verso questo bel cuore [...]' [The world must needs be some significant thing, and similarly it must be that I should not be entirely dead, given how inflamed with love I feel towards this beautiful heart],[13] Giacomo's own soul feels instead frozen ('anima assiderata') and shivering ('abbrividita') as in death. On 19 October 1819, he adds 'non ho più lena di concepire nessun desiderio, neanche della morte' [I no longer have the energy to conceive any desire, not even for death], and on 6 March 1820, he defines himself as definitively 'stecchito' and 'inaridito' [dried up and shrivelled]. Indeed, how can we understand how life can be tolerated without illusions and living affections, and without imagination nor enthusiasm? — only the idea makes him freeze with fright ('m'agghiacciai dallo spavento, non arrivando a comprendere come si possa tollerare la vita senza illusioni e affetti vivi'). He has just turned twenty-one, and youth, he feels, has definitively gone: and with it, the *illusioni* that made life joyful ('insieme con la fanciullezza è finito il mondo per me e per tutti quelli che pensano e sentono' [with youth the world has ended for me and for all those who think and feel]). Life has become like a death, a posthumous affair 'la vita che in questa condizione è piuttosto una morte' [life which in this condition is rather more like death]. Thus, he feels he lived once 'certo d'esser già vissuto', but is now dead, 'io già sento d'esser morto', indeed 'peggio che morto' [worse than dead] and unsuited to the consideration given to the living: 'non mi convengono più gli uffizi che si fanno ai vivi.' Thanking Giordani for his affection and solicitude, he adds, on 14 March 1820, 'fa conto che mi rileverai dal sepolcro' [imagine that you will draw me from my grave].

The metaphor of the body as sepulchre would furthermore surface again in 1825, in a later note in the *Zibaldone*, barely a year after writing the Ruysch.

> *Io sono, si perdoni la metafora, un sepolcro ambulante*, che porto dentro di me un uomo morto, un cuore sensibilissimo che più non sente ecc.' (Zib. 4150; Bologna, 3 novembre 1825).

> [I am, pardon the metaphor, a walking sepulchre, and inside me I carry a dead man, a once very sensitive heart that feels no more, etc.][14]

A poetic self that is either on the threshold of death, or feels already dead dominates in what Lonardi has called a 'linea mortifera' that begins with the *canzoni* pre-Coro, starting with *Ad Angelo Mai* (1820). In dedicating the *canzone* to Leonardo Trissino, Leopardi writes:

> Ma ricordatevi ch'ai disgraziati si conviene il vestire a lutto, ed è forza che le nostre canzoni rassomiglino ai versi funebri.[15]

> [You should remember that mourning garb befits the wretched, and that our canzoni should resemble funerary verse.]

The dedication points to an intent that we have defined elsewhere as 'self-elegiac',[16] articulated by a Subject who feels the very exhaustion and cessation of life in himself: 'grave è il nostro disperato obblio' [when we | have wholly lost | the memory of our heritage] (l. 18); 'Io son distrutto, | né schermo alcuno ho dal dolor, che | scuro m'è l'avvenire' [I'm exhausted, | nothing shields me from suffering, | the way ahead is dark] (ll. 34–36); 'Oh tempi, oh tempi avvolti | in sonno eterno! [Oh times, snowbound in eternal sleep!] (ll. 56–57); 'La vita solitaria' [The Solitary Life] (1821): 'ond'io quasi me stesso e il mondo obblio | sedendo immoto; e già mi par che sciolte | giaccian le membra mia, né spirto o senso | più le commuova' [and sitting still, I seem to forget | myself and the world; my limbs relax, | no longer ruled by mind or spirit] (ll. 34–37); and later in 1826, 'Al Conte Carlo Pepoli', a *canzone* that coincides chronologically with the years of the *Operette*: 'Questo affannoso e travagliato sonno | che noi vita nomiam' [this tortured and tormented | sleep that we call life] (ll. 1–2).[17]

The 'linea mortifera' enervates itself in the 'Ultimo canto di Saffo' — Saffo's future tense in 'Morremo' [We're going to die] (l. 55) provides a classic example of self-elegy, pronounced from the threshold between life and death, which incidentally shows Leopardi's growing interest in *prosopopoeia*; and resurfaces at the other end of the 'Coro', first in the Subject of the 'Ricordanze' [The Recollections]: 'abbandonato, occulto, | senz'amor, senza vita' [secluded here, shut in | with no love and no life] (ll. 38–39), posturing as one who sings a funereal song upon his own dead body: 'a me stesso | in sul languir cantai funereo canto' [sang myself | a song of lamentation, languishing] (ll. 117–18); and would culminate in that 'performance of the posthumous' which is 'A se stesso'.[18] Nowhere, however, does the Leopardian Subject renounce its centripetal position, nor its authority over discourse. Nowhere, that is, except in the 'Coro'.[19]

2. A tragic turn in a comic dialogue

Reading Fontenelle,[20] but also unquestionably in a conversation with his great friend, and personal physician Puccinotti, Leopardi found out about Frederik Ruysch, the Dutch anatomist who pioneered a successful technique of embalming via a liquid that would preserve the plumpness and rosy hue of the corpse — more importantly, from an anatomist's point of view, that would preserve the state of veins and arteries, as when fed by blood circulation. What interests us here is the appearance of these corpses, that would thus look as though they were *still alive*. If Leopardi found the idea of body preservation not merely risible, but profoundly disturbing, nonetheless Ruysch's 'creations' — which were to become part of his most macabre 'cabinet'[21] — provided him with the image of a very peculiar kind of body-sepulchre. The 'mummies' of the *operetta* are not mummies at all, neither in the Egyptian sense (no swaddling) nor in the sense of 'holy' corpses reduced to bones and desiccated skin. Their life-like (and I am using my words carefully here) appearance defines them as beings living a suspended time in which they are *neither one thing nor the other*. Leopardi's choice of this kind of dead is not accidental, and he shows his awareness of the misunderstanding contained in his choice of word, when in the second edition of the *operetta*, he states 'che in linguaggio scentifico si chiamerebbero 'preparazioni anatomiche' [which in scientific language would be called anatomical specimens].[22] It is not even just the product of his interest in, and fierce opposition to, the dubious progress of the science of anatomy. His choice of dead bodies preserving the appearance of life chimes significantly with that condition of suspended existence that he has articulated before, the condition of living as though already dead, yet without the comfort of death: indeed, the very *reversibility* of life and death, and proper death as by far the most preferable of the two.

In full keeping with the 'comic' project of the *Operette*, Leopardi constructs his most hybrid text: a unique bipartite structure of verse and prose (a veritable *hapax* in the *Operette morali*), with a *Coro di morti* as introduction, intoned by an indeterminate number of 'mummies', and a second part, in prose, consisting of an antefact in the form of a brief narrative setting the scene in Ruysch's study, followed by the dialogue 'proper' between Ruysch and the unnamed Dead, now answering with one voice, now collectively, over the physical experience of dying. The dialogue represents an eminent example of that search for a 'comic' style that Leopardi pursues through the *Operette*. It represents a powerfully satirical response to the Romantic myth of progress, and to the widespread, and wide-ranging, culture of scientific experimentation in Leopardi's time, from the preservation of dead tissues for the study of human anatomy, to indeed the hypothesis of an artificial re-creation of life itself. In this respect, it is not so far from being a relative of Mary Shelley's *Frankenstein*, and shares with that text a distinct indulgence in lurid atmospheres and gothic *coups de théâtre*.[23]

The two parts have been recognised as being profoundly, even puzzlingly, different. The Dead's slow, ponderous chant seals within itself, the 'truth' dictated by the locked-in experience of melancholia: that to live is to experience a kind of death, and that death is by far the more preferable of the two as it accords not 'lietezza' but safety from the ancient sorrow/pain of living. It is quite clear that any hope, or any attempt to remedy this irremediable dimension is doomed to failure. The stroke of genius on Leopardi's part lies in placing this text as an episode within a narrative of unquestionable comic flavour, where the scientist Ruysch asks, quite simply, all the wrong questions about the transition between life and death.[24]

This hiatus has been often stressed by critics, and the 'Coro' has been seen to act as a 'controcanto' [countermelody][25] whose purpose is indeed to contrast — in its essentially tragic nature — with the comedy of the dialogue. As a consequence, it has been considered mostly in isolation from the rest of the *operetta*, and explored mainly from a 'poetic' point of view. There are many good reasons for this, as we are about to discover. The idea that this is one of Leopardi's most sublime poetic texts informs its wider reception, too, an eminent example of which is Goffredo Petrassi's musical setting, a meditative *madrigale drammatico* which is considered one of the composer's most accomplished pieces of non-religious music.[26]

Foregoing the satirical and parodic nature of the microtext of the *operetta*, however, in a study of the 'Coro', is arguably risky. Lonardi first, and Natale more recently, have stressed how the model adopted by Leopardi is not the tragic one, but rather more akin to Aristophanean comedy, and to the melodrama of *opera buffa*.[27] If such a position is considered, the microtext can easily be seen as undercutting, through the dialogical (in the Bakhtinian sense) structure, the poetic text's tragic tone. If the idea of 'controcanto' suggests almost a pre-emptive strategy, a more dialogic view of the microtext allows the contrast, and the undercutting to work both ways. What I mean is that when we try to define what kind of text the 'Coro' is, and what it does at poetic level, we should consider what the microtext does to it. Let us consider one major example. The second part of the operetta oscillates between Ruysch's comical colloquialisms ('Chi ha insegnato la musica a questi morti, che cantano di note come galli? [...] Figliuoli, a che gioco giochiamo? [...] che è cotesto baccano?' [...] e quanto dureranno a cantare?') [Who taught music to these dead, that they should sing at night like cockerels [...] come, children, what game are we playing at? [...] what is all this racket [...] and how long will they carry on for?], and the Dead's ironic reply: '[...] tutti i morti, sulla mezza notte, hanno cantato come noi quella canzoncina che hai sentita. [...] Di cantare hanno già finito. Di parlare hanno facoltà per un quarto d'ora. Poi tornano in silenzio per insino a tanto che si compie di nuovo lo stesso anno [all the dead, upon the hour of midnight, sang as we did that little song you have just heard. [...] As for singing, they have finished with it already. As for speaking, they can do it for a quarter of an hour. Then they will return to silence until the same year comes round again]. It is self-evident that the Dead's replies verge on the mock-erudite. The diminutive in 'canzon*cina*' conveys the Dead's mockery of Ruysch's inability to comprehend the conceptual magnitude of the song he has just heard (which he reduces instead to a 'cantare come galli'); furthermore, their telegraphic 'Di cantare hanno già finito. Di parlare hanno facoltà per un quarto d'ora' pre-empts the scientist's pointless questions about the transition between life and death, and above all his preoccupation that the transition may be painful. The diminutive in 'canzoncina' however may be seen perhaps as undercutting not the genre, but the poetic status of the 'Coro'. This inevitably introduces an element of tension between a highly charged philosophical statement about the reversibility of life and death, and the form of the text itself — that is to say, the 'sublime poetry' of the 'Coro' is actually under strain from the very text it belongs to. This has much to do with the choice of genre, but especially, as I am about to discuss, with the unique nature of the text itself: a poetic text that flirts with the dramatic, seemingly refusing the tragic, and ending up with undermining both. The metapoetic implications for the place of the 'Coro' within Leopardi's poetic oeuvre are less hidden than we might think: after all, the form of the 'Coro' is indeed that of a *canzone* — which is reduced, by its singers themselves, to a *canzoncina*, a light form worthy of a vaudeville.

Who — or better, *what* — these Dead are is far from unimportant. *Non solo noi, ma in ogni cimitero, in ogni sepolcro, in fondo al mare, sotto la neve o la rena, a cielo aperto, e in qualsiasi luogo si trovano tutti i morti* [...] [Not only us, but in every graveyard, every sepulchre, at the bottom of the sea, under the snow or the sand, in the open, and in any place all the dead are [...]]. All those who have died have been allowed the 'humic' status that, as Robert Pogue Harrison states, allows them the opportunity to return to the natural state of the earth, to re-enter the cycle of life and death, and to continue to live through nature.[28]

There is no doubt that the experimental hybridity of this text relies on irreconcilable difference: not only are the two parts profoundly different in genre, they actually question the issue of life and death in two very different, almost unrelated ways. The two discourses, the Dead's, and the scientist's, simply cannot meet: even only for fifteen minutes! The alien nature of the singing/speaking Dead forbids any meaningful transaction, for the simple reason that death in itself denies the possibility of language, and entirely precludes communication.

3. The death of the poetic voice, the arrested time of the dead: the 'Coro di morti'

'Coro di morti nello studio di Federico Ruysch'

Sola nel mondo, a cui si volve
Ogni creata cosa,
In te, morte, si posa
Nostra ignuda natura,
Lieta no, ma sicura   5
Dall'antico dolor. Profonda notte
Nella confusa mente
Il pensier grave oscura;
Alla speme, al desio l'arido spirto
Lena mancar si sente: 10
Così d'affanno e di temenza è sciolto,
E l'età vote e lente
Senza tedio consuma.
Vivemmo: e qual di paurosa larva,
E di sudato sogno,   15
Al lattante fanciullo erra nell'alma

Confusa ricordanza:
Tal memoria n'avanza
Del viver nostro: ma da tema è lunge
Il rimembrar. Che fummo?   20
Che fu quel punto acerbo
Che di vita ebbe nome?
Cosa arcana e stupenda
Oggi è la vita al pensier nostro, e tale
Qual de' vivi al pensiero   25
L'ignota morte appar. Come da morte
Vivendo rifuggia, cosi rifugge
Dalla fiamma vitale
Nostra ignuda natura;
Lieta no ma sicura: 30
Però ch'esser beato
Nega ai mortali e nega a' morti il fato.[29]

The 'Coro' consists of a self-contained *stanza di canzone* in hendecasyllables and *settenari* — a closed structure, as I am going to suggest,[30] where closure is achieved through specular repetition, articulating in no uncertain terms the utter reversibility of life and death.[31] The lexis excels in abstraction, intertextually bound to the *Canti*: *natura, dolor, pensier, punto acerbo, speme, desio*, ignoto, arcano (the latter taking us back to Saffo, 'Arcano è tutto, | fuor che il nostro dolor', ll. 46–47). Structurally, it designs a specular structure, with lines 5–6 returning at lines 29–30, with a pivotal turn at line 14, with the laconic 'Vivemmo' [We lived] — again a strong memory of Saffo's 'Morremo', placing the Dead on the opposite shore to her, thus completing the journey from life to death; the second half closing the circle. The gnomic last two lines seal the text with a parallelism that is a summa of Leopardi's views of mortality and the fate of humanity: 'ch'esser beato | Nega ai mortali e nega a' morti il fato' [For to be happy | Is denied to mortals and the dead by Fate'], where 'nega' [is denied] is a not-so-distant echo of *La sera del dì di festa* [The Evening of the Holiday], 'A te la speme | Nego, mi disse, anche la speme' (ll. 14–15) [I deny you hope, she told me, even hope]. And it is Saffo to be echoed here again, but also the *Canto notturno* [Night Song] and the *Operette* themselves, from *Storia del genere umano* [History of Humankind] to the great speech by the Icelander in *Dialogo della Morte e di un Islandese* [Dialogue between Nature and an Icelander]. It is important to realise that there is no progression of argument, and above all no movement but rather a frozen stasis. The sombre tone is monotonous, and monochrome:[32] the verb 'posa' [lies] (an anticipation of *A se stesso*'s 'Posa per sempre' (l. 6) [literally: lie down forever[33]] in particular defines the posture of the Dead, indeed mummified[34] in a time that has no past, let alone a future — memory fails, life is a distant 'confusa ricordanza' [confused recollection]. The Dead simply cannot remember life, and find death infinitely more reassuring: 'Lieta no ma sicura | Dall'antico dolor.' I believe it is possible to speak here of a highly accomplished moment of synthesis for Leopardi, achieved through the subsuming of the Subjective voice to the collective one of the Dead. Subsuming or self-suppressing? Or perhaps achieving what Franco D'Intino calls as 'una imitazione statica di se stesso' [a static imitation of himself].[35]

4. Frozen time

Far from wanting to apply any psychobiography to our reading, it is important to recognise how the images used here have been long acknowledged as characteristic of the melancholia/depression experienced after a major loss. From Burton to Freud, and beyond, feeling dried up inside, and inwardly dead, figuratively defines the feeling induced by a devastating loss, be it of a loved person, or a condition that is now irretrievable, or no longer reproducible (Kristeva); or indeed the Lacanian 'chose', as irretrievably lost as it is indefinable. The subject is affected spatially, and temporally, reducing it to *akinesis*, to immobility. Giacomo's words sound strikingly similar to those used by Denise Riley, writing about the loss of her son Jake: 'I see, as if I am myself dead.' Death, and in particular the death of another, she writes, brings us something much worse than 'thinking sad thoughts' or even mourning as we understand it in its Freudian sense. What it brings us is 'inexorable carnal knowledge': which turns living in the present into the 'timelessness of being dead'.[36] Carnal knowledge suggests that this is indeed a physical experience and not a 'merely' psychological one — something that Giacomo's adjectives, and substantive coinage of the body-sepulchre clearly endorse. The stillness of this deathly space is dominated by 'arrested time', what Riley calls 'private non-time of pure stasis'.[37] Indeed the mourner is no longer 'in' time, despite the fact of being still, inexorably, and atrociously, alive. This forced atemporality, stresses Riley, 'is not to do with any kind of *taking thought*', but, rather, it is prior to it, and, what is worse, 'supremely indifferent to lament and cogitation alike'. Instead, she adds, it feels 'foundational: to do with a change in the entire structure of cognition'.[38] As a result, your own sense of self fades, 'you are pure skin stretched tightly over vacancy. You abide'.[39] You abide, that is, not as an extinguished Self, but as a Self locked out of sequence. For writing, underlines Riley, 'your very condition militates against narrative'. Narrative, but writing in general, is no longer possible because this condition of being both locked in and locked out means that you lack any sense of futurity: 'You can't [...] take the lightest interest in the activity of writing unless you possess some feeling of futurity'.[40]

I find Riley's reflection immensely productive: not because of the personal, biographical dimension (which is nonetheless most powerful and poignant) but because her elaboration of loss and its consequences unlocks for us the notion that writers may not write of/about death, and neither about grief, but *of it*, and *for it*.[41] In Leopardi's specific case, this distinction helps us to measure the distance between experience (of grief experienced, lived, felt, and written about in the intimacy of friendly exchanges) and *scrittura poetica*, which enables the prodigious balancing act of a poetic Self that dares speak where speech is supposed not to be, a Self that dares *to be* in language when language ought to cease. We shall continue to argue next that poetry is unlike narrative, which cannot live without futurity or beyond the locked-out dimension of grief, enacting this identification with the dead and their temporality. Poetry establishes a threshold space from which the self can speak, never quite beyond it (where silence would rule). What unlocks the possibility for the self to speak as fully cognisant of the paradox is the dynamic of apostrophe. Even where the dire dimension of a self that feels dried up like a stick, paralysed by an invisible/non-existent future, unquestionably features in the *Canti*, nonetheless, at either end of the 'Coro', the presence of an addressee guarantees that language will continue as communication with another, alive, or indeed dead. The irreversible dimension of loss, Culler stresses, is restructured by apostrophe, allowing a movement, an alternation of presence and absence 'governed by poetic ingenuity or power'.[42] This is indeed what elegy does: an alternation between mourning and consolation, uttered by a self *in* mourning heading towards some kind of cathartic peak that will release it. In Leopardi, even in the case of 'Ultimo canto di Saffo', a clear example of self-elegy, the identification with *one-who-is-about-to-die* produces a discourse from the edge that can still address, and argue, and formulate some kind of cathartic experience that is yet unaffected by the silencing dimension of death. Such, we have argued elsewhere, is also the experience of 'A se stesso'. And such is, above all else, the discourse in 'A Silvia', where the dialogue with the dead is firmly established, allowing the poetic Subject to identify with the girl-alive, but splitting his immediate destiny from hers. The balance constructed by Saffo and by the first triumphant canto *pisano-recanatese* shows us how *poetry* enables an utterance for grief and of grief, rather than about it.[43]

5. The chorus as mode of the lyric self[44]

One year before writing the Ruysch, Leopardi reflected on the use of the chorus in tragedy:

> Io considero quest'uso come parte di quel vago, di quell'indefinito ch'è la principal cagione dello *charme* dell'antica poesia e bella letteratura. L'individuo è sempre cosa piccola, spesso brutta, spesso disprezzabile. Il bello e il grande ha bisogno dell'indefinito, e questo indefinito non si poteva introdurre sulla scena, se non introducendo la moltitudine. (Zib 2805)

> [I regard this use as part of that vagueness, that indefiniteness which is the principal cause of the *charme* of ancient poetry and fine literature. The individual is always a paltry thing, and often an ugly, often a contemptible one. The beautiful and the great need indefiniteness, and this indefiniteness can only be brought on to the stage by bringing on the multitude.]

The collective and anonymous voice of the chorus, continues Leopardi, 'non era quello degli individui umani' [was not that of human individuals] and its purpose was that of 'far delle profonde e sublimi riflessioni' [to engage in profound and sublime reflections] — as a consequence, even when the Chorus took active part in the action, it was more poetic. It is the very nature of that Subject (indefinite, multitudinous, anonymous) that makes it possible to pronounce 'in grande' the trans-subjective nature of truth, becoming thus its mouthpiece. This, Lonardi stresses, is the difference between the 'canzoni/canto' where a prosopopoeic voice — Saffo's for example — reveals the model of the Homeric *threnos*, vis-à-vis the (equally prosopopoeic) anonymous voice of the shepherd in the 'Canto notturno', whose very anonymity allows him to speak of humanity as a whole, and of its tragic fate.[45] The 'Coro' can be seen to function as a kind of hinge between the two poems, as it points to the beginnings of a transformation 'dell'io lirico che si sta riscoprendo sempre più centripeto, e in grado di forzare i confini del singolo genere' [a transformation of the lyric 'I' that is discovering itself more and more centripetal, and capable of forcing the confines of one single genre].[46] This transition between the pre- and post-'Coro' — a veritable 'aggiramento del soggetto' [a circumvention of the Subject], as Natale writes[47] — is literally dramatised in the 'Coro', where, as we have suggested above, the chorus (which in modernity has very little use) is parodically reduced to the genre of *canzoncina*.

This marks a dangerous point of no return for the lyric, where poetry-as-lyric (could) lose, and could itself be lost.

6. Prosopopoeia, and the corpse poem

Through the prosopopoeic speech of the Dead in the 'Coro', Leopardi attributes a voice (and thus a consciousness) to inanimate bodies temporarily returning to life. This is of course a paradox. In her book *Dying Modern: A Meditation on Elegy*,[48] Fuss underlines how a crucial paradox lies behind the notion itself of a text uttered by the dead, which she calls a 'corpse poem':

> A dead body and a poetic discourse are mutually incompatible, two formal states each precluding the other. A poem implies subjective depth while a corpse testifies to its absence. A poem quickens language while a corpse stills it. The fantastical coupling of 'corpse' and 'poem' denotes an extravagant rhetorical conceit, an impossible literary utterance.[49]

The *Morti* having a voice, here as in any corpse poem 'irretrievably breach the boundary between the place where language intensifies', as Fuss writes, 'and the place where language vanishes'.[50] What is more important, such a poem, in seeking to return authority/authoriality to the dead, risks to 'contaminate' and indeed to 'kill' poetry as the utterance of the poet's subjectivity. This is also a point made by Paul De Man, as

> [...] by succumbing to the fiction that the dead may speak, we give voice to the haunting within ourselves, which ensures that we are also deprived of our own voice.[51]

While we may consider that Leopardi might be ventriloquising with his dead self, thus performing a lyric utterance from inside the place where the dead dwell, it must be recognised that what we have before us is what Fuss calls 'an insensate figure'[52] that challenges the modality of elegy. And indeed, this is the most important difference, in our view, between the electively elegiac intent of the *Canti*, and this most extraordinary text. For a start, it does not 'mourn' but rather enacts (not merely declaring it) the absolute reversibility of life and death. Indeed, the Dead are, as we said above, keen to return to death, as it guarantees, between the two, safety and certainty ('lieta no ma sicura' [not glad but certain]). Life is nullified, made insubstantial, by the lack of remembrance. As Antonella del Gatto has pointed out, the dead cannot see, thus cannot identify material objects that will take them back to a recognition of life through *rimembranza*.

7. Poetry mummified and the paradox of perfect balance: by way of a conclusion

We would argue, then, that the loss of memory as a vehicle and as a process between A and B, in favour of an absolute state where the object itself is virtually absent, makes elegy (and eventually poetry) virtually impossible. The non/anti-elegiac dimension of the 'Coro' relies on another paradox: whilst elegy replaces 'an irreversible temporal disjunction, the movement from life to death, with a reversible alternation between mourning and consolation',[53] the perfectly balanced a-temporality of the 'Coro', its crystallised, indeed mummified, 'mortifero' dimension, declares the death of poetry, a speaking from the beyond, and not merely about it.

The 'Coro' thus manages to perform 'un atto mortifero' which contaminates, even 'kills' poetry — despite or indeed precisely because of its 'admirable' perfection. We may want to consider here, as we move towards a conclusion, some of the crucial passages from the *Zibaldone* on the subject of *equilibrium*, explored by Franco D'Intino in his masterly book *La caduta e il ritorno*. 'L'uguale' in Leopardi, D'Intino writes, 'indica un universo immobile, mortuario, impoetico' [points to a universe that is immobile, deathly, and impoetic'].[54] Romantic reflection (of which Leopardi is unquestionably an exponent) is not, as we have already stressed, a tired imitation of oneself, but rather 'una autoduplicazione del principio vitale in un soggetto rappresentante e in un oggetto rappresentato dalla cui continua tensione scaturisce l'energia creativa del poeta' [a self-duplication of the vital principle into a representing subject and a represented object, and from the tension between the two is born the creative energy of the poet].[55] The mortiferous self-identification between the voice of the poet and that of the Dead constructs the veritable sepulchre that the 'Coro' is. Its admirable form leaves our affects in perfect equilibrium. But as Leopardi writes:

> [...] una poesia che lascia gli affetti dei lettori o uditori in pienissimo equilibrio, si chiama poesia? Produce un effetto poetico? che altro vuol dire essere in pieno equilibrio, se non esser quieti senza tempesta né commozione alcuna? E qual altro è il proprio uffizio e scopo della poesia se non il commuovere, così o così, ma sempre commuover gli affetti? (Zib 3455)

> [And can a poem which leaves the feelings of its readers or listeners in perfect equilibrium, other than to be calm, and without any agitation or turmoil? And what else is the proper office of poetry than to move the feelings, this way or that but [3456] always to move them?]

Where the pathos should be, there is almost only form, in a near-bureaucratic balancing of the books:

> [...] Le partite sono uguali, l'affare è finito, il negozio è terminato, gli interessi pareggiati: voi chiudete il vostro libro de' conti e non ci pensate più. (Zib 3455–3457).

> [The entries are balanced, the deal is struck, the negotiation is completed, the interests matched equally: you shut your ledger book and think no more of it.]

This may indeed be the desire of the Dead, for whom Death means safety and protection. At the end of the poem (because a poem, after all, it is!) we can only hear the sound of a marble slab slamming their grave shut, to protect their millennial sleep. But poetry does, and would do, something else. It would return to that most ancient of role of lyric poetry, as admirably argued by Giovanni Nencioni, which is the funerary rite, the address to the lost one, their evocation — in other words, elegy.[56] The voice lost among the Dead would be found again in 'A Silvia', where the self-duplication that D'Intino speaks of is embodied in the split between the poet-survivor, and the dead girl; where identification with Silvia's fate is not mortiferous, but rather poured into the singing of the funerary song. In 'A Silvia', even in 'A se stesso', the poet reserves for himself that role of witness, removed from and yet utterly bound up in the tragedy of grief. But he is not trapped in its time; his voice is his own.

Bibliography

CULLER, JONATHAN, *Theory of the Lyric* (Cambridge, MA: Harvard University Press, 2015)

DAVIS, COLIN, 'Can the Dead Speak to Us? De Man, Levinas and Agamben', *Culture, Theory and Critique*, 45:1 (2004), 77–89

D'INTINO, FRANCO, *La caduta e il ritorno: Cinque movimenti dell'immaginario romantico leopardiano* (Macerata: Quodlibet, 2019)

DEL GATTO, ANTONELLA, *Uno specchio d'acqua diaccia. La struttura dialogico-umoristica del testo leopardiano: dalle 'Operette morali' ai 'Canti' pisano-recanatesi* (Florence: Cesati, 2001)

FUSS, DIANE, *Dying Modern: A Meditation on Elegy* (Durham: Duke University Press, 2013)

HARRISON, ROBERT POGUE, *The Dominion of the Dead* (Chicago: University of Chicago Press, 2003)

LEOPARDI, GIACOMO, *Ad Angelo Mai, quand'ebbe trovato i libri di Cicerone della Repubblica*, ed. by Pietro Brighenti (Bologna: Marsigli, 1820)

—— *Canti*, trans. by Jonathan Galassi (London: Penguin, 2010)

—— *Operette Morali: Essays and Dialogues*, translated with introduction and notes by Giovanni Cecchetti (Berkeley: University of California Press, 1982)

—— *Operette morali*, ed. by Laura Melosi (Milan: Bompiani, 2008)

—— *Zibaldone: The Notebooks of Leopardi* (London: Penguin, 2013)

LONARDI, GILBERTO, 'Il "Coro di morti" nel sistema poetico leopardiano (fra intenzione antica e modello cinquecentesco)', in *Leopardi e la letteratura italiana dal Duecento al Seicento, Atti del IV convegno internazionale di studi leopardiani*, Recanati, 13–16 September 1976 (Florence: Olschki, 1978), pp. 655–79

MAZIERSKI, DAVE, 'The Cabinet of Federick Ruysch and the Kunstkamera of Peter the Great: Past and Present', *Journal of Biocommunication*, 38 (2012), <www.jbiocommunication.org>

NATALE, MASSIMO, 'Il coro, modo dell'io lirico: fra Manzoni e Leopardi', in *Il curatore ozioso: Forme e funzioni del coro tragico in Italia* (Venice: Marsilio, 2013), pp. 349–73

NENCIONI, GIOVANNI, 'Antropologia poetica?', *Strumenti critici*, 19 (1972), 243–58; now in *Tra grammatica e retorica* (Turin: Einaudi, 1983), pp. 161–75

RILEY, DENISE, *Time Lived, Without its Flow*, with intro. by Max Porter (London: Picador, 2019)

TANDELLO, EMANUELA, 'A Note on Elegy and Self-elegy in the *Canti*', *Appunti leopardiani*, 4:2 (2012), <http://www.appuntileopardiani.cce.ufsc.br/edition04/artigos/a-note-on-elegy-and-self-elegy-in-the-canti.php>

—— 'Percorsi di lettura tra *Operette morali* e *Frankenstein*', *Rivista internazionale di studi leopardiani*, 12 (2019), pp. 87–114

Notes to Chapter 1

1. All translations are by Jonathan Galassi, from Giacomo Leopardi, *Canti* (London: Penguin, 2010).
2. These are the *Canti* written between Leopardi's sojourn in Pisa (1828) and his last period of residence in Recanati (end of 1830), formerly known as 'grandi idilli', a definition that has recently been recognised by scholars as being both imprecise, and misleading.
3. From here onwards, 'Ruysch'.
4. From here onwards, 'Coro'.
5. Gilberto Lonardi, 'Il "Coro di morti" nel sistema poetico leopardiano (fra intenzione antica e modello cinquecentesco)', in *Leopardi e la letteratura italiana dal Duecento al Seicento*, Atti del IV convegno internazionale di studi leopardiani, Recanati 13–16 September 1976 (Florence: Olschki, 1978), pp. 655–79.
6. Lonardi uses the term 'crocicchio' [crossroads] to describe this pivotal position of the 'Coro' within the Leopardian poetic universe, in 'Il "Coro di morti" nel sistema poetico leopardiano', p. 655.
7. Massimo Natale, 'Il coro, modo dell'io lirico: fra Manzoni e Leopardi', in *Il curatore ozioso: Forme e funzioni del coro tragico in Italia* (Venice: Marsilio, 2013), pp. 349–73 (p. 359).
8. As well as Lonardi above, see also Natale, 'Il coro, modo dell'io lirico'.
9. Lonardi, 'Il "Coro di morti" nel sistema poetico leopardiano', p. 674.
10. Denise Riley, *Time Lived, Without its Flow*, intro. by Max Porter (London: Picador, 2019).
11. Diana Fuss, *Dying Modern: A Meditation on Elegy* (Durham, NC: Duke University Press, 2013).
12. Franco D'Intino, *La caduta e il ritorno: Cinque movimenti dell'immaginario romantico leopardiano* (Macerata: Quodlibet, 2019).
13. The translations from Leopardi's letters are my own.
14. Giacomo Leopardi, *Zibaldone di pensieri*, ed. by Giuseppe Pacella (Milan: Garzanti, 1991). Translations are drawn from Giacomo Leopardi, *Zibaldone: The Notebooks of Leopardi*, ed. and trans. by Franco D'Intino (London: Penguin, 2013).
15. Giacomo Leopardi, *Ad Angelo Mai, quand'ebbe trovato i libri di Cicerone della Repubblica*, ed. by Pietro Brighenti (Bologna: Marsigli, 1820). My translation.
16. Emanuela Tandello, 'A Note on Elegy and Self-elegy in the *Canti*', in *Appunti leopardiani*, 4:2 (2012), <http://www.appuntileopardiani.cce.ufsc.br/edition04/artigos/a-note-on-elegy-and-self-elegy-in-the-canti.php> [accessed 10 October 2021].
17. Lonardi, 'Il "Coro di morti" nel sistema poetico leopardiano', p. 656.
18. Tandello, 'A Note on Elegy and Self-elegy in the *Canti*'.
19. And eventually, in 'Il tramonto della luna'.
20. Fontenelle's *Eloge de mons. Frederick Ruysch* is given by Leopardi as the original source for the 'Dialogo'.
21. In 1716, Czar Peter I purchased the entire collection for 30,000 Dutch florins; see <http://www.kunstkamera.ru/en/museum/kunst_hist/5/5_2> [accessed 29 July 2019]. See also Dave Mazierski, 'The Cabinet of Federick Ruysch and the Kunstkamera of Peter the Great: Past and Present', *Journal of Biocommunication*, 38 (2012), <www.jbiocommunication.org> [accessed 29 July 2019].
22. Added to the second edition of the *Operette morali* (*seconda edizione con molte aggiunte e correzioni dell'autore, Firenze, presso Guglielmo Piatti, 1834*).
23. See Emanuela Tandello, 'Percorsi di lettura tra *Operette morali* e *Frankenstein*', *Rivista internazionale di studi leopardiani*, 12 (2019), pp. 87–114.
24. Leopardi depicts Ruysch as a kind of sorcerer's apprentice rather than innovator and scientist, spying on his mummies from the keyhole, taking a fright, and threatening to 'kill' them again if they do not stop making a racket in the middle of the night with their 'canzoncina' [cradle song]. Leopardi tackles here the obsession, experienced right across Europe, with the possibility

of restoring life, or indeed recreating it through scientific means. Ruysch was a pioneer of body preservation based on the injection of an embalming fluid that would make the corpse look plump and rosy, like that of a living person. In particular, preservation of body parts served the purpose of making body parts available to anatomists without the risk of them wasting and rotting away, thus allowing the detailed and leisurely study of the human body.

25. Lonardi, 'Il "Coro di morti" nel sistema poetico leopardiano', p. 653.

26. Goffredo Petrassi, *Partita / Divertimento / 4 inni sacri / Coro di morti*, conductor Francesco La Vecchia, performed by Nuovo Coro Lirico Sinfonico Romano and the Orchestra Sinfonica in Rome with Carlo Putelli (tenor) and Davide Malvestio (bass) (Naxos, 2013).

27. 'Sarebbe di una qualche utilità guardare al Coro del Ruysch come al compimento di una linea di coralità deformi o parodiche [...]' [It would be useful to consider the Coro of Ruysch as the completion of a line of deformed and parodic uses of chorality], which the scholar traces back to Aristophanes, Natale, 'Il coro, modo dell'io lirico', p. 360.

28. Robert Pogue Harrison, *The Dominion of the Dead* (Chicago: University of Chicago Press, 2003). Harrison explains: 'A humic foundation is one whose contents have been buried so that they may be reclaimed by the future. The humic holds in its conserving element the unfinished story of what has come to pass. If it is true that we move forward into the future only by retrieving the past, it is because, through burial, we consign the future of our legacies to this humic element, with its vast, diversely populated underworlds' (p. 19).

29. *Chorus of Mummies in Frederick Ruysch's Study*: 'Alone in the world, eternal, toward whom does move | Every created thing, | In you, Death, finds rest | Our naked nature; | Not joyous, but secure | From ancient suffering. Profound | Night in our confused mind | Obscures our grave thought; | Towards hope, desire, the shriveled spirit | Feels it strength wane; | Thus from affliction and from fear is freed | And the empty slow years | Unbored whiles away. | We lived; and as the confused memory | Of a frightening ghost | And of a sweating dream | Wanders in the souls of infants, | So in us remembrance lingers | Of our lives: but far from fear | Is our remembering. What were we? | What was the bitter point called life? | Stupendous mystery is today | Life to our minds, and such | As to the minds of the living | Unknown death appears. As when living | From death it fled, now flees | From vital flame | Our naked nature | Not joyous but secure; | For to be happy | Is denied to mortals and the dead by Fate'; translation by Giovanni Cecchetti, in Giacomo Leopardi, *Operette Morali: Essays and Dialogues*, trans., intro. and notes by Giovanni Cecchetti (Berkeley: University of California Press, 1982), pp. 271–73.

30. Here I dissent from Laura Melosi's suggestion that it is a 'forma aperta'. Laura Melosi, note to 'Dialogo di Federico Ruysch e le sue mummie', in Giacomo Leopardi, *Operette morali*, ed. by Laura Melosi (Milan: Bompiani, 2008), p. 325.

31. '*reversibilità* fra condizione vitale e condizione funeraria'; Natale, 'Il coro, modo dell'io lirico', p. 359.

32. Lonardi speaks of 'effetto di monotonia, tempo fermo o assenza del tempo, riduzione al minimo della vitalità' [an effect of monotony, a *tempus firmus* or lack of time, a reduction of vitality to its minimum degree], in 'Il "Coro di morti" nel sistema poetico leopardiano', p. 657.

33. My translation.

34. Antonella Del Gatto speaks precisely of 'mummificazione' of discourse, in her book *Uno specchio d'acqua diaccia: Sulla struttura dialogico-umoristica del testo leopardiano: dalle 'Operette morali' ai 'Canti' pisano-recanatesi* (Florence: Cesati, 2001), p. 168.

35. D'Intino, *La caduta e il ritorno*, p. 291.

36. Riley, *Time Lived, Without its Flow*, p. 15.

37. Ibid., p.16

38. Ibid., p. 59.

39. Ibid., p. 67.

40. Ibid., p. 16.

41. Max Porter, Introduction to Riley, *Time Lived, Without its Flow*, p. 5.

42. Jonathan Culler, *Theory of the Lyric* (Cambridge, MA: Harvard University Press, 2015), p. 227.

43. It was not meant to last, as the final *canto* 'Il tramonto della luna' [The Setting of the Moon] testifies.

44. I am adopting here Natale's own formula of the chorus as a 'mode' for the lyric self, in 'Il coro, modo dell'io lirico', p. 349.
45. Lonardi, 'Il "Coro di morti" nel sistema poetico leopardiano', p. 666.
46. Natale, 'Il coro, modo dell'io lirico', p. 350.
47. Ibid., p. 349.
48. Fuss, *Dying Modern*, p. 44.
49. Ibid., p. 44.
50. Ibid., p. 44.
51. Colin Davis, 'Can the Dead Speak to Us? De Man, Levinas and Agamben', *Culture, Theory and Critique*, 45:1 (2004), 77–89 (p. 79).
52. Fuss, *Dying Modern*, p. 42.
53. Culler, *Theory of the Lyric*, p. 227.
54. D'Intino, *La caduta e il ritorno*, p. 319.
55. Ibid., p. 319.
56. Giovanni Nencioni, 'Antropologia poetica?', *Strumenti critici*, 19 (1972), 243–58; now in *Tra grammatica e retorica* (Turin: Einaudi, 1983), pp. 161–75.

CHAPTER 2

❖

Carlotta's Ghost

Fabio Camilletti

Guido Gozzano wrote 'L'esperimento' [The Experiment] in 1908, published it in 1909 in the periodical *Il Viandante* [The Wanderer], and then revised it in 1911 for the magazine *La donna* [The Woman].[1] The poem was meant to be a sequel and a parody to his most famous 'L'amica di nonna Speranza' [Grandmother Speranza's Friend], which had appeared in 1907.[2] In both texts, the poetic subject tries to establish a contact with his grandmother's schoolfriend Carlotta Capenna, who had lived in the 1850s, before being forced to admit that the past is lost forever. Both poems, therefore, display a process of mourning, which refers both to Carlotta and to the age she epitomises — the Romantic generation and its illusion, its ideals, and even its bad taste. Still, they exhibit quite different strategies, and would meet different fates.

'L'amica di nonna Speranza', one of the most famous poems of twentieth-century Italian literature, moves from the tangible experience of grandmother Speranza's parlour room in order to unbridle a chain of free associations, bringing the poetic subject to experience the mid-nineteenth century in an almost physical way, as if in a sort of psychometric incident ('il cúcu dell'ore che canta, le sedie parate a damasco | chermisi... rinasco, rinasco del mille ottocento cinquanta!', ll. 13–14) [the singing cuckoo clock, the chairs clothed in crimson damask... I return, I return to 1850].[3] The enumeration of 'obsolete objects' outlined in the first stanzas enables him to visualise the room at the times of the 'zii molto dabbene' (l. 73) [most respectable uncle and aunt], before shifting to the conversations of Carlotta and Speranza and, finally, to the album of photos that has plausibly inspired the whole imagining fantasy.[4] Here, we behold a photo of Carlotta as well as a very precise date. The enthralling power of the image goes in parallel with the historicisation of the scene it depicts, and therefore, implicitly, with the awareness of its absence, following a connection between photography and loss that characterises the new medium since its invention.[5] That of Speranza and Carlotta is fully, from this viewpoint, a present perfect — a past that can be remembered or reconstructed, which does not cease to hold its power into the present, yet which remains past (that is to say, dead) nonetheless.[6]

Ti fisso nell'albo con tanta tristezza, ov'è di tuo pugno
la data: vent'otto di Giugno del mille ottocento cinquanta.
Stai come rapita in un cantico; lo sguardo al cielo profondo,
e l'indice al labbro, secondo l'atteggiamento romantico.
Quel giorno — malinconia! — vestivi un abito rosa
per farti — novissima cosa! — ritrarre in fotografia...

Ma te non rivedo nel fiore, o amica di Nonna! Ove sei
o sola che — forse — potrei amare, amare d'amore? (ll. 102–09)

[So sadly, I behold you in the album, with the date written by your hand: twenty-eighth of June, 1850. You look as if enraptured in a canticle: your gaze towards the deep sky, the forefinger on your lip in the Romantic fashion. On that day — so melancholy! — you wore a pink dress, in order — what a most novel thing! — to be portrayed in a photograph... And yet I do not see you in your bloom, o grandma's friend! Where are you, the only one I could perchance love, love of true love?]

'L'esperimento' too opens with a citation of Carlotta's name in its material concreteness as a grapheme:

'Carlotta'... Vedo il nome che sussurro
scritto in oro, in corsivo, a mezzo un fregio
ovale, sui volumi di collegio
d'un tempo, rilegati in cuoio azzurro... (ll. 1–4)

['Carlotta'... I see the name I whisper written in gold, in cursive, within an oval tailpiece, on the college books of long ago, bound in blue leather...]

Similarly, the setting is the 'salone ove par morto da poco | il riso di Carlotta' (ll. 5–6) [dining room where Carlotta's smile seems just to be dead]. Here, a far more literal conjuration will take place, this time by the means of an intermediary (a medium?). An otherwise unnamed lover will have to perform Carlotta, disguising herself in mid-nineteenth century clothing, singing a song that might be popular in 1850, and offering herself on the sofa, thereby giving concreteness to the subject's phantasms: 'pel mio rimpianto voglio che tu finga | una commedia: tu sarai Carlotta' (ll. 11–12) [for my regret, I want you to stage a piece: you will be Carlotta]. The 'piece', however, cannot resist the impact of truth: in the moment of sexualisation ('Alterno, amica, un bacio ad ogni grido | della tua gola nuda e palpitante', ll. 85–86 [I alternate, my friend, a kiss with every moan of your naked, beating throat]), the subject understands the illusory nature of Carlotta's phantasm (or ghost?).

Carlotta non è più! Commedïante
del mio sognare fanciullesco, rido!
Rido! Perdona il riso che mi tiene,
Mentre mi baci con pupille fisse...
Rido! Se qui, se qui ricomparisse
lo Zio con la Zia molto dabbene!
Vesti la gonna, pettina le chiome,
Riponi i falbalà nel canterano.
Commediante del tempo lontano,
di Carlotta non resta altro che il nome. (ll. 87–96)

[Carlotta is no more! O actress, I laugh of my childish dream! I laugh! Please pardon my persistent laugh while you kiss me with your fixed eyes... I laugh! What if, what if there would reappear here my most respectable Uncle with my Aunt! Put on your skirt, comb your hair, put the falbala back in the commode. You who are acting some long-gone time, only Carlotta's name now remains]

In a circular way, the poem closes with the same quatrain as that it opened with:

> Il nome!... Vedo il nome che sussurro,
> scritto in oro, in corsivo, a mezzo un fregio
> ovale, sui volumi di collegio
> d'un tempo, rilegati in cuoio azzurro... (ll. 1–4)

[The Name!... I see the name I whisper written in gold, in cursive, within an oval tailpiece, on the college books of long ago, bound in blue leather...]

It may be worth noticing that Gozzano was not satisfied with 'L'esperimento'. On 15 January 1908 he wrote to Carlo Vallini:

> Ho abbozzato una stiticissima poesia su Carlotta Capenna, dove finisco per chiavare la medesima sul divano chermisi, ma non riesco a partire dalla paura che entrino da un momento all'altro li zii molto dabbene... L'idea, come vedi, è sublime: ma non ho saputo ridurla in bei versi e ne sono contrariatissimo.[7]

[I sketched a most stingy poem about Carlotta Capenna, where I end up by fucking the aforementioned on the crimson sofa, and still I cannot refrain from fearing that the most respectable uncle and aunt may appear at any moment... It is a sublime idea, you see: but I couldn't reduce it into beautiful lines, and I am most annoyed]

The incongruous coarseness of such verb as 'chiavare' is revealing, inasmuch as it is the substantial misrepresentation of the poem's subject matter as outlined here. On the one hand, the subject's intercourse with his mistress is not interrupted by the fear of the aunt and uncle, but rather stems from a sudden perception that Carlotta has vanished ('Carlotta non è più'); on the other, it is very telling that, in the letter to Vallini, there is no mention of any mistress at all, and Gozzano describes himself (in person) in the act of 'chiavare' Carlotta Capenna (in person). In other words, the letter reiterates the identification that is denied in the poem: at the same time, 'sublime' as the poem's subject might be, it is difficult not to equalise the *sexual* impotence of Gozzano the subject on the sofa and the *textual* impotence of Gozzano the poet in rendering such a situation 'in bei versi' [beautiful lines]. The coitus interruptus with Carlotta Capenna, therefore, reverberates in an equally 'interrupted' poem, whose potential cannot be brought to full maturation: both the sexual and the textual spheres testify to the impossibility of possessing Carlotta's ghost, being a way (albeit a trivial one) of coping with her loss.

One problem emerges here for our consideration. Is Carlotta actually lost? Roughly speaking, in order for loss to be experienced, there must have been some kind of possession. This self-evident consideration underlies the psychoanalytic distinction between mourning and melancholia. As 'two conditions' whose 'correlation [...] seems justified by the general picture', mourning (*Trauer*) and melancholia are primarily defined in relation to loss, and as two ways — as

Sigmund Freud put it in 1917 — of 'react[ing] to the loss of a loved person, or to the loss of some abstraction which has taken the place of one'.[8] The difference between the two conditions lies in the perception, from the subject's viewpoint, of what has been lost. Whereas mourning reacts to (and works through) the loss of an object that is perfectly identifiable by the subject who mourns it, the melancholy, Julia Kristeva writes, 'has the impression of having been deprived of an unnameable, supreme good, of something unrepresentable, that perhaps only devouring might represent, or an *invocation* might point out, but no word could signify'.[9] As a consequence, as Giorgio Agamben points out, 'with respect to the genetic process of mourning, melancholia presents a relationship to its origin that is especially difficult to explain. [...] although mourning follows a loss that has really occurred, in melancholia not only it is unclear what object has been lost, it is uncertain that one can speak of a loss at all'.[10]

Both conditions presuppose, however, an element in common: that the lost object, albeit unacknowledged as such, was once known by the subject. In other words, the mourning or melancholic subject would suffer from their own loss: of something they once owned, of which they have been deprived. But what if the loss was someone else's, and the subject mourned or melancholically beheld something that could not ever possibly be theirs?

The problem has been addressed from different angles, and principally by the psychoanalytic theory of Nicolas Abraham and Maria Torok. Through their analysis of the Freudian case of the 'Wolf Man', initially published in French in 1976, and later in the essays collected in *L'Écorce et le noyau* [The Shell and the Kernel] (first edition in 1978), Abraham and Torok developed the concept of the 'phantom' (*fantôme*), distinguished from the *fantasme* of Lacanian psychoanalysis. Unlike the latter, partially translating the Freudian notion of *Phantasie*, the *fantôme* denotes 'the gaps left within us by the secrets of others', normally parents or grandparents:

> Since the phantom is not related to the loss of an object of love, it cannot be considered the effect of unsuccessful mourning, as would be the case with melancholics or with all those who carry a tomb in themselves. It is the children's or descendants' lot to objectify these buried tombs through diverse species of ghosts. What comes back to haunt are the tombs of others. The phantoms of folklore merely objectify a metaphor active in the unconscious: the burial of an unspeakable fact *within the love-object*.[11]

From this viewpoint, the phantom haunts in that it stems from a process of mourning that remains, by definition, impossible to be worked through: for those who are haunted by 'the tombs of others' inherit the symptom without the associations that are attached to it, and which are the sole means to unpack it through the process of analysis. It is no coincidence that Abraham's and Torok's work caught the attention of Jacques Derrida, who in 1976 wrote a long preface to their book on the Wolf Man,[12] triggering a reflection on spectrality that would lead, in 1993, to *Spectres de Marx* and the coinage of the notion of 'hauntology'.[13] Tellingly, the subtitle of Derrida's book is *The State of the Debt, the Work of Mourning, and the New International*: the phantom/spectre, in Derrida's terms, is not (only) the haunting remnant of some past trauma, but principally the mourning for a loss one cannot account for, if not for the fact that the unknown, lost object is perceived as a gap in the potential of the present.

Such consideration, I believe, is particularly valid for Gozzano, whose poetic and prose work seems to be dominated by one single, obsessive image: the shadow of nineteenth-century Turin, an unreal realm that he could not know in person (Gozzano was born in 1883) and which, as Edoardo Sanguineti puts it, can only be recuperated 'per via di fantasia, di sogno' [by means of imagination and dream].[14] Significantly, when defining the power of such image, Sanguineti recurs to oxymora that evoke the duplicity of the Freudian uncanny: Gozzano's conjuration of the past is a 'incubo gradevole' [pleasing nightmare], enabling the poetic subject to go up the flow of time and communicate with the dead.[15] From this viewpoint, the return of the past as outlined in Gozzano's oeuvre is fully a phantasmal return of something dead, haunting someone who has not experienced its loss (and, we may add, *precisely* because of it). As I will explain in the following, in the poems relating to Carlotta Capenna, the past is, at the same time, a *fantasme* of desire, a *fantôme* of the beyond, and a *spectre* of a disappeared world, which does not cease to return in a 'hauntological' way.

Fantasme: both 'L'amica di nonna Speranza' and 'L'esperimento' describe a process of intentional self-deception, by which the subject imagines, conjures, and beholds a scene from 1850. There, and there only, his desire can be fulfilled ('L'amica di nonna Speranza', ll. 108–09: 'Ma te non rivedo nel fuore, o amica di Nonna! Ove sei | o *sola* che — forse — potrei amare, amare d'amore?', my emphasis). As such, they both fall within the category defined by Freud as *Phantasie*: normally translated as 'fantasy' or 'phantasy', but more correctly meaning 'daydreaming', *Phantasie* has the specific function, in Freudian theory, of creating a setting in which desire — exactly as happens in dreams — can be fulfilled.[16] However, as Jean Laplanche and Jean-Bertrand Pontalis highlight, fantasy in itself is not the object of desire: 'in fantasy the subject does not pursue the object or its sign', but rather 'he appears caught up himself in the sequence of images'.[17] As a consequence, 'the subject, although always present in the fantasy, may be so in a desubjectivised form — that is to say, in the very syntax of the sequence in question', so that if 'desire is not purely an upsurge of the drives, but is articulated into the fantasy', fantasy happens to be 'a favoured spot for the most primitive defensive reactions, such as turning against oneself, or into an opposite, projection, negation'.[18] The impasse of desire as described in 'L'esperimento' appears, from this viewpoint, to be particularly telling. Rather than being the unexpected interruption of the phantasmatised intercourse with the medium/Carlotta, the impossibility of coitus underlies the whole fantasy, revealing itself to be a fantasy of castration. As Jacques Lacan reminds us, *Phantasie* (which he translates as *fantasme*) has primarily a protective function: Lacan, Dylan Evans writes, 'compares the fantasy scene to a frozen image on a cinema screen; just as the film may be stopped at a certain point in order to avoid showing a traumatic scene which follows, so also the fantasy scene is a defence which veils castration. The fantasy is thus characterised by a fixed and immobile quality'.[19] In

'L'esperimento', the past, no matter how vividly conjured it may be, reveals itself to be ultimately stranger and alien to the subject. As a consequence, it remains fixed and inaccessible as a cinema screen or a phantasmagoria slide, and communication with Carlotta appears to be castrated from the beginning.

At the same time, as a 'femme de l'au-delà' [woman of the beyond],[20] Carlotta is fully a *fantôme* — both literally and metaphorically. Both 'L'amica di nonna Speranza' and 'L'esperimento' describe a conjuration that comes tellingly close to the evocations of spiritualist séances. Both take place in a parlour room, a convivial space that holds, from the second half of the nineteenth century to the first half of the twentieth, specific connotations. As Bruno Capaci reminds us, the period between the *fin de siècle* and the interwar years, the parlour is, among other things, the place where spiritualist séances are held. As such it is the setting for the two most famous séances in Italian literature: at the Paleari house in Luigi Pirandello's *Il fu Mattia Pascal* (1904), and at the Malfenti house in Italo Svevo's *La coscienza di Zeno* (1923).[21] As the space where family memory is preserved in a tangible form — through the kitsch of travel souvenirs, or the photos of the dead — the parlour is a liminal space between past and present, enabling intergenerational communication. In both poems, the object triggering the conjuration is a photo album. Photos and daguerreotypes are a constant presence in Gozzano's oeuvre, and are normally connected to erotic desire (for example in the ghost stories 'Novella romantica' [Romantic Tale] and 'Un sogno' [A Dream]).[22] The history of photography, however, has strong connections with the metamorphoses undergone by the idea of death throughout the nineteenth century. By creating a liminal space between reality and mimesis, Daguerre's creation — as will happen later with Edison's phonographs[23] — captures Victorian concerns for continuity between life and the hereafter, giving birth to a multifaceted use of daguerreotypes as a means of survival, and often crossing pathways with the Spiritualist movement (whose origins date two years before the year 1850 in which Gozzano's fantasy is set).[24] As two girls of 1850, Speranza and Carlotta cannot help but recall Kate and Maggie Fox, the two American teenage sisters who in 1848 had 'invented' modern spiritualism by attempting to communicate with a spirit by means of raps.[25] Most of all, whereas 'L'amica di nonna Speranza' describes (as we have seen) an experience that comes close to the psychic one of psychometry, 'L'esperimento' outlines a series of ritual gestures that seem to be a prelude to a veritable evocation. While the woman's voice starts singing a ballad that used to be 'dolce a Carlotta, sessant'anni fa' (l. 36) [pleasing to Carlotta, sixty years ago], all of a sudden 'Carlotta appare' (l. 54) [Carlotta appears]: the 'fantasma vano' [vain ghost] gains in corporeal concreteness 'qui dove in sogno già ti vidi e udii' (ll. 57–58) [here where I already saw and heard you]. In other words, like the mediums of Spiritualism, the 'commediante' (l. 30) [actress], once introduced in the parlour, mutates her voice, and transforms herself into Carlotta. Moreover, the *cantata* she sings is Giovanni Prati's poem *Convegno degli spiriti*, the story of two spectral lovers who are doomed forever to bid each other 'il tormentoso addio' [the excruciating farewell], rather than enjoy together the glory of Heaven.[26] Such a choice, other than homage paid to the literary bad taste of 1850, is also, perhaps, a cryptic reference to the fate of the poetic subject and of Carlotta, divided by the barriers of time. At the same time, it is a textual clue enabling us to read, beneath the ironic tone of the poem, a reference to the semantic sphere of spectrality and of the ghostly survival of the past.

Finally, Carlotta is a phantom in that she exists merely as a gap in the emotional potential of the present. Never having been technically lost, if not for the simple fact that the subject never had the opportunity to possess her, she may be present, poetically and phantasmatically, only insofar as she is absent. By relying on the repertoire of courtly love — in Lacan's terms, the interplay of those 'detours and obstacles' that are erected 'in opposition to the purposes of the pleasure principle', and resulting in 'techniques of holding back, of suspension, of *amor interruptus*'[27] — these poems expose the phantasmal nature of love, so to say, degree zero. But whereas the courtly love tradition erected obstacles of social or geographical nature — a husband, the community of gossipy courtiers, the distance of *amor de lonh* — the barrier here is the most unsurmountable one, that of time. Carlotta's realm is an 'absolute, inscrutable Otherness' not because of 'her uncanny, monstrous character [as] the Other which is not our "fellow-creature"':[28] Carlotta is instead a remarkably familiar figure — a host of the family — that time and history have made distant and unreachable.

Such contiguity — both social and spatial — between Carlotta's 1850 and the poetic subject, underlies the third aspect by which the past manifests itself in the poems: its *spectral* nature, which endows these poems with a peculiarly hauntological value. The object of the subject's mourning without loss is not only Carlotta: it is the Italy of 1850 — or, rather, its aura, with all the resonances endowed to this term by Walter Benjamin's thought. It is no coincidence that 'L'amica di nonna Speranza' opens with the famed enumeration of the parlour's kitschy furnishings, or that 'L'esperimento' includes a detailed description of a 'collana di città' (a necklace made of miniatures of Italian cities), by which the subject recapitulates a nostalgic psychogeography of the Risorgimento:

> Oh! La collana di città! Viaggio
> lungo la filza grave di musaici:
> dolce seguire i panorami arcaici,
> far con le labra tal pellegrinaggio!
> Come sussulta al ritmo del tuo fiato
> Piazza San Marco e al ritmo d'una vena
> come sussulta la città di Siena...
> Pisa...Firenze... tutto il Gran Ducato!
> Seguo tra i baci molte meraviglie,
> colonne mozze, golfi sorridenti:
> Castellamare... Napoli... Girgenti...
> Tutto il Reame delle Due Sicilie!
> Dolce tentare l'ultime che tieni
> Chiuse tra i seni piccole cornici:
> Roma papale! Palpita tra i seni
> la Roma degli Stati Pontifici! (ll. 69–84)

[Oh! The cities' necklace! I travel across the whole series of thick mosaics: it is sweet to follow these ancient landscapes, and to make such a pilgrimage with my lips! How the Piazza San Marco shakes at the rhythm of your breath, and how the city of Siena leaps at the rhythm of a vein... Pisa... Firenze... the whole Grand Duchy of Tuscany! So many marvels I follow with my kisses, broken columns, smiling gulfs: Castellamare... Naples... Agrigento... the whole Kingdom of the Two Sicilies! And sweet it is to force the small frames you keep in the end enclosed within your breasts: the Pope's Rome! There beats, between your breasts, the Rome of the Papal States!]

And so in both poems, the tactile experience of objects allows an illusory phantasmagoria to be created, lending the past fleeting concreteness: the aura of the age that dissolved the aura by means of technical reproduction not incidentally, 'L'amica di nonna Speranza' derives from a photo, which in 1850 was a 'novissima cosa' [the newest invention] (l. 107) — something which could be captured, and made an object of knowledge, only through the spectral value of its bric-à-brac. The purpose of such knowledge, however, is not historical, but rather hauntological: the world of 1850 — Mazzini, Verdi, *Le ultime lettere di Jacopo Ortis* [The Last Letters of Jacopo Ortis], the King of Sardinia — is only evoked in that its loss is perceived as a vacuum in the loss of ideals and illusions of the present. Both poems are very explicit in this respect, and 'L'amica di nonna Speranza' strongly underlies the fact that the past is not beholden as it was, but through the self-consciousness of the present:

> Romantica Luna fra un nimbo leggero, che baci le chiome
> dei pioppi arcata siccome un sopracciglio di bimbo,
> il sogno di tutto un passato nella tua curva s'accampa:
> non sorta sei da una stampa del Novelliere Illustrato? (ll. 84–87)

[Romantic Moon in a light cloud, who kisses the crowns of the poplars like a child's eyebrow, the dream of an entire past age is encamped in your curve: did you rise from an engraving of the *Novelliere illustrato*?]

As mentioned above, both 'L'amica di nonna Speranza' and 'L'esperimento' end with the image of the photo album: 'di Carlotta non resta altro che il nome' ('L'esperimento', l. 96). An inescapable conclusion, if we consider how the attempted operation was intimately paradoxical. An object of possession as a living creature and at the same time excluded from possession as a sign, the lover/medium remains ungraspable. The fictionality of the whole operation is pitilessly revealed, a fictive mourning pursued through a careful exercise in self-deception.

Hence, what Pierre Klossowski would call the subject's 'cursed virility' (*virilité maudite*) is doomed to express itself only in the incessant, inescapable loss of its object.[29] This loss is due on the one hand to the intrinsic paradox underlying the practice of courtly love itself, and, on the other, to the impossibility of signifying, and therefore of working through, the mourning for something one has not known, and which perhaps never existed as such (Carlotta, the Savoy and liberal dream of Italy, the Romantic generation...). It is thus, most of all, a text that cannot but bear the stigmata of such an impasse: the idea of mourning the loss of a fake

Risorgimento through the conjuring of a fake Carlotta and the consummation of a fake engagement, may well have been sublime, but a 'bad' poem — or, at least, one disowned by its author as such — is all we might expect, and is perhaps quite appropriate as an outcome.

Bibliography

ABRAHAM, NICOLAS, 'Notes on the Phantom: A Complement to Freud's Metapsychology' (1975), in Nicolas Abraham and Maria Torok, *The Shell and the Kernel. Renewals of Psychoanalysis*, ed. and trans. by Nicholas T. Rand (Chicago: The University of Chicago Press, 1994), pp. 171–76

——, and MARIA TOROK, *The Wolf Man's Magic Word: A Cryptonymy*, trans. by Nicholas Rand (Minneapolis: University of Minnesota Press, 1986)

AGAMBEN, GIORGIO, *Stanzas: Word and Phantasm in Western Culture*, trans. by Ronald L. Martinez (Minneapolis: University of Minnesota Press, 1993)

CAMILLETTI, FABIO, 'Present Perfect: Time and the Uncanny in American Science and Horror Fiction of the 1970s (Finney, Matheson, King)', *Image and Narrative*, 11:3 (2010), 25–41

CAPACI, BRUNO, 'Salotto', in *Luoghi della letteratura italiana*, ed. by Gian Mario Anselmi and Gino Ruozzi (Milan: Bruno Mondadori 2003), pp. 319–29

DAVIS, COLIN, *Haunted Subjects: Deconstruction, Psychoanalysis and the Return of the Dead* (Basingstoke: Palgrave Macmillan, 2007)

DERRIDA, JACQUES, 'Foreword: Fors: The Anglish Words of Nicolas Abraham and Maria Torok', in Nicolas Abraham and Maria Torok, *The Wolf Man's Magic Word: A Cryptonymy*, trans. by Nicholas Rand (Minneapolis: University of Minnesota Press, 1986), pp. xi–xlviii

DOUGLAS-FAIRHURST, ROBERT, *Victorian Afterlives: The Shaping of Influence in Nineteenth-Century Literature* (Oxford: Oxford University Press, 2002)

EVANS, DYLAN, *An Introductory Dictionary of Lacanian Psychoanalysis* (London: Routledge, 1996)

FREUD, SIGMUND, 'Mourning and Melancholia' (1917), in Id., *The Standard Edition of the Complete Psychological Works*, ed. and trans. by James Strachey, 24 vols (London: The Hogarth Press), XIV, pp. 243–58

GOZZANO, GUIDO, *Poesie*, ed. by Edoardo Sanguineti (Turin: Einaudi, 1973)

—— *Tutte le poesie*, ed. by Andrea Rocca (Milan: Mondadori 1980)

HARVEY, JOHN, *Photography and Spirit* (London: Reaktion Books, 2007)

KLOSSOWSKI, PIERRE, *Sade My Neighbour*, trans. by Alphonso Lingis (Noyes St. Evanston: Northwestern University Press, 1991)

KRISTEVA, JULIA, *Black Sun: Depression and Melancholia*, trans. by Leon S. Roudiez (New York: Columbia University Press, 1989)

LACAN, JACQUES, 'Jeunesse de Gide ou la lettre et le désir' (1958), in *Écrits* (Paris: Seuil, 1966), pp. 739–64

—— *Le Séminaire. Livre XIV, La logique du fantasme, 1966–1976* (unpublished)

—— 'The Youth of Gide, or the Letter and Desire', in Id., *Écrits*, trans. by Bruce Fink with Héloïse Fink and Russell Grigg (New York: Norton, 2006), pp. 623–44

—— *The Seminar Book VII: The Ethics of Psychoanalysis 1959–1960*, ed. by Jacques-Alain Miller, trans. by Dennis Porter (New York: Norton, 1997)

LAPLANCHE, JEAN, and JEAN-BERTRAND PONTALIS, 'Fantasy and the Origins of Sexuality', in *Formations of Fantasy*, ed. by Victor Burgin, James Donald, and Cora Kaplan (London: Routledge, 1986), pp. 5–34

——— *The Language of Psychoanalysis*, trans. by Donald Nicholson-Smith (London: The Hogarth Press, 1973)

ORLANDO, FRANCESCO, *Obsolete Objects in the Literary Imagination: Ruins, Relics, Rarities, Rubbish, Uninhabited Places, and Hidden Treasures*, trans. by Gabriel Pihas and Daniel Seidel with Alessandra Grego (New Haven: Yale University Press, 2006)

PRATI, GIOVANNI, *Opere edite e inedite*, 4 vols (Milan: Casa Editrice Italiana, 1862), I, pp. 263–67

SANGUINETI, EDOARDO, '"Torino d'altri tempi"', in Id., *Guido Gozzano. Indagini e letture* (Turin: Einaudi, 1973), pp. 13–26

STÄUBLE, ANTONIO, *Sincerità e artificio in Gozzano* (Ravenna: Longo, 1972)

WEISBERG, BARBARA, *Talking to the Dead: Kate and Maggie Fox and the Rise of Spiritualism* (New York: HarperCollins, 2004), Kindle edn.

ŽIŽEK, SLAVOJ, 'Courtly Love, or, Woman as Thing', in Id., *The Metastases of Enjoyment: Six Essays on Woman and Causality* (London: Verso, 1994), pp. 89–116

Notes to Chapter 2

1. All English translations are my own.

2. 'L'amica di nonna Speranza': I quote from the text as included in *I Colloqui* [The Talks] (1911): the poem, however, had already appeared in *La via del rifugio* [The Way to the Refuge] (1907) and, even before, in the magazine *La donna* (1907). I cite from the edition Guido Gozzano, *Poesie*, ed. by Edoardo Sanguineti (Turin: Einaudi, 1973) pp. 155–64 (see pp. 31–36 for the version included in *La via del rifugio*). 'L'esperimento': I quote from ivi, pp. 348–52. It should be added that Sanguineti's edition does not testify to the text's troubled history, and includes textual variants that have been arbitrarily introduced after Gozzano's death. See Andrea Rocca's note to the text in Guido Gozzano, *Tutte le poesie*, ed. by Andrea Rocca (Milan: Mondadori 1980), pp. 746–48.

3. Psychometry was a branch of psychical research that was very popular in Gozzano's time. The term had been coined in 1849 by American MD Joseph Rhodes Buchanan and had been popularised in 1863 by geologist and naturalist William Denton. Psychometry enables the psychic to relive a scene of the past by merely touching an object that has 'witnessed' the events in question. In Gozzano's time, psychometry-related questions were common for Italian psychical research, including Enrico Morselli and Ernesto Bozzano (who published his essay *Gli enigmi della psicometria* [The Psychometry's Riddles] between 1920 and 1921 in the periodical *Luce e Ombra* [Light and Shadow]).

4. For the notion of 'obsolete objects' I refer to Francesco Orlando, *Obsolete Objects in the Literary Imagination: Ruins, Relics, Rarities, Rubbish, Uninhabited Places, and Hidden Treasures*, trans. by Gabriel Pihas and Daniel Seidel with Alessandra Grego (New Haven: Yale University Press, 2006). 'L'amica di nonna Speranza' is, not incidentally, one of Orlando's initial examples (pp. 21–23).

5. In the following chapter, Francesco Giusti discusses the role played by photographs in Roland Barthes's mourning for his mother and the theoretical reflections triggered by them, as exposed in *La Chambre Claire* [Camera Lucida] (1980). We may add, here, that Barthes's attraction for his mother's childhood photos exposes an attitude that is similar to Gozzano's — the wish of living a time preceding one's own birth, with all the Oedipal resonances that might not be obvious in 1907, but certainly were in 1980 (without the need of recurring to a 'friend' of one's 'grandmother').

6. On this point see Fabio Camilletti, 'Present Perfect: Time and the Uncanny in American Science and Horror Fiction of the 1970s (Finney, Matheson, King)', *Image and Narrative*, 11:3 (2010), 25–41. Orlando raises a similar point: 'the choice of grandma's day was not made at random. Fifty or sixty years — the space of two generations — are as far back as an individual can go to summon up a still concrete image through family memories' (as quoted in Orlando, *Obsolete Objects in the Literary Imagination*, p. 22).

7. Cit. in Gozzano, *Poesie*, ed. Sanguineti, *ad loc.*

8. Sigmund Freud, 'Mourning and Melancholia' (1917), in Id., *The Standard Edition of the Complete Psychological Works*, ed. and trans. by James Strachey, 24 vols (London: The Hogarth Press), XIV, pp. 243–58 (p. 243).

9. Julia Kristeva, *Black Sun: Depression and Melancholia*, trans. by Leon S. Roudiez (New York: Columbia University Press, 1989), p. 13.

10. Giorgio Agamben, *Stanzas: Word and Phantasm in Western Culture*, trans. by Ronald L. Martinez (Minneapolis: University of Minnesota Press, 1993), p. 20.

11. Nicolas Abraham, 'Notes on the Phantom: A Complement to Freud's Metapsychology' (1975), in Nicolas Abraham and Maria Torok, *The Shell and the Kernel: Renewals of Psychoanalysis*, ed. and trans. by Nicholas T. Rand (Chicago: The University of Chicago Press, 1994), pp. 171–76 (pp. 171–72). Abraham's and Torok's work on the Wolf Man is collected in their *The Wolf Man's Magic Word: A Cryptonymy*, trans. by Nicholas Rand (Minneapolis: University of Minnesota Press, 1986), with a foreword by Jacques Derrida.

12. Jacques Derrida, 'Foreword: *Fors*: The Anglish Words of Nicolas Abraham and Maria Torok', in Abraham and Torok, *The Wolf Man's Magic Word*, pp. xi–xlviii.

13. Derrida's 'hauntology has virtually removed Abraham and Torok from the agenda of literary ghost studies; or to be more precise, when Abraham and Torok are now discussed by deconstructive-minded critics their work is most frequently given a distinctly Derridean inflection'. Colin Davis, *Haunted Subjects. Deconstruction, Psychoanalysis, and the Return of the Dead* (Basingstoke: Palgrave Macmillan, 2007), pp. 9–10.

14. Edoardo Sanguineti, '"Torino d'altri tempi"', in Id., *Guido Gozzano: Indagini e letture* (Turin: Einaudi, 1973), pp. 13–26 (p. 17).

15. Ibid., p. 18.

16. 'Imaginary scene in which the subject is a protagonist, representing the fulfilment of a wish (in the last analysis, an unconscious wish) in a manner that is distorted to a greater or lesser extent by defensive processes'; Jean Laplanche and Jean-Bertrand Pontalis, *The Language of Psychoanalysis*, trans. by Donald Nicholson-Smith (London: The Hogarth Press, 1973), *ad voc.* 'Phantasy'.

17. Jean Laplanche and Jean-Bertrand Pontalis, 'Fantasy and the Origins of Sexuality', in *Formations of Fantasy*, ed. by Victor Burgin, James Donald, and Cora Kaplan (London: Routledge, 1986), pp. 5–34 (p. 26).

18. Ibid., pp. 26–27.

19. Dylan Evans, *An Introductory Dictionary of Lacanian Psychoanalysis* (London: Routledge, 1996), p. 61. Lacan elaborates the notion of *fantasme* from the late 1950s, and devotes to it the seminar of 1966–67, *La logique du fantasme* [The Phantasm's Logic]. To date, there is no critical edition of this seminar.

20. Jacques Lacan, 'The Youth of Gide, or the Letter and Desire', in Id., *Écrits*, trans. by Bruce Fink with Héloïse Fink and Russell Grigg (New York: Norton, 2006), pp. 623–44 (p. 635); 'Jeunesse de Gide ou la lettre et le désir' (1958), in *Écrits* (Paris: Seuil, 1966), pp. 739–64 (p. 755).

21. Bruno Capaci, 'Salotto', in *Luoghi della letteratura italiana*, ed. by Gian Mario Anselmi and Gino Ruozzi (Milan: Bruno Mondadori 2003), pp. 319–29.

22. Antonio Stäuble, *Sincerità e artificio in Gozzano* (Ravenna: Longo, 1972), pp. 73–79.

23. See Robert Douglas-Fairhurst, *Victorian Afterlives: The Shaping of Influence in Nineteenth-Century Literature* (Oxford: Oxford University Press, 2002), pp. 5–6.

24. On the relationship between photography and Spiritualism see John Harvey, *Photography and Spirit* (London: Reaktion Books, 2007).

25. See Barbara Weisberg, *Talking to the Dead: Kate and Maggie Fox and the Rise of Spiritualism* (New York: HarperCollins, 2004), Kindle edn.

26. In Giovanni Prati, *Opere edite e inedite*, 4 vols (Milan: Casa Editrice Italiana, 1862), I, pp. 263–67.

27. Jacques Lacan, *The Seminar Book VII: The Ethics of Psychoanalysis 1959–1960*, ed. by Jacques-Alain Miller, trans. by Dennis Porter (New York: Norton, 1997), p. 152.

28. Slavoj Žižek, 'Courtly Love, or, Woman as Thing', in Id., *The Metastases of Enjoyment. Six Essays on Woman and Causality* (London and New York, NY: Verso, 1994), pp. 89–116 (p. 90).

29. Klossowski introduces this notion in relation to Sade, see Pierre Klossowski, *Sade My Neighbour*, trans. by Alphonso Lingis (Noyes St. Evanston, IL: Northwestern University Press, 1991).

CHAPTER 3

❖

Mourning Over Her Image: The Re-enactment of Lyric Gestures in Giorgio Caproni's 'Versi livornesi'

Francesco Giusti

1. Digging up the 'seed of weeping'

According to later discussions and revisions of the pattern illustrated by Sigmund Freud in his 1917 essay *Trauer und Melancholie* [Mourning and Melancholia],[1] 'healthy' or 'successful' mourning cannot be so easily conceived as a single prescriptive and teleological procedure. Nonetheless, it seems that a set of transhistorically recognisable *gestures* can be detected in different literary presentations of experiences of bereavement, at least as long as the cultural practices of a certain tradition maintain a degree of continuity through the centuries. As far as the practice of lyric poetry is concerned (let us take the notion of 'lyric' as a given for now), the praise of the dead beloved, the evocation of their presence, and the apostrophe to them are a few gestures that come immediately to mind for their evident recurrence throughout the Western tradition.

In this context, there are two main reasons for focusing on Giorgio Caproni's 'Versi livornesi' [Livorno verses, my trans.], the first section of his 1959 book *Il seme del piangere* [The seed of weeping; my trans.].[2] Firstly, this celebrated section is openly devoted the poet's mother, Anna Picchi, who died in 1950. Written between 1950 and 1958, the collection directly involves the work of mourning, or rather, to echo Roland Barthes, *la blessure du deuil*, the 'wound of mourning'.[3] This wound keeps bleeding, not continuously but immutably.[4] Secondly, *mourning* and *melancholia* — if they can really be set apart as two different psychic conditions in this context — are pervasive in Caproni's entire poetic production as thematic content, a perspective on human experience, and a condition of language.[5] In the series 'Versi livornesi', therefore, the reader finds a particular episode of personal bereavement — in the lyric form of a *canzoniere in morte*[6] — within a life-long experience of mournful writing. It will become clear the sense in which I mobilise the idea of 'mournful writing': for both Barthes and Caproni, grief and grieving radically alter not only the subject matter of their writing, but also the very modality of writing.

In recent scholarship, the pre-twentieth-century love elegy has often been reproached for constructing an image of the beloved, usually a woman, which is exploited by the male elegist as a means to his own ends and, above all, for the sake of poetry.[7] The singularity of the other 'flesh and blood' person is thus obscured, internalised, and somehow consumed by the poet in order to gain a new and even stronger voice. In broad terms, this is the crime with which Orpheus has often been charged. In writing his poems of mourning, Caproni seems to travel precisely this well-trodden path. The poems collected in *Il seme del piangere*, however, allow the reader to push interpretation beyond this apparent traditionalism, and to bring to the fore what the grief for the loss of his mother actually *does* in these verses. In order to do so, some of Barthes's meditations on the death of his mother Henriette, who died on 25 October 1977, collected in his *Journal de deuil: 26 octobre 1977–15 septembre 1979*, will prove helpful. The *Journal* was published posthumously in 2009. It is a proper diary, that is to say, a collection of annotations about feelings, thoughts, and experiences, in which the principle of organisation is calendar time. It is neither a retrospective narration of the painful experience nor a structured essay on an object of analysis.[8] Therefore, certain similarities will emerge more on the level of writing practice than on the level of theoretical reflection.[9]

The title of Caproni's collection, a quotation from Dante's *Purgatory* XXXI, 46, reveals immediately the issue at stake. As Francesca Southerden points out about Dante's passage, 'Moving beyond or out of melancholia becomes possible only if the "seme del piangere" or "seed of weeping" can be relinquished'. In other words, the 'voice of grief [...] which threatened to draw the (poetic) voice away from the "beatitudine" of praise, put into crisis by her physical absence from the world, toward a kind of lyric lament' must be transcended. How could this be achieved? 'By forcing the "I", in Eden, to confront again the reality of that loss, Dante suggests that the negativity of language and desire can, and must, be overturned, redeeming the sign and restoring the subject to himself'.[10] What does the retrieval of Dante's 'seed of weeping' mean in Caproni? Does the speaker bring his mourning to an end, or rather does he fall inexorably into irreparable melancholy? Does he even try to restore his (previous) *self*? Where does the beatitude of praise reside? Is there an Eden? Where is it located? In order to provide potential answers to these questions, one has to pay close attention to the poems' multidirectional temporality.

Many of the poems collected in 'Versi livornesi' present an idealised image of Annina as a beautiful and sensual young woman.[11] Of this attractive woman, the speaker can imaginatively be both son and lover. He is almost associated with the young men in whom she triggers erotic interest when walking or riding her bicycle down the streets of Livorno. This appears to be just another instance of the inscription of a masculine self in a long poetic tradition: the male subject can voice his affection and desire for an objectified woman only as a distant observer and lover. This relationship, indeed, could be seen as almost superimposed on the unfulfilled relationship Caproni had with his fiancée Olga Franzoni, who died in 1936.[12] Yet something undermines the easy frame of the introjection of the female beloved by the male lover. The reader can sense immediately that the apparently recalled memories do not really belong to the poet-speaker. How could he remember his mother's wedding? The memory-bearer images that he depicts, then, seem rather to belong to his mother's memory. He cannot bear first-hand witness to those events; he can only attest the effort to re-enact them. The poet-speaker reconstructs scenes that are generic enough to have possibly happened and which, at the same time, are plausibly located within a precise context: the Livorno of the first decade of the twentieth century. The lively and unconventional young woman is part of a world that the First World War will soon wipe away both in reality and in the poet's imagination. A terrible menace looms, in retrospect, over that world, but at that half-imaginary and half-real time, it appears still untouched by the catastrophe.[13]

One could venture that, in both recognising and creating a time-space in which his mother had (or could have had) a life of her own before or outside the speaker's memory, the poet-speaker is not simply internalising her in the form of a safe and compensating figure, but also exteriorising her as an autonomous other. Something similar seems to happen in Barthes's obsession with the photograph of *maman* as a little girl in the Winter Garden, an image that points to her past existence, to where she once was, well before the now sorrowful child was born.[14] In Caproni's case, though, the poem-image points to where she could have been; the speaker has no photograph as unquestionable evidence of the event. In the diary entry of 29 December 1978, Barthes notes how he cannot bear the visual presence of the reproduction of the Winter Garden photograph, because it is 'too painful', 'intolerable'. The photograph is in conflict with his actual daily life, because it does not recall an *identity*, but 'rather, within that identity, a rare *expression*, a "virtue".' The image of the past thus becomes 'a measure, a judge' of the present.[15] Caproni's images of his mother's past perform quite a similar function: they are the (ideal) measure by which to judge the fallen present. In both cases, moreover, the images point to a time that precedes the mourning subject's existence, and in different fashions, are at the roots of the effort to write in order to establish a connection with their mother. Other features of these poems reflect such an attempt at *exteriorisation*, or perhaps, in terms closer to Jacques Derrida's account of mourning, at the interiorisation of the other as radical alterity.[16] As Derrida puts it,

> Faithfulness prescribes to me at once the necessity and the impossibility of mourning. It enjoins me to take the other within me, to make him live in me, to idealize him, to internalize him, but it also enjoins me not to succeed in the work of mourning: the other must remain the other. He is effectively, presently, undeniably dead, but, if I take him into me as part of me, and if, consequently, I 'narcissize' this death of the other by a successful work of mourning, I annihilate the other, I reduce or mitigate his death. Infidelity begins here, unless it continues thus and is aggravated further.[17]

Undoubtedly, both Caproni's and Barthes's mothers undergo a strong idealisation, but mourning them also compels the sons to generate a new (writing) self, not to simply restore the previous one.[18] For the former, Annina becomes the physical embodiment of an Edenic human being; for the latter, Henriette becomes the embodiment of the highest values. From the very first days of his mourning, Barthes is urged to give birth to a new human being who matches those high values: 'a *moral* being, a subject of *value* — not of integration' must come out of the work of mourning (27 October).[19] Yet, through mourning, Barthes has to recognise the impossibility of such a rebirth of the self as a reincarnation of the other. Caproni, instead, has to recognise the lost ideal Eden as already contaminated by history. After the death of *maman*, her photograph does not only point to her existence at some point in the past, to her having been alive; retrospectively, it also points to her *will having been dead*, to her future anterior absence. The photograph enacts the temporality of psychoanalytic *Nachträglichkeit* or *après-coup*. Something similar perhaps happens in Caproni's poetic 'images', where the youthful Eden, retrospectively, bears the sign of the future disaster, which has already happened in the speaker's present. It is indicative that the Winter Garden photograph does not enter the essay as an object of analysis, even though the painful image haunts it from beginning to end. Writing seems to be an operation that cannot easily accommodate that particular image. The act of writing does not fully repair the loss. The *punctum* — the detail that pricks the viewer, pierces the general cultural interest of the *studium*, and elicits personal interest — can never be wholly narrated nor symbolised. In his later poetry, indeed, Caproni will progressively resist metaphorisation in favour of a language that hosts, performs, and exposes mourning in its linguistic failures, shortages, and blanks. Barthes's fragmentary, repetitive, and sometimes inconsistent diary, to a certain extent, performs mourning in a similar manner: it is not so much a coherent reflection on the topic, as an embodiment of the act of mourning in words.

It suffices to think of the problematic and obsessive role of *maman*'s words '*Mon Roland! Mon Roland!*' in Barthes's diary to understand how his mourning involves a dialogue both interrupted and unremitting. 'I begin crying when I think of *maman*'s words that lacerate me still: my R! my R! (I've never been able to tell this to anyone)', Barthes writes on 20 July 1978.[20] The return of these final words of direct address haunts the project of the novel he intends to write: 'I am writing my course and manage to write *My Roman*. And then I think with a certain laceration of one of *maman*'s last utterances: *Mon Roland! Mon Roland!* I feel like crying' (15 December 1978).[21] The dialogue continues after her death as an interruption: words and expressions keep coming back and call for an urgent and impossible reply.[22]

Another effort pursued in Caproni's collection should be pointed out. At least since Dante's *Vita nuova*, mourning in poetry is often associated with a linguistic crisis, in particular with a failure of the representational power of language. Indeed, the appropriateness of language to the experience of grief is directly and radically questioned. As in Dante, so in Caproni, the poet has to find a different language in order to speak of the young woman he is trying to portray. For his *style of praise*, to use Dante's well-known expression, the poet-speaker of 'Versi livornesi' seeks a simple, delicate, and common language.[23] If it does not want to betray Annina's unpretentious glory, language must match her (extraordinarily) ordinary qualities. Such a new poetry must therefore resound of her own voice. It needs light, elegant but commonplace rhymes, in *-are* ('Per lei' [For Her]), and rhyming couplets as fresh and lively as the young voices of Annina and her two friends Elettra and Ada ('Barbaglio' [Flare, my trans.]). Poetry must bear the traces of her passage through the streets of Livorno and through life. It must embody as much as possible the effects that the woman had, and perhaps can still have through poetry, on people ('Battendo a macchina', [Typewriting, my trans.]).

Barthes faces a similar problem when, on 31 October, he notes: 'I don't want to talk about it, for fear of making literature out of it — or without being sure of not doing so — although as a matter of fact literature originates within these truths.'[24] Sam Ferguson notices that 'the practical consequence of these attitudes towards the writing of mourning is that a privileged role is granted to the diary's treatment of the words that emerges spontaneously and painfully into consciousness, so that the diary becomes the continuation in writing of the unconscious work of mourning'.[25] In order to avoid generalisation and thus alienation, Barthes relies on a form of writing which is as close as possible to the unformed unconscious mourning; Caproni, instead, looks for a poetic diction which should be as close as possible to his mother's attitudes and language.

In 'Preghiera' [Prayer], the soul, identified with the poem itself, is exhorted to go with its timid candle to the place where Annina used to be, in the hope of finding her still there. The poem-soul is urged to connect not the lover with the hesitant beloved, but rather the present of bereavement with the past time-space where the speaker cannot go any longer — if he was ever able to go there. The soul-poetry could help to remember what the poet-speaker cannot remember; it could meet again the woman whom he can no longer meet on the familiar streets. As in Dante's 'Tanto gentile e tanto onesta pare' [Such sweet decorum and such gentle grace],[26] the sonnet recognised as the closest to a full embodiment of his new *style of praise*, this evocation through poetry entails the effacement of the 'I'.[27] Also in Caproni's 'L'uscita mattutina' [Morning Exiting, my trans.], the 'I' makes himself totally absent to allow for the self-presentation of the woman. This poem is all about the absolute but repeatable event of Annina leaving her house and walking down Corso Amedeo. Her early morning passage enlivens and enlightens the neighbourhood.

2. Being T/here Together: Mourning as a Problem of Reference

Even though Annina is partially externalised and recognised as other, the poems about her as a young woman still operate in a dimension of the evocation of presence. Something quite different happens in 'Ad portam inferi'. The title provides a setting to the scene. Though narrated in the third person, the poem is all about Annina's actions and perceptions in a smoky and disturbing railway station, identified with the entrance to the underworld.[28] She is uncomfortably sitting at a bar table and waiting, in tears, for 'l'ultima coincidenza | per l'ultima destinazione' [the last transfer | to the last destination] (ll. 9–10). She intends to write a postcard to her child, but she tries in vain to recollect him. In a state of profound disorientation, she cannot remember whether her son is dead or alive. Moreover, she has no pencil in her purse; it has been left somewhere with the house keys. She also wants to write a message to her husband as she used to when she went to Colle Salvetti, a village in the area of Livorno. She reminisces about what she used to say to her husband at that time, but then suddenly realises that she no longer has a ring on her finger.

Without managing to accomplish any of those actions, her thought meanders among scattered and incomplete memories. Words such as 'son' and 'husband' do not indicate any clear referent; memory does not assist her in connecting words to definite mental images and even less to real objects.

At lines 74–86, there is an overlapping of what she could have been thinking, but cannot actually think, with her poet-son's sense of guilt. She does not remember that her son has grown up now, that he has betrayed her and flees all over the world 'morso | dal cane del suo rimorso | inutile' [bitten by | the dog of his futile | remorse] (ll. 79–81). Now he has his own family to feed with countless faults. As usual in mourning, the survivor is in despair not only for his sense of guilt, but also for the now impossible recognition of this guilt by the dead other. Annina is not even able to distinguish her husband from her son. The blur of past and present in her mind resembles the speaker's inability to fully recall and be faithful to the past, but sheds a new light on the attempt. Mourning 'cuts our life'[29] in two, but what changes the second half is not so much the burden of memory, but rather the anxiety of forgetting and being forgotten. The mysterious little bundle Annina puts on the floor at the beginning of the second stanza is the only thing she brings with her to her last destination. In the nightmarish station, dogs smell the little bundle, then look at her with tearful eyes from a corner (ll. 91–95). She cannot sense 'ch'è proprio negli occhi dei cani | la nebbia del suo domani' [that in the dog's eyes is | the fog of her tomorrow] (ll. 128–29). It is hard to make plain sense of these disquieting elements, but the obfuscation of her future seems to be also in the eyes of the quasi-infernal observers. Like Dante at the beginning of *Purgatory* XXXI, 7–9, at the end of the poem she is so confounded in the smoky station that it is impossible for her to articulate even one word.[30] Words get stuck in her throat.

The following poem, 'Eppure...' [Yet..., my trans.], signals that no linear progress is clearly detectable in the collection and seems to embody, once again, the speaker's attempt to remember and speak on Annina's behalf. In opposition to Beatrice's exhortation to Dante, Caproni's speaker keeps going to where Annina once was fully, bodily alive. Barthes repeats many times to feel a very similar urge. Since those places are not completely real, this process cannot be easily assimilated to Freud's reality-testing (*Realitätsprüfung*), which should assist in the subject's progressive detachment from the lost object. Caproni does not even stop sowing (in) tears.[31] In praising her, he seems, rather, to be digging up the 'seed of weeping'. The poem is about the woman's happiness on the day of her wedding with Attilio; the promise of a future waiting for her; a very different train, the one which takes her on honeymoon; a farewell to all the places where she spent her cheerful youth, all of them carefully mentioned. At that time, she believed that life was an eternal cycle always leading to spring as first and last destination.[32] She was not aware, as the last lines of the poem make clear, that that time was already wounded: '[I]l seme della guerra' [the seed of war, my trans.] (l. 90), was already in her and in that world.

If the young Annina is the token of the very possibility of a prelapsarian age untouched by the 'seed of weeping', the speaker can now see, retrospectively, that the menace was already there. The cyclical time is not really made linear, but it does not lead to a new spring.[33] It is true that the straight rail of life heads to a permanent winter of death for the singular being, but retrospectively, the departure shows traces of the arrival. The seed of weeping — ingrained in both personal loss and collective disaster — cannot be fully relinquished to embrace the fullness of being. This seed lies at the creative core of these poems, because it does not generate a remembrance that should instead be abandoned, but rather it activates an oblivion. The loss expands: the seed from which mourning grows was already there, planted in that imaginary Eden. The speaker casts his mind back to the beginning only to discover that the beginning reverberates the end. This discovery puts the very possibility of the existence of Eden at risk. Eden, indeed, might be possible only as long as the young mother preserves and offers an exteriority, the very possibility of alterity. Annina at the railway station, instead, is dangerously close to the 'I'.

Annina's state of not being able to remember and to connect unequivocally signs to their referents is the position the poet will take up in his later poetry.[34] Mourning as a disposition, and not as a Freudian work to be carried out, becomes a melancholic perspective on experience in general. In the transience of every living being and the unavoidable lack of clear meaning, this world seems to become the smoky railway station where Annina is sitting. Poetry, thus, will progressively fall back into inarticulate language, almost into silence.[35] It is not properly a melancholic attachment to the lost love object nor to desire itself. The concrete object can change, but the modalities of its perception are mournful from now on. There is no transcendence to grant any grace. Caproni's lyric speaker will retain this peculiar detachment from (referential) reality — which, in Freudian terms, can be considered as one of the stages in the 'healthy' work of mourning — in all his subsequent poetic production. Not even phantasms are preserved. The extreme outcome of this position is embodied in Caproni's unfinished poem 'Res amissa'. Its very title announces that something — some thing — has been lost and is radically unrecoverable.[36] In Caproni's later poetry the loss will in all likelihood become a sort of primal lack, but the peculiar condition of the voice presented in 'Ad portam inferi' is not yet fully identifiable with Lacan's *manque* [lack]. It is not yet ontological as the *manque*, a universal lack in which every individual is always already inscribed. It is still a personal perspective on experience and a dimension of writing that preserves a historical experience, but at the same time shatters the imaginary unity of the self as a linear autonomous trajectory, as a hoard of retrievable memories, and as an agent of intentional actions and knowledge.[37]

In *Il seme del piangere*, Caproni's speaker remains, at least partially, a sort of bereft young boy, a weeping child who goes time and time again to Livorno to look for a presence which is no longer there. In some poems, indeed, the loss is displaced onto a dismayed boy who weeps without being able to say 'il seme del mio morire' [the seed of my dying, my trans.] ('Il becolino' [The Barge], ll. 53–54, in the section 'Altri versi' [Other Verses]). He is still in the process of dying as much as Annina at the gates of the afterlife. That boy, however, is part of the poet-speaker. Within the collection, even the poems that more joyfully describe the young woman bear a nostalgic desire for the unfulfilled promise of an Eden to which those same poems as 'messages' desperately try to reach out. The speaker's messages to Annina in the fullness of her youth reveal themselves to be too close to Annina's aborted messages to her almost forgotten husband and son, now uncertain addressees and missing referents. They cannot heal the wound by restoring a prelapsarian state that could compensate for the loss or by restoring any self-identity and full signification.

3. Repeating the last prayer

As mentioned at the beginning, the praise of the dead beloved, the evocation of their presence, and the apostrophe to them are gestures that recur throughout the European lyric tradition. The 'Versi livornesi' re-perform some of these gestures, which seem to pertain not only to a language of mourning, but also to the lyric as such. The connections with medieval poetry, and with Guido Cavalcanti in particular, that Caproni's poems exhibit will prompt some reflections about the transhistorical re-enactment of certain lyric gestures. Both Barthes and Caproni bring to the fore the ways in which personal mourning radically changes their modalities of writing, but the idea of mournful writing is not understood here as a kind of writing that works through the loss of an individuated object or a psychic condition of the writer, but rather as a peculiar relationship of language with its referents.

In 'Versi livornesi', the speaker's fantasy of his mother as a young girl pushes a specific feature of the lyric to its extreme: language has no definite and stable external referent, not even an experience-derived image in the speaker's memory. As Jonathan Culler argues, a lyric poem is not the *representation* of an event that has previously occurred.[38] Indeed, it never did occur in Caproni's case; or, at least, there is no tangible evidence of its having occurred. It is a *presentation* — or rather a (repeatable) attempt at presentation — in the 'now' of the time of speech. It is an event in the present of performance. But, what would then be the difference between Annina and a character in a novel? 'Versi livornesi' as a macro-text has sometimes been referred to as Annina's *poema* emphasising its narrative dimension. One should distinguish, though, between the character projected in the reader's imagination by the sequence of interconnected poems and the inner workings of each individual poem.[39] If there is such a thing as a use of language that can be called 'lyric', some of its parameters could be sought in the gestures that frame the utterance. A lyric poem can obviously include narrative or descriptive parts, and often does, but they are usually inserted in a rather different frame.

The poem 'Ultima preghiera' [Last Prayer] condenses many of the motifs of the sequence 'Versi livornesi' and its title seems to indicate immediately a specific gesture. The poem opens with an apostrophe to the speaker's own soul:[40]

> Anima mia, fa' in fretta.
> Ti presto la bicicletta,
> ma corri. E con la gente
> (ti prego, sii prudente)
> non ti fermare a parlare
> smettendo di pedalare. (ll. 1–6)

[My soul, oh hurry up. | I'll lend you my bike, but | run. And don't ever stop | (I implore you, be cautious) | your pedalling to talk | to people.]

More than simply evoking the soul into presence as an external object of contemplation, the opening apostrophe leads into an exhortation: the soul should hasten to reach Annina, careful to avoid being distracted by other people. The woman is distant not only geographically, but also temporally. Yet 'distance' is not the appropriate word, because the woman is nowhere.

In the second stanza, the soul has to arrive in Livorno before dawn and wait for Annina to leave the house to go to the market:

> Arriverai a Livorno
> vedrai, prima di giorno.
> Non ci sarà nessuno
> ancora, ma uno
> per uno guarda chi esce
> da ogni portone, e aspetta
> (mentre odora di pesce
> e di notte il selciato)
> la figurina netta,
> nel buio, volta al mercato. (ll. 7–16)

[You will see, | you'll get to Leghorn before morn. | Nobody will be there | yet, but look at each one | as they come out of | the door, and await | (as the pavement gives off | odours of fish and the night) | the clear-cut silhouette, | in the darkness, bound for market.]

The description of Livorno and the events that take place there are subordinated to both the main action of the stanza — the soul's travelling away in space and back in time — and the mode of enunciation — the exhortation to perform that action. The stanza is not so much *about* Annina or Livorno, as it is the movement itself of going back to Livorno to look for Annina. The utterance is situated in the present of the speaker and it is only in that present that it can conjure something of the alleged past.

The 'I' appears as the first word of the following stanza, and it appears as the bearer of some sort of knowledge. Yet such knowledge, one may infer, does not derive from experience (the 'I' has never been to Livorno at that time); rather, it is an affirmation of his own desire:

> Io so che non potrà tardare
> oltre quel primo albeggiare.
> Pedala, vola. E bada
> (un nulla potrebbe bastare)
> di non lasciarti sviare
> da un'altra, sulla stessa strada. (ll. 17–22)

[I know she won't be later | than the first dawning. | Pedal away. Fly. Watch | (a trifle might be enough) | that you be not waylaid | by another on the road.]

The conviction that Annina will not be late is not an absolute certainty — after all the soul is going to arrive in Livorno, if it does, at the dawn of no precise day. The impossibility of Annina's being late that morning has evidently more to do with the speaker's desire not to miss that meeting than with prearranged appointments.

The soul has to arrive on time because, as the day brightens, Livorno becomes crowded with young, lively women who could enthral and hijack it:[41]

> Livorno, come aggiorna,
> col vento una torma
> popola di ragazze
> aperte come le sue piazze.
> Ragazze grandi e vive
> ma, attenta!, così sensitive
> di reni (ragazze che hanno,
> si dice, una dolcezza
> tale nel petto, e tale
> energia nella stretta)
> che, se dovessi arrivare
> col bianco vento che fanno,
> so bene che andrebbe a finire
> che ti lasceresti rapire. (ll. 22–35)

[Leghorn, as the light breaks, | with wind takes hold | of a bevy of young girls | flung open like its squares. | Big girls, alive, but mind you!, | with such delicate loins | (girls who, they say, have such | tenderness in their breasts, | such energy in their hugs) | that should you arrive | with the white wind they generate, | I know you would end up | letting yourself be trapped.]

The risk of missing the encounter with Annina on the doorstep is equated with the risk of losing the woman again. Or, conversely, the meeting of the soul with Annina, if successful, could be a substitute for the now impossible meeting between Annina and the speaker:

> Mia anima, non aspettare,
> no, il loro apparire.
> Faresti così fallire
> con dolore il mio piano,
> e io un'altra volta Annina,
> di tutte la più mattutina,
> vedrei anche a te sfuggita,
> ahimè, come già alla vita. (ll. 36–43)

[My soul, don't wait for them | to show up. That way you | would painfully upset | my plan, and once again | I would see Annina, the earliest | of them all, flee from you, | alas, as she fled life.]

At this point in the poem, the reader is informed that Annina is dead, and therefore the desired encounter between the speaker's soul and the woman is intended to take place in an imaginary past. This past is not identified with any singular moment or event in linear calendar time, but with the recurrent appearance of the woman at the door of her house, ready to go to the market early in the morning: this is an image repeating itself in the speaker's mind.

The soul has to remember the reason of its mission:

> Ricordati perché ti mando;
> altro non ti raccomando.
> Ricordati che ti dovrà apparire

> prima di giorno, e spia
> (giacché, non so più come,
> ho scordato il portone)
> da un capo all'altro la via,
> da Cors'Amedeo al Cisternone. (ll. 44–51)

[Remember why I'm sending you; | nothing else, please. | Remember that she's bound | to sight you before dawn, | and keep an eye (since, I don't know how, | I have forgotten the door) | on both sides of the street | from Amadeo Avenue | to the big Water Tower.]

To a certain extent, the memory that the soul is invited to keep is contrasted with the speaker's forgetfulness of the front door. Yet another juxtaposition underlies this stanza: the memory of what could still be experienced in the present because it is still objectively there — the street that runs from Cors'Amedeo to the Cisternone — and the front door, which belongs to a past and unrepeatable experience. The reader can assume that the accomplishment of the task assigned to the soul would compensate for the speaker's inability to remember.

What the soul needs at this point, in order to recognise Annina, is a description of her:

> Porterà uno scialletto
> nero, e una gonna verde.
> Terrà stretto sul petto
> il borsellino, e d'erbe
> già sapendo e di mare
> rinfrescato il mattino,
> non ti potrai sbagliare
> vedendola attraversare. (ll. 52–59)

[She'll be wearing a black | scarf and emerald skirt. | She'll hold her wallet tight | to her breast, and since morning | already tastes like grass | and fresh sea water, | you cannot miss her when | she crosses over.]

The speaker knows what she will wear on that past future day. The poem articulates in the present exhortation a future meeting that could happen only as the encounter with the young Annina of an uncontaminated imaginary past. The only event mentioned in the poem that belongs to a past experienced by the speaker is the woman's death, which is equated with the dreaded case of misrecognition.

The soul should follow Annina with circumspection and approach her only when it will hear from afar — and apparently from the future — the speaker weeping heavily at the bottom of his heart:

> Seguila prudentemente,
> allora, e con la mente
> all'erta. E, circospetta,
> buttata la sigaretta,
> accòstati a lei soltanto,
> anima, quando il mio pianto
> sentirai che di piombo
> è diventato in fondo
> al mio cuore lontano. (ll. 60–68)

[Follow her with discretion, | then, and with an alert | mind. And, circum-
spectly, | after dropping your cigarette, | get close to her only when, | soul,
you can hear | my weeping turned to lead | in my faraway heart.]

The desired contact with the woman must coincide with the moment of deepest
grief. Such a level of grief is not constant; evidently, the emotion of the subject in
mourning goes through peaks of intensity. The distance that the soul is called to
overcome is a matter of age, too: paradoxically, the 'I' of the present is too old to
connect to the young woman of the past.[42] So, the soul, apparently unaffected by
ageing or more precisely outside of linear time, has to take up its role of mediator
not only across time and space, but also between two individuals of different age.
The soul can do what the speaker could not, without making the young woman
blush: to put its arm around her waist, to whisper into her ear, to talk to her.

> Anche se io, così vecchio,
> non potrò darti mano,
> tu mórmorale all'orecchio
> (più lieve del mio sospiro,
> messole un braccio in giro
> alla vita) in un soffio
> ciò ch'io e il mio rimorso,
> pur parlassimo piano,
> non le potremmo mai dire
> senza vederla arrossire. (ll. 69–78)

[Even if I, so old, | can't give you a hand, | you whisper into her ear | (but
lighter than my sigh, | after putting an arm | around her waist) what I | and
my remorse | could never tell her, even | speaking so softly, | without seeing
her blush.]

The *congedo* [envoy] of this Cavalcantian *ballata* takes a sudden turn and gives
unexpected colour (but is it really so?) to all that precedes:

> Dille chi ti ha mandato:
> suo figlio, il suo fidanzato.
> D'altro non ti richiedo.
> Poi, va' pure in congedo. (ll. 79–82)

[Tell her who sent you: | her son, her fiancé. | From you I want nothing else.
| Then you may well depart.]

Firstly, the soul is clearly identified with the poem itself: they share the same task
and are called to bridge the same distances. Secondly, as in many medieval poems,
the main message assigned to the poem-messenger is the disclosure of the sender:
here he is both son and fiancé of the beloved receiver. This is, ultimately, what
the soul-poem is meant to accomplish. Something similar happens in Cavalcanti's
ballata 'Perch'i' no spero di tornar giammai' [Because I do not hope to turn again],
which constitutes a long envoy in which, as Domenico De Robertis has pointed
out, the message is personified and the voice, which comes out of the suffering
heart, has to go to the beloved Lady together with the soul and the poem (ll.
37–39).[43] At its very end, the poem is still in an exhortative mode: as in Caproni,

and so in Cavalcanti, the last lines seem to postpone the accomplishment at an indefinite point in the future. In Caproni, only after having delivered its message can the soul-emissary take its leave and be discharged: the meta-poetic move of deploying the word 'congedo' in the final portion of the poem, which is called *congedo* in medieval poetry and is intended to perform the function of taking leave, arrests the poem at a point of indecision. Has the encounter happened in the poem itself, or is the poem an endless effort to reach out to the addressee (and referent) of the utterance?

There is a specific reason why this question is relevant. If, following Culler, one agrees that the lyric is an event that happens in each 'now' of its performance as a *script*, then a question arises: what is actually actualised by the poem? Its object or the utterance itself? Culler aptly distinguishes between *performativity* in J. L. Austin's sense,[44] the capacity of an utterance to actualise what it is about (as in a promise or an oath), proper to literature in general as a discourse that creates fictional objects and worlds, and *performance*, which is a feature specifically ascribable to the lyric: the actualisation of the poem itself as a lyric event, 'the poem's functioning in the world'.[45] In the first case — the poem as a performative speech act — 'Ultima preghiera' would bring forth the encounter it describes and for which it yearns; in the second case — the poem as performance — 'Ultima preghiera' would actualise only the utterance itself, and no encounter would happen within the poem. The second model seems to correspond better to what happens here: the encounter that constitutes the poem's content is deferred in every act of reading the text in order to re-perform the *last prayer* itself and the desire it embodies.

The conflation of son and fiancé in the last lines (*congedo*) could suggest the idea of an 'incestuous sublimation' of desire; however, Giorgio Agamben's response to such a critical stance appears to be substantially correct:

> One cannot, however, grasp the poetic task that is fulfilled here as long as one considers this poetry in the context of the psychological and biographical question of the incestuous sublimation of the mother-son relationship — which is to say, as long as one does not recognize the anthropological change that takes place in these verses. For here there are neither figures of memory nor even *amor de lonh*. Rather, love, in a kind of temporal (and hence not merely spatial, as in the Dolce Stil Novo poets) shamanism, encounters *for the first time* its love object in another time. This is why there can be no trace of incest: the mother is truly a girl, 'a cyclist,' and the 'betrothed' poet literally loves her *at first sight*.[46]

Nonetheless, I would not claim that love actually *encounters* its object, but rather that that *first time* is indefinitely deferred. I would state that this deferral of the encounter between love and its individuated object, as well as between language and its particular referent, allows the poem to maintain its iterability and its shareability. In the temporal paradox of the poem, if the encounter happened, that would be evidence that such a past actually existed.

In a certain sense, 'Ultima preghiera' as a poem functions differently from Barthes's photograph in *Camera Lucida*. Any photograph, including the one of the Winter Garden, unavoidably points to the fact that its referent was there at some point in time. That particular referent is so pervasive that the observer needs a *punctum* to have a point of entrance and to engender an affective reaction to the photograph, a detail inexplicable in terms of *studium* which allows to find a subjective way into the image. 'Ultima preghiera', and perhaps the lyric in general, allows for the re-enactment of the utterance and for the inscription of different subjects in the performance, because its referents — both the speaking 'I' and 'Annina' — have undergone a process of subtraction. Annina is not fully in the poem with her individuality; she is not fully manifested in it. Even her proper name, tinged with affection, points to her more than it makes her present. Since the action that animates a lyric poem is not fully accomplished within the limits of its utterance, a lyric poem could be conceived as a suspended and repeatable gesture more than as a completed action. The verbal gesture that frames 'Ultima preghiera' is an exhortation and, as with prayer,[47] the speaker will never know if his request will be heard, acknowledged, and eventually fulfilled. This request does not change the state of things in this world, as a performative utterance in Austin's sense would do; it can only keep asking for its voice to be heard.[48]

Such an iterable verbal gesture that ends up in a state of suspension every time it is performed has interesting implications. On the one hand, it needs a 'world' external to the poem in which to take place and, in this way, each time it happens as an event in this world, as Culler maintains. On the other hand, however, being an act of will or desire, more than a direct statement about the world,[49] the lyric does not rely on a principle of correspondence to reality nor does it need an individuated referent and a precise positioning in linear time. Mourning in the lyric has to do with this suspension of both the performative, in Austin's sense, and the assertive power of language. If Cavalcanti's poem was an exhortation to the *ballatetta* itself to speak to the woman as soon as it is before her, Caproni's *ballata* is asked to follow the woman, and only when the speaker's grief reaches its peak it must speak to her. If we look at poetic mourning as a discourse that has lost not only its addressee but also its referent, the idea of looking for and then following the woman acquires a particular significance. One can find descriptions of both Livorno and Annina in 'Ultima preghiera', as well as narrative fragments, but the poem is framed as an exhortation and is bound to this movement of going towards its referent, more than to an affirmation of its presence or an evaluation of its qualities. The use of the diminutive *Annina*, not unlike *maman* in Barthes's diary, not only manifests the affective dimension of the relationship, but seeks also to compensate for the lack of the referent.[50]

In the note dated 29 October, Barthes writes: 'In the sentence "She is no longer suffering", to what, to whom does "she" refer? What does that present tense mean?'[51] The issue Barthes is raising here, in the first days of his mourning, is not only the generic linguistic issue of the empty shifters in Émile Benveniste's terms.[52] That sentence sounds too general, and repeatable as received common sense, to be immediately applicable to the singular case without feeling uncomfortable. But Barthes is also addressing the painful loss of his own personal referent for that pronoun, the present absence of the cherished referent of that 'she' who is meant to be no longer suffering. Throughout the diary, indeed, Barthes always calls his mother *maman*. This 'private' word once used in intimate conversations between him and his mother should now probably compensate for the actual lack of external reference with an emotional investment on the act of address. For the speaker, *maman* cannot be anyone else. All the speech acts beginning with *maman*, one can assume, were addressed to her and to no one else.

At the same time, as Agamben maintains, mourning in Caproni's poem is not simply reduced to the outpouring of an individual distress or psychological case. 'Ultima preghiera' embodies the collision between the individual and the general (which is not necessarily to say the universal) that can be often found in poetry of mourning. Caproni does not only de-personalise mourning by locating the potential encounter with his mother in a space-time where he could not have been entirely himself, but as one of the admiring beholders of Annina, he also inscribes his poetic gesture in a long tradition as a conscious re-enactment of that tradition. Poetry, after all, can go back into the past and retrieve old and disused forms. Critics usually acknowledge that in *Il seme del piangere* Caproni achieves 'un linguaggio sciolto e quotidiano'[53] [an easy and everyday language] and attains some of the *leggerezza* [lightness] that Italo Calvino recognised as proper to Cavalcanti's style. Such a critical stance, however, appears to be in partial contradiction with the adoption, admitted by the poet himself, of rhetorical structures proper to medieval poetry. Moreover, such traditional language seems to be in conflict with the privacy of personal loss and with the irrecoverable uniqueness of Annina. 'Ultima preghiera' and 'Versi livornesi' in general seem to deploy 'everyday language', if one can call it so, inasmuch as they want to keep together the individual case and the transhistorical gesture without reconciling them. They could be perhaps reconciled in some sort of universality (as a law of nature or a piece of abstract knowledge: the 'she is no longer suffering' that so puzzled Barthes), but this is precisely what the (lyric) poet refuses to do in Freud's 1916 essay *Vergänglichkeit* [*On Transience*].[54] Language, in lyric poetry, keeps seeking its unrecoverable unique referent.

Indeed, the collision between the particular and the general lies at the centre of poetic attempts at mourning, and probably of any work of mourning. To this extent, all the forms structuring mourning — rhythmic, phonic, rhetorical, and behavioural — are highly problematic: they allow grief to be culturally formalised and socially recognised while, at the same time, something of the real singular loss gets irremediably lost. Readers find the subject's grief in 'Ultima preghiera' in so far as they detect identifiable devices of poetic mourning in the poem. Mourning is thus both a position from where to speak and a set of iterable forms. This position can be also found in poetry which does not concern any particular lost object; indeed, Caproni's subsequent poetic work will exhibit a language of mourning — and to a certain extent, the mourning of language — up until the unfinished 'Res Amissa'.

4. Mourning a future past

In conclusion, let me suggest a few more speculative considerations elicited by the relevance given, in 'Ultima preghiera', to the deferred moment of the encounter between the poem-soul and Annina, when the speaker could ideally be in touch with his mother, or at least the poem could convey the speaker's message to the beloved woman. The poem itself, in fact, is not identified as the message, but rather as the messenger or vehicle of a (full) communication that is (always) yet to take place. If the iterative temporality in which the woman keeps leaving the house every morning and the poem should follow her is the time of what *could have been*, that is to say the time of the poem, what would eventually happen at the moment of the encounter? The time of the encounter, when the soul-poem will actually whisper into Annina's ears, could be the future moment that will prove the fantasised epoch of Annina's youth to be real, or rather to *have been* real. What the speaker seems to be endlessly mourning is not so much a lost past, but a potential future that never took place in the past.

Somehow, it seems to be the reverse of *Realitätsprüfung* [reality-testing], a fundamental mechanism in Freud's early linear account of mourning. It is not the impact of perceptual reality on the mourning subject that confirms the present absence of the dead and thus enables the progressive detachment of libidinal energies from the lost object. The speaker in 'Ultima preghiera' is rather conjecturing on and invoking an event that would confirm that his image of the mother — which, it is worth repeating, does not come from his own experience and memory — and his personal grief are indeed real. Because, as identified earlier when discussing 'Ad portam inferi', what terrifies the mourner is the very idea that grief could be unreal, that the actual mother could be betrayed or forgotten, and her son with her. The encounter may be related to the imaginary event in the anterior future, what *will have been*, which maintains a certain degree of conditionality and characterises the temporality of psychoanalytic *après-coup*. It seems that the very potentiality of that event validates the peak(s) of grief in the present of the speaker's mourning: when the 'I' is seized with the deepest sorrow, the verbal contact with his mother should be established and his message communicated. The potentiality of this future past communication, never actualised nor negated within the poem, allows for both mourning and poetic writing in the present, while at the same time keeping them open and unfinished.

Jean Laplanche distinguishes his concept of *après-coup* (*afterwardness* in his own English translation) from both Freud's 'deterministic' *Nachträglichkeit* (the past real scene determines later events) and Carl Gustav Jung's 'retroactive' *Zurückphantasieren* (a fantasy projected in retrospect upon the past).[55] Rejecting both the deterministic and the hermeneutic position, Laplanche proposes a less ipso-centric notion of *afterwardness* based on the priority of the implantation of the other's 'enigmatic message' in the infant. This message, which comes from the other, is 'afterward retranslated and reinterpreted':

> Even if we concentrate all our attention on the retroactive temporal direction, in the sense that someone reinterprets the past, this past cannot be a purely factual

one, an unprocessed or raw 'given'. It contains rather in an immanent fashion something that comes before — a message from the other. It is impossible therefore to put forward a purely hermeneutic position on this — that is to say, that everyone interprets their past according to their present — because the past already has something deposited in it that demands to be deciphered, which is the message of the other person.[56]

About the temporal dynamics entailed in his notion of *afterwardness*, Laplanche writes:

> I want to account for this problem of the different directions, to and fro, by arguing that, right at the start, there is something that goes in the direction of the past to the future, from the other to the individual in question, that is in the direction from the adult to the baby, which I call the implantation of the enigmatic message. This message is then retranslated, following a temporal direction which is, in an alternating fashion, by turns retrogressive and progressive (according to my general model of translation — detranslation — retranslation).[57]

Of course, the rigid application of psychoanalytic models to literary texts is always problematic, because they presuppose the existence of an unconscious. Therefore, the analysis risks relying too heavily on the author, instead of restricting its scope to an understanding of what happens within the poem. The focus here, however, is not on the unconscious operations of Caproni's psyche, but on poetic phenomena detectable in 'Ultima preghiera', and Laplanche's approach could help to shed some light on those phenomena, especially because on the one hand it disconnects the temporality of *afterwardness* from trauma, on the other hand it involves communication and the notion of translation. For Laplanche the ties that should be un-woven in the work of mourning are communicational. Those ties bear the other's message, a message laden with meanings that require translation, and it is as a message that they can outlast the other's life. This translation, however, remains always partial because there is an enigmatic part that was transmitted unconsciously by the lost other. It is, in fact, an enigma for the sender too. Laplanche explains how the work of mourning relates to a communication with the other which is now both lost, because of death, and missing, because of the insolvable enigma. The dead is now absent, but their messages remain:

> What are the threads that are unwoven which this work of untying bears upon? Freud spoke of 'memories' and 'expectations' attaching us to the other. What he doesn't take account of, but which is rarely absent — precisely in the fabric, the *context* of those memories and expectations — is the place for the *message* of the other. For the person in mourning, that message has never been adequately understood, never listened to enough. Mourning is hardly ever without the question: what would he be saying now? What would he have said? hardly ever without regret or remorse for not having been able to speak with the other enough, for not having heard what he had to say.[58]

Caproni's poem, one could venture, enacts the effort of maintaining the potentiality of that full communication. At the same time, the priority and non-assimilability of the woman as other seems to be addressed in the poem through the double temporal dislocation of the beloved subject to a time to which the mournful speaking subject does not belong. On the one hand, Annina was an attractive young woman, who manifests her own sensuality, well before the appearance of the desiring subject who is now mourning her. On the other hand, in order to translate the immemorial scene of the encounter with his mother, the speaker of 'Ultima preghiera' resorts to a trope, the encounter with the beloved woman in the street, and to rhetorical structures, the envoy, of medieval poetry. Moreover, by partially displacing the poem's speaker from the position of Annina's grown-up son to the position of her excited beholder, one amongst others ('Barbaglio'), the poet-speaker achieves a certain degree of impersonality in the celebration of her qualities, whose appreciation is shared by a community in Livorno (as, for instance, in Dante's 'Tanto gentile e tanto onesta pare'). Yet he could be also exposed to the implantation of what one may call — borrowing the term from Laplanche — the 'enigmatic message' that the future speaker-son will attempt to translate in his time of mourning.

Such an endless poetic re-translation can only be conducted by retrieving a certain degree of that initial impersonality through the adoption of another language, or a language of the other. This language, which is as 'past' as the Livorno of pre-war times, on the one hand intends to embody Annina's own qualities of candour and clarity, and on the other inscribes the operation in a poetic tradition which dates back to the thirteenth century. In this way, it helps to detach the speaker's voice from the absolute and unsayable uniqueness of his own grief. Otherwise, the speaker would inexorably fall into the silence of radically individual and unshareable sorrow. In Laplanche's *translation*, the enigma is never to be revealed. It is not a mystery that can be solved and thus exhausted. If the poem's speaker wants to keep open the possibility for him (again and, in Agamben's words, *for the first time*) to get in touch with the woman, and for his message to be delivered to her and recognised by his readers, he must find a shareable, yet not completely general, code into which continually to translate the message and its enigmatic core. The lyric as a transhistorical and transcontextual repertoire of recognisable gestures and rhetorical structures,[59] which offer themselves for re-enactment in different contexts and for the inscription of different subjectivities before conveying any specific contextual meaning, seems to provide such a code.

Bibliography

Agamben, Giorgio, 'Expropriated Manner', in *The End of the Poem: Studies in Poetics*, trans. by Daniel Heller-Roazen (Stanford: Stanford University Press, 1999), pp. 87–101

Alighieri, Dante, *Dante's* Vita Nuova: *A Translation and an Essay*, new edn, ed. and trans. by Mark Musa (Bloomington: Indiana University Press, 1973)

Austin, John L., *How to Do Things with Words* (Cambridge, MA: Harvard University Press, 1975)

Barthes, Roland, *La Chambre Claire: note sur la photographie* (Paris: Gallimard-Seuil, 1980)

—— *Camera Lucida: Reflections on Photography*, trans. by Richard Howard (New York: Vintage, 1980)

—— *Journal de deuil: 26 octobre 1977–15 septembre 1979*, ed. by Nathalie Léger (Paris: Seuil, 2009)

—— *Mourning Diary*, ed. by Nathalie Léger, trans. by Richard Howard (London: Notting Hill Editions, 2011)

BENVENISTE, ÉMILE, *Problems in General Linguistics*, trans. by Mary Elizabeth Meek (Miami: University of Miami Press, 1971)

CAMON, FERDINANDO, *Il mestiere di poeta* (Milan: Lerici, 1965; expanded edn, Milan: Garzanti, 1982)

CAPRONI, GIORGIO, *L'opera in versi*, ed. by Luca Zuliani, intro. by Pier Vincenzo Mengaldo, chronology and bibliography by Adele Dei (Milan: Mondadori, 1998)

—— *The Earth's Wall: Selected Poems 1932–1986*, trans. by Ned Condini (New York: Chelsea Editions, 2004)

CAVALCANTI, GUIDO, *The Selected Poetry of Guido Cavalcanti: A Critical English Edition*, ed. by Simon West (Leicester: Troubador Publishing, 2009)

—— *Rime*, ed. by Roberto Rea and Giorgio Inglese (Rome: Carocci, 2011)

COMPARINI, ALBERTO, 'Giorgio Caproni Between Poetry and Prayer: *Il muro della terra*', *Italica*, 92:1 (2015), 83–101

CULLER, JONATHAN, 'Apostrophe', in *The Pursuit of Signs: Semiotics, Literature, Deconstruction*, 2nd edn (London: Routledge, 2001), pp. 149–71

—— *Theory of the Lyric* (Cambridge, MA: Harvard University Press, 2015)

DEI, ADELE, *Giorgio Caproni* (Milan: Mursia, 1992)

DE MAN, PAUL, 'Lyrical Voice in Contemporary Theory', in *Lyric Poetry: Beyond New Criticism*, ed. by Chaviva Hošek and Patricia Parker (Ithaca, NY: Cornell University Press, 1985), pp. 55–72

DERRIDA, JACQUES, *The Work of Mourning*, ed. by Pascale-Anne Brault and Michael Naas (Chicago: The University of Chicago Press, 2001)

—— and ELISABETH ROUDINESCO, *For What Tomorrow... A Dialogue*, trans. by Jeff Fort (Stanford: Stanford University Press, 2004)

DOLFI, ANNA, 'Caproni, la cosa perduta e la malinconia', in *"Il mio nome è sofferenza": Le forme e la rappresentazione del dolore*, ed. by Fabio Rosa (Trento: Dipartimento di Scienze Filologiche e Storiche, 1993), pp. 323–46

DONZELLI, ELISA, *Giorgio Caproni e gli altri: Temi, percorsi e incontri nella poesia europea del Novecento* (Venice: Marsilio, 2016)

FERGUSON, SAM, 'Diary-writing and the Return of Gide in Barthes's "Vita Nova"', *Textual Practice*, 30:2 (2016), 241–66

FRABOTTA, BIANCAMARIA, '"Lutto" della ripetizione e "malinconia" della differenza: il terzo libro di Giorgio Caproni', *Rassegna della letteratura italiana*, 90 (1986): 414–28

—— *Giorgio Caproni. Il poeta del disincanto* (Rome: Officina Edizioni, 1993)

FREUD, SIGMUND, 'Mourning and Melancholia', in *The Standard Edition of the Complete Psychological Works of Sigmund Freud*, trans. by James Strachey in collab. with Anna Freud, assisted by Alix Strachey and Alan Tyson (1914–1916), XIV: *On the History of the Psycho-Analytic Movement, Papers on Metapsychology and Other Works* (London: Hogarth Press and Institute of Psycho-Analysis, 1957), pp. 237–58

GIUSTI, FRANCESCO, 'Il meriggio nella natura: Riflessioni estetiche su un'utopia poetica', *Enthymema*, 9 (2013), 302–22

—— *Canzonieri in morte: Per un'etica poetica del lutto* (L'Aquila: Textus Edizioni, 2015)

—— 'Antologizzare il proprio passato: Macrostrutture liriche e temporalità del lutto', *Enthymema*, 7 (2017), 79–91

—— 'Temporalità liriche: Ripetizione e incompiutezza tra Dante e Caproni, Montale e Sanguineti', *California Italian Studies*, 8:1 (2018), <https://escholarship.org/uc/item/87x199p7>

—— 'Rispondere solo a Beatrice: "Tanto gentile e tanto onesta pare" e il rischio della ripetizione lirica', *Revue des études dantesques*, 2 (2018), 87–109

—— 'Transcontextual Gestures: A Lyric Approach to the World of Literature', in *The Work of World Literature*, ed. by Francesco Giusti and Benjamin Lewis Robinson (Berlin: ICI Berlin Press, 2021), pp. 75–103

GRAGNOLATI, MANUELE, and FRANCESCA SOUTHERDEN, 'Dalla perdita al possesso: Forme di temporalità non lineare nelle epifanie liriche di Cavalcanti, Dante e Petrarca', *Chroniques italiennes web*, 32:1 (2017), 136–54

HARRISON, ROBERT POGUE, *The Body of Beatrice* (Baltimore: Johns Hopkins University Press, 1988)

LAPLANCHE, JEAN, *Essays on Otherness*, ed. by John Fletcher (London: Routledge, 1999)

MILLER, PAUL ALLEN, *Lyric Texts and Lyric Consciousness: The Birth of a Genre from Archaic Greece to Augustan Rome* (London: Routledge, 1994)

RAMAZANI, JAHAN, *Poetry of Mourning: The Modern Elegy from Hardy to Heaney* (Chicago: University of Chicago Press, 1994)

RUSHWORTH, JENNIFER, *Discourses of Mourning in Dante, Petrarch, and Proust* (Oxford: Oxford University Press, 2016)

SOUTHERDEN, FRANCESCA, 'Lost for Words: recuperating Melancholy Subjectivity in Dante's Eden,' in *Dante's Plurilingualism: Authority, Knowledge, Subjectivity*, ed. by Sara Fortuna, Manuele Gragnolati, and Jürgen Trabant (Oxford: Legenda, 2010), pp. 193–210

—— 'Performative Desires: Sereni's Re-staging of Dante and Petrarch', in *Aspects of the Performative in Medieval Culture*, ed. by Manuele Gragnolati and Almut Suerbaum (Berlin: De Gruyter, 2010), pp. 165–96

TESTA, ENRICO, 'Con gli occhi di Annina: La morte della distinzione', in *Giorgio Caproni: Lingua, stile, figure*, ed. by Davide Colussi and Paolo Zublena (Macerata: Quodlibet, 2014), pp. 45–57

TAMIOZZO GOLDMANN, SILVANA, 'Il dialogo con le ombre: Note sulla poesia di Giorgio Caproni', in *'Vaghe stelle dell'Orsa...': L'io' e il 'tu' nella lirica italiana*, ed. by Francesco Bruni (Venice: Marsilio, 2005), pp. 321–42

WATERS, WILLIAM, *Poetry's Touch: On Lyric Address* (Ithaca, NY: Cornell University Press, 2003)

ZUBLENA, PAOLO, *Giorgio Caproni. La lingua, la morte* (Milan: edizioni del verri, 2013)

—— 'Qualcosa di opaco. Barthes, il lutto e la scrittura,' *il verri*, 59 (2015), 36–56

Notes to Chapter 3

1. Sigmund Freud, 'Mourning and Melancholia', in *The Standard Edition of the Complete Psychological Works of Sigmund Freud*, trans. by James Strachey with Anna Freud, assisted by Alix Strachey and Alan Tyson, xiv (1914–1916): *On the History of the Psycho-Analytic Movement, Papers on Metapsychology and Other Works* (London: The Hogarth Press and the Institute of Psychoanalysis, 1957), pp. 237–58.

2. All the quotations of Caproni's poems are from Giorgio Caproni, *L'opera in versi*, ed. by Luca Zuliani, intro. by Pier Vincenzo Mengaldo, chronology and bibliography by Adele Dei (Milan: Mondadori, 1998). *Il seme del piangere* is at pages 181–235. Translations are from Giorgio Caproni, *The Earth's Wall: Selected Poems 1932–1986*, trans. by Ned Condini (New York: Chelsea Editions, 2004), pp. 73–99. Translations of poems not included in Condini's selection and of secondary sources are mine.

3. Roland Barthes, *Journal de deuil: 26 octobre 1977–15 septembre 1979*, ed. by Nathalie Léger (Paris: Seuil, 2009); *Mourning Diary*, ed. by Nathalie Léger, trans. by Richard Howard (London: Nothing Hill Editions, 2011), p. 95 (18 February 1978).

4. On the intermittence of mourning, see Jennifer Rushworth, *Discourses of Mourning in Dante, Petrarch, and Proust* (Oxford: Oxford University Press, 2016), pp. 96–102.

5. Paolo Zublena, 'Cartoline da Vega: Il tema della morte nella poesia di Caproni: dal lutto alla

meditatio mortis' [1999], now in Id., *Giorgio Caproni: La lingua, la morte* (Milan: edizioni del verri, 2013). See also Biancamaria Frabotta, '"Lutto" della ripetizione e "malinconia" della differenza: il terzo libro di Giorgio Caproni', *Rassegna della letteratura italiana*, 90 (1986), 414–28; Anna Dolfi, 'Caproni, la cosa perduta e la malinconia', in *"Il mio nome è sofferenza": Le forme e la rappresentazione del dolore*, ed. by Fabio Rosa (Trento: Dipartimento di Scienze Filologiche e Storiche, 1993), pp. 323–46.

6. This is a particular form of lyric collection, a recurrent sub-genre in the Western poetic tradition, which I theorise in my *Canzonieri in morte: Per un'etica poetica del lutto* (L'Aquila: Textus Edizioni, 2015).

7. On the refusal of aesthetic reparation or compensation in modern elegy, see Jahan Ramazani, *Poetry of Mourning: The Modern Elegy from Hardy to Heaney* (Chicago: University of Chicago Press, 1994).

8. See Sam Ferguson, 'Diary-writing and the Return of Gide in Barthes's "Vita Nova"', *Textual Practice*, 30:2 (2016), 241–66.

9. For an analysis of Barthes' reflections, see Paolo Zublena, 'Qualcosa di opaco: Barthes, il lutto e la scrittura', *il verri*, 59 (2015), 36–56.

10. Francesca Southerden, 'Lost for Words: recuperating Melancholy Subjectivity in Dante's Eden', in *Dante's Plurilingualism: Authority, Knowledge, Subjectivity*, ed. by Sara Fortuna, Manuele Gragnolati, and Jürgen Trabant (Oxford: Legenda, 2010), pp. 193–210 (pp. 194–95). For a notion of *performance* similar to the one mobilised here, see also Francesca Southerden, 'Performative Desires: Sereni's Re-staging of Dante and Petrarch', in *Aspects of the Performative in Medieval Culture*, ed. by Manuele Gragnolati and Almut Suerbaum (Berlin: De Gruyter, 2010), pp. 165–96.

11. Years later, Caproni will say: 'Tentar di far rivivere mia madre come ragazza [...] mi parve un modo, certo ingenuo, di risarcimento contro le molte sofferenze e contro la morte' [The attempt to revive my mother as a young woman [...] was a way, of course naïve, to compensate for the many pains and for death], in Ferdinando Camon, *Il mestiere di poeta* (Milan: Lerici, 1965; expanded edn, Milan: Garzanti, 1982), p. 103, quoted in Zublena, 'Cartoline da Vega', p. 45.

12. See Zublena, 'Cartoline da Vega', pp. 14–43, where the author reconsiders also previous interpretations by Biancamaria Frabotta and Adele Dei. In a later interview, Caproni states: 'All'origine dei miei versi, più che una donna, direi che c'è la giovinezza e il gusto quasi fisico della vita, ombreggiato da un vivo senso della labilità delle cose, della loro fuggevolezza: *coup de cloche*, come dicono i francesi, o continuo avvertimento della presenza, in tutto della morte' [I would say that, at the origin of my poetry, more than a woman, there is the youth and the almost physical joy of life, shadowed by a deep sense of the lability of all things, of their transience: *coup de cloche*, as French say, or the constant feeling of the presence of death in everything], in Camon, *Il mestiere di poeta*, p. 102, quoted in Zublena, 'Cartoline da Vega', p. 15.

13. I will not explore in detail here the association of mourning for Annina with mourning for the lost world represented by Livorno before World War I. Interesting considerations about mourning for a place (Ferrara) and an epoch (before World War II and racial persecution) can be found in Martina Piperno's investigation of Giorgio Bassani's poetry included in this volume.

14. Barthes, *Mourning Diary*, p. 168 (July 24, 1978), p. 220 (29 December 1978). *Maman*'s photograph will be at core of his essay *La Chambre Claire: note sur la photographie* (Paris: Gallimard-Seuil, 1980); *Camera Lucida: Reflections on Photography*, trans. by Richard Howard (New York: Vintage, 1980).

15. Barthes, *Mourning Diary*, p. 220.

16. The idea recurs in several of Derrida's writings, see especially Jacques Derrida, *The Work of Mourning*, ed. by Pascale-Anne Brault and Michael Naas (Chicago: University of Chicago Press, 2001).

17. Jacques Derrida, Elisabeth Roudinesco, *For What Tomorrow... A Dialogue*, trans. by Jeff Fort (Stanford: Stanford University Press, 2004), p. 160.

18. On the generation of a new 'poet' and a new 'poetry' by opening one's writing to the dead other and their language (a form of poetic hospitality), see Giusti, *Canzonieri in morte*, pp. 100–26, and Francesco Giusti, 'Antologizzare il proprio passato: Macrostrutture liriche e temporalità

del lutto', *Enthymema*, 17 (2017), 79–91 <https://riviste.unimi.it/index.php/enthymema/article/view/8581> [accessed 1 September 2019].

19. Barthes, *Mourning Diary*, p. 8.

20. *Ibid.*, p. 166.

21. *Ibid.*, p. 216. The English translation reads '*My Novel*', thus missing the consonance in French between '*Mon Roman*' and '*Mon Roland*'.

22. Ferguson points out that 'the diary cannot completely relinquish a language of interpretation' and this form of metalanguage 'relegate[s] the words of mourning to a past time that does not coincide with the moment of writing, and frame[s] it within a second voice closer to the linguistic subject of the diarist', in 'Diary-writing and the return of Gide', pp. 249–50.

23. As Dante defines it in the *Vita nuova* (XVII–XIX), the *style of praise* is a new form of writing that renounces the physical presence of the beloved and any expectation of a response from her, in order to find its pleasure in the very words that praise the beloved. See Dante Alighieri, *Dante's 'Vita Nuova': A Translation and an Essay*, new edn, ed. and trans. by Mark Musa (Bloomington: Indiana University Press, 1973), pp. 30–37.

24. Barthes, *Mourning Diary*, p. 23.

25. Ferguson, 'Diary-writing and the Return of Gide', p. 249.

26. Alighieri, *Dante's Vita Nuova*, p. 57.

27. See Robert Pogue Harrison, *The Body of Beatrice* (Baltimore: Johns Hopkins University Press, 1988), pp. 42–46; Manuele Gragnolati and Francesca Southerden, 'Dalla perdita al possesso: Forme di temporalità non lineare nelle epifanie liriche di Cavalcanti, Dante e Petrarca', *Chroniques italiennes web*, 32:1 (2017), 136–54; Francesco Giusti, 'Rispondere solo a Beatrice: "Tanto gentile e tanto onesta pare" e il rischio della ripetizione lirica', *Revue des études dantesques*, 2 (2018), 87–109.

28. On Annina as the Latin *larva*, 'an intermediate status between the world of the living and the world of the dead', see Enrico Testa, 'Con gli occhi di Annina: La morte della distinzione', in *Giorgio Caproni: Lingua, stile, figure*, ed. by Davide Colussi and Paolo Zublena (Macerata: Quodlibet, 2014), pp. 45–57 (pp. 53–54). Zublena points out that with *Stanze della funicolare* (1952) Caproni's poetry 'enters the milky Erebus which will increasingly constitute an exclusive territory of comparison with the mortal fate', in 'Cartoline da Vega', pp. 40–41. See also Silvana Tamiozzo Goldmann, 'Il dialogo con le ombre: Note sulla poesia di Giorgio Caproni', in *'Vaghe stelle dell'Orsa...': L''io' e il 'tu' nella lirica italiana*, ed. by Francesco Bruni (Venice: Marsilio, 2005), pp. 321–42.

29. Zublena, 'Qualcosa di opaco', p. 36.

30. Southerden, 'Lost for Words', pp. 195–97. Referring to Dante's statements about the *lingua confusionis* in *De vulgari eloquentia* (I, vi, 6), Southerden understands this 'language of confusion' as 'a fallen or (post-)Babelic language, one that had been "confounded", in distinction to the pure language of grace' (p. 197). In Caproni, we cannot explain Annina's inability to speak with an excess of memory. If she stands for a melancholy position here, her melancholia resides in the disconnection between remembered words and forgotten referents. Some attachment is preserved, but the objects are falling into oblivion.

31. 'They that sow in tears shall reap in joy' (Psalm 126:5) in the King James Bible.

32. For Dolfi, Annina and Olga are conflated into a lost thing that can be identified as a 'youth-innocence' which absorbs 'the pure female characters'; this shadow on the I generates 'melancholy more than mourning', in 'Caproni, la cosa perduta e la malinconia', p. 337, quoted in Zublena, 'Cartoline da Vega', p. 44. Both Dolfi and Zublena read the quotation from Dante as a marker of the threshold between the weeping for the personal loss(es) and 'a new path of comprehension' (Dolfi, 'Caproni, la cosa perduta e la malinconia', p. 336).

33. On cyclic time, see Adele Dei, *Giorgio Caproni* (Milan: Mursia, 1992), p. 126.

34. Testa notices how the status of the *larva* mirrors the mourner's condition, which is 'opaque, thick, immobile, with no possible substitutes nor symbolizations — a condition in which time has no power to soften or stop the continuity of sadness and in which stasis is marked by the recurrence of the identical. And thus — we add — it is marked by the regime of indistinction' ('Con gli occhi di Annina', p. 55). 'Ad portam inferi' can thus be considered as the 'germinal core' of Caproni's fundamental theme of the 'death of distinction' (p. 46).

35. Ferguson notices a sort of closure in the diary, 'a change towards a minimal state of language and then its eventual extinction' ('Diary-writing and the Return of Gide', p. 251). In Barthes's words, 'I write my suffering less and less but in a sense, it grows stronger, shifting to the realm of the eternal, since I no longer write it' (*Mourning Diary*, 4 December 1978, p. 215). About the final entry (15 September 1979, p. 244), Ferguson observes that it 'comes closer than any other entry to assuming the univocal and fully present subject of the words of mourning' ('Diary-writing and the Return of Gide', p. 251). The 'subject of the words of mourning' has been absorbed into the writing subject and those words stop here because any future word would be mournful. Mourning is no longer an object to be transferred into writing by an I ('I write my suffering'), but a perspective from which to write ('I no longer write it').

36. See Paolo Zublena, 'L'oggetto perduto tra silenzio della morte e fantasma della scrittura: Lettura di *Res amissa*', in *Giorgio Caproni. La lingua, la morte*, pp. 143–79.

37. Referring to the entry dated 1 May 1978, in which Barthes links the thought that his mother 'is dead *forever and completely*' to the knowledge that 'I too will die *forever and completely*' (*Mourning Diary*, p. 119), Testa stresses that after such a personal realisation, 'the survivor cannot be but one *departing [trapassante]*'. Even though there is a movement towards a 'chronic mourning', this is not 'a completely intellectual achievement'; the 'primal loss' is conveyed by 'a personal and concrete event' ('Con gli occhi di Annina', pp. 52–53). In Caproni's later poetry, mourning may be 'almost oblivious of the very object of its own sorrow' (Dolfi, 'Caproni, la cosa perduta e la malinconia', p. 337), and for Zublena, *Il seme del piangere* 'marks a crucial turning point in the process of detachment from mourning, and at the same time the transformation of mourning with its radical internalisation as a melancholic foundation of the subject' ('Cartoline da Vega', p. 44); yet, following Barthes, Testa raises doubts about the abandonment of the personal loss that has generated the chronic mourning ('Con gli occhi di Annina', note 25, p. 56).

38. Jonathan Culler, *Theory of the Lyric* (Cambridge, MA: Harvard University Press, 2015).

39. Paul Allen Miller locates the birth of the modern lyric subject in the production of authorial books of poetry in Augustan Rome, which allows the projection of a poet-subject through the series of poems, in his *Lyric Texts and Lyric Consciousness: The Birth of a Genre from Archaic Greece to Augustan Rome* (London: Routledge, 1994), pp. 1–7.

40. On apostrophe, see Culler, *Theory of the Lyric*, pp. 211–43; Jonathan Culler, 'Apostrophe', in *The Pursuit of Signs: Semiotics, Literature, Deconstruction*, 2nd edn (London: Routledge, 2001), pp. 149–71; Paul de Man, 'Lyrical Voice in Contemporary Theory', in *Lyric Poetry: Beyond New Criticism*, ed. by Chaviva Hošek and Patricia Parker (Ithaca, NY: Cornell University Press, 1985), pp. 55–72; William Waters, *Poetry's Touch: On Lyric Address* (Ithaca, NY: Cornell University Press, 2003).

41. See Biancamaria Frabotta, *Giorgio Caproni: Il poeta del disincanto* (Rome: Officina Edizioni, 1993), p. 98.

42. On childhood and youth, as well as the image of the mother, see Elisa Donzelli, *Giorgio Caproni e gli altri: Temi, percorsi e incontri nella poesia europea del Novecento* (Venice: Marsilio, 2016), pp. 114–44 and 145–55.

43. Guido Cavalcanti, *Rime*, ed. by Roberto Rea and Giorgio Inglese (Rome: Carocci, 2011), pp. 194–99. De Robertis is quoted in the introduction to the poem (p. 194). English translation *The Selected Poetry of Guido Cavalcanti: A Critical English Edition*, ed. by Simon West (Leicester: Troubador Publishing, 2009), pp. 67–69.

44. John L. Austin, *How to Do Things with Words* (Cambridge, MA: Harvard University Press, 1975).

45. Culler, *Theory of the Lyric*, p. 131. In 'Versi livornesi', the creation of scenes in which the young Annina is protagonist can be seen as performative. Yet the performance by which the lyric institutes itself as an artefact available for repetition in the present — the poem as a message sent to the other's time-space — seems to undermine the very fictional world that performativity is meant to create. This conflict discloses a 'work' of mourning more complex than the attempt at compensation Caproni notes in the statement quoted in note 11.

46. Giorgio Agamben, 'Expropriated Manner', in *The End of the Poem: Studies in Poetics*, trans. by Daniel Heller-Roazen (Stanford: Stanford University Press, 1999), pp. 87–101 (pp. 94–95).

47. On the relation between poetry and prayer in Caproni's later book *Il muro della terra* (1975), see

Alberto Comparini, 'Giorgio Caproni Between Poetry and Prayer: *Il muro della terra*', *Italica*, 92:1 (2015), 83–101.

48. Francesco Giusti, 'Temporalità liriche: Ripetizione e incompiutezza tra Dante e Caproni, Montale e Sanguineti', *California Italian Studies*, 8:1 (2018) <https://escholarship.org/uc/item/87x199p7> [accessed 1 September 2019].

49. Culler, *Theory of the Lyric*, p. 128.

50. On the empty deictics in Caproni's later poetry, see Paolo Zublena, 'Segnali di vuoto: La lingua dell'ultimo Caproni: opacità referenziale di anaforici e deittici', in *Giorgio Caproni: La lingua, la morte*, pp. 79–109.

51. Barthes, *Mourning Diary*, p. 15.

52. Emile Benveniste, *Problems in General Linguistics*, trans. by Mary Elizabeth Meek (Miami: University of Miami Press, 1971), pp. 217–22.

53. Dei, *Giorgio Caproni*, p. 125.

54. Sigmund Freud, *On Transience*, in *The Standard Edition of the Complete Psychological Works of Sigmund Freud*, vol. xiv, pp. 303–08. In this essay, the impossibility for the poet (a lyric poet if the identification with Rainer Maria Rilke is correct) to transcend singular losses in order to subsume them into an intellectual understanding of the cycle of life leaves the psychoanalyst quite perplexed. See Francesco Giusti, 'Il meriggio nella natura: Riflessioni estetiche su un'utopia poetica', *Enthymema*, 9 (2013), 302–22.

55. Jean Laplanche, 'Notes on Afterwardness', in *Essays on Otherness*, ed. by John Fletcher (London: Routledge, 1999), pp. 264–69.

56. Laplanche, 'Notes on Afterwardness', p. 269.

57. *Ibid.*

58. Laplanche, 'Time and the Other', trans. by Luke Thurston, in *Essays on Otherness*, pp. 238–63 (pp. 257–58).

59. Francesco Giusti, 'Transcontextual Gestures: A Lyric Approach to the World of Literature', in *The Work of World Literature*, ed. by Francesco Giusti and Benjamin Lewis Robinson (Berlin: ICI Berlin Press, 2021), pp. 75–103 <https://doi.org/10.37050/ci-19_04> [accessed 16 October 2021].

CHAPTER 4

❖

Giorgio Bassani, the Poet-Ghost, and the Memorial Duty of the Survivor

Martina Piperno

When Giorgio Bassani first approached poetry and started to write verses by imitating a fellow student in the first years of high school (*ginnasio*), he was somehow resurrecting an art that belonged to the past. He did not believe that writing poetry was possible in the modern day. Poets are characters who belong to history, and literary handbooks: 'nella mia dabbenaggine non supponevo che se ne facessero più di versi: le poesie appartenevano al passato, i poeti erano già tutti accaduti' [I was so gullible I believed that writing verse was old-fashioned: poems belonged to the past, all poets were long gone].[1] Poetry itself, therefore, was no longer in fashion in modernity, which forces a dialogue with dead, celebrated models, and, more generally, with the past.

During his lifetime, writing and mourning became fatally intertwined. It is widely known that Bassani's works, particularly his world-famous novels, are dominated by a need to remember the dead — specifically, the members of the Jewish community of his native town, Ferrara, and his own acquaintances, who were decimated by the deportations to Nazi concentration camps during the Second World War. This desire is rooted in Bassani's ethos of remembrance and recollection, perhaps enhanced by survivor guilt. This was made clear directly by him, echoing the duty of the survivor that had already been evoked by Primo Levi a few years previously:

> Il pericolo che incombe sui giovani di oggi è che si dimentichino di ciò che è accaduto, dei luoghi donde tutti quanti siamo venuti. Uno dei compiti della mia arte (se l'arte può avere un compito), lo considero soprattutto quello di evitare un danno di questo tipo, di garantire la memoria, il ricordo. Veniamo tutti quanti da una delle esperienze più terribili che l'umanità abbia mai affrontato. Pensi ai campi di sterminio. Niente è mai stato attuato di più atroce e di più assoluto. Ebbene i poeti sono qua per far sì che l'oblio non succeda. Un'umanità che dimenticasse Buchenwald, Auschwitz, Mauthausen, io non posso accettarla. Scrivo perché ci se ne ricordi.[2]

> [The danger looming over young people today is that they forget what happened, the places where we all came from. One of the duties of my art (if art can have duties), is first of all to avoid damage of this kind, to guarantee

memory and remembrance. We all come from one of the most horrible experiences that humanity has ever faced. Think of the extermination camps. Nothing more atrocious and more absolute was ever done. Well, poets are here to avoid oblivion. I can't accept that the humankind can possibly forget Buchenwald, Auschwitz, Mauthausen. I write so that we can all remember them.]

Bassani's *oeuvre* is largely the work of a survivor: it testifies to the obsession of the survivor of offering testimony and posthumous compensation to those who have died in the Nazi-Fascist persecution. However, unlike Primo Levi, he is not a witness of the concentration camps, as, thankfully, he was never deported. It is possible that his being one of the lucky few who escaped deportation to concentration camps complicates his survivor's guilt, and perhaps even amplifies it. This is suggested by the fact that Bassani's literary works are somehow reticent about the Nazi concentration camps: his writing stops just before a deportation (*Il giardino dei Finzi-Contini* [The Garden of the Finzi-Continis]) and starts up again just after their disappearance, with the victims' return (*Una lapide in via Mazzini* [Memorial Tablet in Via Mazzini]). Bassani chooses therefore the role of the voice of a community rather than that of the witness, recounting life before the war rather than what happened during the war. This essay claims for Bassani the role of survivor and of witness of the largest historical trauma of the twentieth century; or rather, it aims to suggest that Bassani claimed it for himself.

Bibliography on the theme of historical trauma and its representations is immense and giving a full account of it goes beyond the aims of this essay. However, I have considered, among other bibliographical references, the work of Cathy Caruth and Ruth Leys on the definitions of and reactions to historical trauma[3] and Fabio Camilletti's and Katherine Astbury's[4] work about the representations of trauma in modern literature. While the bibliography on the witnesses who were actually deported is endless, the testimonial value of the experiences of those who, instead, faced prison or lived in hiding is still to be explored. This essay attempts to trace this testimonial value in Bassani's works.

Bassani is most known for his novels (in particular for *Il giardino dei Finzi-Contini*, 1962, later popularised by a homonymous movie by Vittorio De Sica), whose elegiac nature was immediately highlighted by an insightful reader as Franco Fortini.[5] His poetry, instead, is scarcely known outside a relatively small network of specialists. This essay aims to discuss the role of mourning in Bassani's poetry, which is linked to the all-encompassing theme of death and remembrance.

1. Bassani's Mournful Dimension

Bassani's poetry books were published in 1982 in a Mondadori volume entitled *In rima e senza* [With and Without Rhymes], winner of the Bagutta Prize in the same year. As the title suggests, Bassani's earlier poetry books fall into two symmetrical sections, one characterised by the use of rhymes, the other by their absence: the first includes *Storie dei poveri amanti* [Stories of Poor Lovers], 1945, *Te lucis ante* [To Thee Before the Close of Day], 1947, and Bassani's translations from Paul-Jean

Toulet, René Char, and Robert Louis Stevenson (1959); the second part includes his collections from the Seventies: *Epitaffio*, [Epitaph], 1974 and *In gran segreto* [Secretly], 1978. The bipartition of *In rima e senza* in two very different sections follows the chronological distance of the four collections, and evidences even further the formal difference between Bassani's juvenile poetry (1940s) and his mature poetry (1970s).

Epitaffio, as the title openly remarks, and *In gran segreto*, are both made up of poems that, despite the variety of themes and situations displayed, systematically play with a sepulchral dimension. They do so not only on semantic and thematic levels, but also through an optic device: the compositions are laid out in the centre of the page, just as epitaphs are inscribed on gravestones. As Luca Lenzini notes, even the form of these poems is in mourning.[6] According to Lenzini, this kind of pagination is not entirely new for 1900 poetry, Jahier and Pasolini having used it, while Portia Prebys[7] and Martin Rueff[8] stress the novelty of Bassani's metrics. Certainly Bassani exploits the potential of the form of the epigraph/epitaph quite radically. He uses the distribution of the text on the page to strengthen the traditional technique of *enjambement* (sometimes separating article and substantive, very unusual for Italian poetry) which makes selected words stand out; secondly, the almost complete absence of punctuation (we only find exclamation and question marks) gives the poems a sense of suspension and incompletion.[9] However, it should also be noted that this unusual form is used to produce deformation: some poems alternate extremely long and extremely short verses, sometimes consisting of just one word, sometimes as short as 'ti' or 'è', to the point that critics doubt whether they really are verses.[10] The alternation of short and long verses and an emphasised use of the *enjambement*, therefore, do not only create a distinctive visual effect, but also play with sound patterning, determining the prosody of the reading, and building a very unique structure for these poems both from a visual and a melic point of view.[11] Like other modern poets interested in the forms of poetic mourning, Bassani offers his own attack on conventions, challenging traditional and established models.[12]

Finally it is noticeable that, in both *Epitaffio* and *In gran segreto*, epitaphs — carved in stone, remaining there, perennially memorable — are entrusted to collect and remember fragments of a poetics of the ephemeral, the irrelevant, the instantaneous, which is corroborated by an insistent search for the minimal, most insignificant occasion; see for example 'Carta igienica' [Toilet Paper].[13] This minimalistic selection of objects confirms the paradoxical nature of the metrical choice: instances of ordinary life, habitual as well as trivial situations, are elevated from their everyday dimension and carved in a commemorative plaque. Borrowing from Culler's discussion of the trans-historical features of the lyric, we might define this element as the 'hyperbolic character' of Bassani's poetry: Culler identifies hyperbole as a longstanding element of the lyric, an 'underlying convention' of the genre based on the fact that 'apparently trivial observations' are represented as 'of considerable significance'.[14]

With its evident allusion to the sphere of the burial, Bassani plays with the ritual dimension which is also an essential feature of the lyric in Culler's theory. By choosing the form of the epitaph, Bassani proposes a model of poetry in mourning that differs from the established category of elegy, which has so far dominated critical perspectives on literary mourning.[15] Bassani expresses mourning not so much in the form of lament, but rather in the more composed, solemn form of epigraph: his poetry mimics the imposing resonance of liturgy rather than the affectionate notes of elegy.

Overthrowing the epitaph's original function, Bassani mocks the redundant rhetoric of memorial plaques, a genre of texts familiar to the Italian audience especially after the boastful rhetorical strategies of the Risorgimento and Fascism. Those had acquired a dramatically different connotation after World War II: Bassani himself, in 'Una lapide in via Mazzini', refers to a plaque being prepared for the one hundred and eighty-three Ferrarese Jews who never returned from the Nazi concentration camps.[16] Bassani adopts a form that belongs to the sphere of memory and commemoration, but forces said form to the point that it becomes caricatural. It should be noted too that Pier Paolo Pasolini warned the reader that *Epitaffio*'s main tone is one of mockery: light irony permeates the whole book and distorts every character and theme.[17] By so doing, Bassani takes on a 'posthumous' mask: the sardonic laughter of those who gave up hope. As Giacomo Leopardi words it after the publication of his own ironic book, the *Operette morali* [Moral Tales, 1827], 'terribile ed *awful* è la potenza del riso: chi ha il coraggio di ridere è padrone degli altri come chi ha il coraggio di morire' [The power of laughter is terrible and awful: anyone who has the courage to laugh is master over others, in the same way as anyone who has the courage to die] (*Zibaldone* 4321, 23 September 1828).[18] Bassani most certainly reclaimed for himself the courage of having 'died', coming back to the world to tell his story, implicitly incorporating the archetypical role of Orpheus, or rather that of Dante, as we will see: 'i poeti che cosa fanno, se non morire e tornare di qua per parlare?' [What do poets do, if not die and then come back here to talk?].[19] It should be noted, however, that despite the fact that he reclaimed the uniformity of his style across the genres,[20] Bassani came back from 'death' with (at least) two poetic *langues*: the elegiac, the tone of the novels and of some of his poetry, and the ironic, which permeates Bassani's late poetry.

The difference in the choice of metrics, however, is not the only macroscopic difference between the two sections of Bassani's collection. The twofold structure has important antecedents in Italian literature, and Petrarch's *Rerum Vulgarium Fragmenta*, a division which is read back onto Dante's *Vita Nova*. As is well known, the death of the women to whom the poems are dedicated, Beatrice and Laura, divides both fundamental books in two parts: 'in vita' and 'in morte'. As Francesco Giusti has demonstrated, the 'canzoniere in morte' is a form of lyric collection that has survived into modernity, with examples ranging from Eugenio Montale, Milo De Angelis and Patrizia Valduga, to focus only on the Italian tradition.[21] Can Bassani's mature poetry, specifically the 'senza rima' section, be considered a 'canzoniere in morte', even if it was left unsaid by the poet? The fracture dividing *In rima e senza* in two parts, excluding the small collection of translations, does not correspond exactly to the fracture between the time before the war and the time after the racial laws and the persecution of the Jews — the incurable wound that marks the entirety of Bassani's works, as Roberto Cotroneo[22] and Giulio Ferroni[23] among others have remarked on. *Te lucis ante* was indeed published in 1947, collecting poems belonging to the time of Bassani's incarceration and persecution; additionally, Bassani himself identified the essential difference between *Storie* and *Te lucis ante*.[24] The structure of *In rima e senza* is therefore not so much determined by the war, a breach that belongs to the collective dimension that determines a new paradigm of historicity: it is instead a more personal, intimate watershed. I would like to suggest that it may consist of the completion of the monument to the memory of antebellum Ferrara that is the famous series of Bassani's novels, all composed in Rome between 1951 and 1972, far away in time and space from Ferrara where they are all set.[25]

It is probably not a coincidence that the first edition of the complete edited series of Bassani's Ferrara novels, entitled *Il romanzo di Ferrara* [The Novel of Ferrara] was published in the same year as *Epitaffio*. Additionally, the previous year he had revised and republished the *Cinque storie ferraresi* [Five Ferrarese Stories], as indicated above: both may be read as signals of a new phase of Bassani's memorial work. The *celebration* of the mourning of Bassani's youth, acquaintances, and environment has come to an end. In other words, he passed from *objectification of grief*, as Robert Pogue Harrison puts it (with a term borrowed from Benedetto Croce),[26] to a new stage of mourning, where instead the subject's perspective prevails. Harrison also details that the objectification of grief, as a coping mechanism, involves a *separation* from the world of the dead, and a *verbalisation* of this separation. By analysing a ritual song collected by Ernesto de Martino in his *Morte e pianto rituale* [Death and Ritual Cry], Harrison observes that a key passage involves the singer and the dead parting ways, one towards life, the other towards afterlife, echoing the archetypal model of Orpheus and Eurydice.[27] Bassani performed this ritual separation in *Il giardino*, which is considered not only the cornerstone of his monument to Ferrara, but also the most autobiographical of his novels. As Bassani himself commented, in *Il giardino* those destined to live and those destined to die walk in opposite directions: 'Nel romanzo, Micòl simboleggia la Vita, e per questo muore, sceglie di morire. Giorgio, l'Arte; e per questo vive, sceglie di sopravvivere, e quindi, di scrivere' [In the novel, Micòl symbolises Life, and for this reason she dies, she chooses to die. Giorgio symbolises Art; that is why he lives, he chooses to survive, and therefore to write].[28]

The novels monumentalise memory, while poetry maintains fragments in their fragmented form. The Ferrara novels are pieces of a memorial dedicated to the city which Bassani in the mid-seventies viewed as an entire, almost concluded, work (however, this did not last for long: his obsession for rewriting led to a new revised edition to be published in 1980). It is therefore possible that for Bassani it was then time to give space to a new voice, that of the paradoxical, irreverent, elusive voice of *Epitaffio*. That is a voice that springs from the completion of a fifteen-year long memorial operation encapsulated in *Il romanzo di Ferrara*: 'la seconda parte di *In rima e senza*, quella cioè che raccoglie due libri, *Epitaffio* e *In gran segreto*, è stata dettata dal bisogno fondamentale di dire in versi tutto ciò che di me, nel *Romanzo di Ferrara*, non avevo detto esplicitamente' [the second part of *In rima e senza*, which includes two books, *Epitaffio* and *In gran segreto*, was dictated by the fundamental need to say in verses everything about myself that, in *The Novel of Ferrara*, I was not able to say explicitly].[29] The title of *Epitaffio* can also be read as a tentative farewell to the world of the novels, to Ferrara and to the poet's youth, finally enclosed in a complete memorial series. As we shall see, however, that lost world will find unexpected ways to haunt the poet in the lyrical dimension as well.

The second part of *In rima e senza* bears some similarities with the genre of the 'canzonieri in morte': here and there, fragments of an archive of memory[30] find their space in Bassani's poetry, a poetry dominated by the here and now. It happens in 'La cuginetta cattolica' [The Catholic Little Cousin], when the poet remembers his happy childhood and adolescence at his grandparents' house.[31] The memory is both visual and aural, as the poet remembers the sunset over Bologna and his grandfather singing and crying. In 'Al telefono' [On the Phone], he questions the location of his inner child, who sometimes resurfaces in his tone of voice: 'possibile? Vivo e sepolto in me | così e da tanti anni?' [Can it be true? Alive and yet buried inside me | like this for all these years?]. The hope that this child, lost in a primitive age when the poet lived in harmony with his city and environment, before adulthood and the racial laws, has somehow survived, is immediately contradicted by the feeling of the looming death of his old self: 'ma allora cosa gli accadrà che ne sarà di lui misero | tra poco?' (ll. 12–15) [But now what will become of him? What's going to happen to him, poor thing | before long?].[32] In 'Le leggi razziali' [The Racial Laws] he recalls the event that marked his whole life and correlates it to an object, the magnolia tree planted by his family in 1939 'pochi mesi dopo la promulgazione | delle leggi razziali [...] tutti quanti abbastanza allegri se Dio | vuole | in barba al noioso ebraismo | metastorico' (ll. 6–12) [a few months after the promulgation | of the racial laws [...], everyone was cheerful enough, | thank God, | despite boring metahistorical | Judaism].[33] In 'La Porta Rosa', he celebrates his archaeological search for resurrecting the ruins of his lost city of Ferrara: 'non lasciarmi solo a scavare nella mia città a resuscitare | grado a grado alla luce | ciò che di lei sta sepolto là sotto il duro | spessore di ventimila e più giorni' (ll. 49–51) [do not leave me alone digging in my city resuscitating | step by step to the light | what is buried of her there under the solid | depth of twenty thousand and more days].[34] In 'Parafrasando Engels' [Paraphrasing Engels], while travelling by car towards Ferrara, he exclaims 'eccola là già in vista la grande la tiepida | dimora | eccola là la mia | gioventù' (ll. 18–21) [there it is already visible the big the aloof | abode | there it is my | youth].[35] Ferrara is his only motherland, as he details in 'Dove vivi?' [Where do you live?]: of all the places and cities on earth, he writes, 'non ne hai abitato in fondo che | uno' (ll. 10–11) [in the end you lived in only | one].[36] Harrison reminds us that a house, in antiquity, was conceptualised as the place where the *manes*, that is to say the ancestral graves, were placed: 'to inhabit the world humanly one must be a creature of legacy. [...] To house [...] means to open the place of an afterlife.'[37] There is little doubt that Bassani's *manes* remained in his home-town Ferrara throughout his life. Bassani's poetry, while it does not mourn the loss of a partner, shows a backward tension towards a past innocence that is lost not only because of the passing of time, but because of the irredeemable fracture of the trauma experienced in his youth.

Bassani's novels cherish immutability and durability, something that is evident for example in the famous *Prologo* to *Il giardino*. While visiting an Etruscan necropolis, the narrator is inspired by the sense of peace and quiet that surrounds the tombs: the afterlife does not seem so bad from this perspective. Scholars agree that this *Prologo* recounts Bassani's approach to memory and the inspiration to write: the novel is a monument, a space where the past can survive unchanged, untouched and preserved from the ruinous passage of history. As Fortini commented, in the *Prologo*:

> *C'è un desiderio di immutabilità che finisce col credere che valore e immutabilità coincidano,* ma la nascita di quella rovinosa persuasione avviene proprio nel momento in cui le ruote dentate della storia si mettono in moto e cominciano ad afferrarti. [...] La 'magna domus' non è solo il materno ghetto, il *taléd* sotto cui rifugiarsi dalla tempesta imminente; è la difesa della storia e anche dalla propria storia, interiore, la difesa della 'pigra brace che è tanto spesso il cuore dei giovani' (p. 174). 'Almeno lì nulla sarebbe cambiato', (p. 16), questa frase detta per le tombe etrusche vale ovviamente per lo studio dei Finzi-Contini.[38]

> [*There is a desire of immutability which leads to the belief that value and immutability coincide,* but this ruinous belief is born precisely when the cogged wheels of history start rotating and chasing you. [...] The [Finzi-Contini's] 'magna domus' [house] is not just the maternal ghetto, the *tallit* [scarf or cape used by male fellows of Jewish communities] under which it is possible to seek refuge from the looming storm; it is the protection of history and also of one's own story, the protection of the 'kind of slow-burning ember which the hearts of the young so often are' (p. 174). 'There, at least, nothing could ever change' (p. 16). This sentence, referring to the Etruscan tombs, is also valid for the study of the Finzi-Contini.][39]

In *L'airone* [The Heron] we find a similar example of cherished durability and intactness. In this novel, we follow Edgardo Limentani, a Jew who escaped the racial laws by marrying a Catholic woman, as he goes hunting in his car. His wandering about the Ferrara countryside and his helpless carrying around of dead birds, which he does not even want to keep, symbolises the sense of guilt for the cowardice that saved his life. Towards the end of his inconclusive wandering in the hunting area, he stops by the window of a taxidermist:

> Si arrestò sui due piedi, affascinato. Fucili da caccia, cartuccere gravide di munizioni, canne da pesca, reti, specchietti per le allodole, richiami da valle, stivaloni di gomma, roba di lana, di fustagno, di velluto, nonché, si capisce, animali imbalsamati, uccelli, i più, ma c'era anche una volpe, una faina, qualche scoiattolo, alcune tartarughe: stracolma di oggetti [...] la vetrina gli splendeva dinanzi come un piccolo, assolato universo a sé stante, contiguo ma inattingibile. Lo sapeva bene: c'era la lastra, in mezzo, a renderlo tale. E allora siccome la lastra [...] gli rimandava qualcosa della sua immagine (appena un'ombra, è vero, però fastidiosa), allo scopo di cancellarla completamente, questa lieve ombra residua, e di illudersi che la lastra medesima non esistesse, si avvicinò ancora di più, fin quasi a toccare il vetro con la fronte [...]. *Di là dal vetro il silenzio, l'immobilità assoluta, la pace.*[40]

[He stopped there, fascinated. Hunting rifles, belts full of cartridges, fishing rods, nets, lark mirrors, decoys for the valleys, gumboots, woollen fabrics as well as fustian and velvet, and of course the stuffed animals, mainly birds, but there was also a fox, a marten, some squirrels, the odd tortoise: full to the brim [...] the window shone before him like a small, sunny, self-sufficient universe, parallel but unreachable. He was well aware that the pane of glass between him and the interior was what rendered it so. And since the pane of glass [...] reflected a part of his own image — barely a shadow, it was true, but still annoying — in order to be completely rid of this faint residual shadow and to pretend the glass itself wasn't there, he drew even closer, almost touching the window with his forehead [...]. *Beyond the windowpane, silence, absolute immobility, peace.*][41]

This passage depicts an image of death that is similar to that of the Etruscan necropolis in *Il giardino*: death, immobility and stillness as an image of silent and peaceful rest in good company ('accanto ai padri');[42] death that offers no reward other than this peacefulness as a cure for the damage of time. Death that the survivor of the Nazi-Fascist persecutions cherishes almost as a gift, as it provides calm but also dignifies and monumentalises the once living: 'tutto ciò che esiste è degno di morire' [everything that exists has the right to die], he synthesises in a late poem.[43] Bassani's novels take up the challenge of creating a collective memory of the extermination of the Jews, and in this sense his novels seek to construct what Walter Benjamin calls an 'eternating memory'. Memory (*Gedächtnis*), argues Benjamin, is the original inspiration ('the musal principle') of epics, but different types of memory characterise different types of narration. 'Eternating memory' (*verewigende Gedächtnis*) characterises the novel as the heir of ancient epic; while a 'short-lived' or 'diverting memory' (*kurzweilige Gedächtnis*: diverting; pleasant in an ephemeral way; funny; distracting) characterises short stories or tales.[44]

This second kind of memory seems to inform Bassani's poetry, mostly dedicated, as discussed above, to the ephemeral and the instantaneous: as one might expect, therefore, images of ephemerality, decomposition, and decay are frequent in his late poetry. In 'Invettiva' [Invective], he ironically attacks an older woman because she wears tight jeans.[45] A poem about a lost member of the family is entitled 'Gli spettri (frammento)' [Spectres, Fragment], which at the same time recalls the ghostly nature of the dead, the necessity of remembering before it is too late ('prima che sia troppo tardi | prima che gli anni via via più | rapidi | sottraggano alla mia memoria troppi particolari' (ll. 27–29) [before it's too late | before the years more and more | rapid | steal too many particulars from my memory]) and the fragmented and almost completely lost nature of this story.[46] This poem might hint at the fact that Bassani, around 1977, started to lose his memory[47] — a cruelly ironic final chapter for a poet whose *ethos* and poetics were built on memory, remembering and monumentalising. It might not be a coincidence that after the first symptoms of memory loss, Bassani stopped publishing poetry.

In 'Danse macabre' [Macabre dance], Bassani's taste for grimace comes fully into play. Here he portrays several senior members of the upper class, 'appartenenti | — ovverossia appartenuti fra '30 e '40 — alla migliore società' [belonging | — or rather who once belonged to the Thirties and Forties — to the jet set of society], as they attend a lavish lunch: 'tutti quanti stasera resi un po'pazzi | all'idea della prossima | baldoria a base di boli | succulenti' [all of them are a bit crazy tonight | about the idea of the forthcoming | revelry based on succulent | cud]. The scene rapidly transforms into a ridiculous and disgusting jest where the old people fight over the food, choosing the most delicate bites: 'di roba tenera insomma la quale resta | sempre l'ottima per chiunque non ha | più denti' (ll. 6–9; 17–19) [in sum tender stuff which still is | the best for those who have lost | their teeth].[48] The characters, which might have been Fascist sympathisers (we are told that they were part of the elite in the Thirties and Forties), are therefore portrayed almost as zombies, half-dead, and ridiculed for their gluttony. Furthermore, the fact that they have lost their teeth, as the poet points out, renders them unarmed as the victims of the racial persecution had once been. This poem closely recalls a parallel passage from *Il giardino*, where, in the night of the Jewish holiday of Pesach, the members of the narrator's family gather together in a sad, depressed state ('tristi e pensierosi come dei morti'), like in a convention of ghosts:

> Guardavo in giro ad uno ad uno zii e cugini, gran parte dei quali di lì a qualche anno sarebbero stati inghiottiti dai forni crematori tedeschi, e certo non lo immaginavano che sarebbero finiti così, né io stesso lo immaginavo, ma ciò nondimeno già allora [...] mi apparivano avvolti della stessa aura di misteriosa fatalità statuaria che li avvolge adesso, nella memoria. [...] Perché non mi sottraevo subito a quel disperato e grottesco convegno di spettri?[49]

> [I looked around, one by one, at uncles and aunts and cousins, a great number of whom, within a few years from then, would be swallowed up by German crematoria ovens, and never would they have dreamt of ending up like that, nor would I myself have dreamt it, but all the same, then, that evening [...] already then they seemed to me swathed in the same aura of statue-like, mysterious fate that still, in memory, encircles them today. [...] Why didn't I immediately leave that grotesque and desperate gathering of ghosts?][50]

The realism of both scenes is fierce. At the same time the scenes take on allegorical value, as in late-Medieval macabre dances: the human race is doomed to mortality. In 'Odradek', Bassani provides one further image of ephemerality in the form of a dog-like creature made of white thread (drawn directly from Kafka's homonymous work) on the verge of being eradicated by a stroke of brush: 'supplica di durare solo un pochino | di più' (ll. 7–9) [it begs to last just a moment | more].[51] Ephemeral is also the fast passage of the car in the poem 'Passo veloce come il vento' [I race like the wind], in which speed fades into inconsistency and inexistence: 'Di me e di te cos'altro rimarrà | negli occhi di chi ci avrà visti? | Un'immagine così | un flash e | basta | insomma niente' (ll. 8–13) [What else will remain of me and of you | in the eyes of those who saw us? An image like this | a flash and | stop | in a word nothing].[52] Ephemeral also is the wet newspaper page that flies away in the rain, dancing 'una specie di estremo valzer avanti di cedere | d'arrendersi a diventare informe e bigia | poltiglia | a ridursi a | niente' (ll. 11–15) [a sort of extreme waltz before collapsing | surrendering and becoming shapeless grey mush | reduced to | nothing].[53]

Ephemerality and a sense of decay also haunt the poet's self-representation. The following sections will detail how Bassani portrays himself as a phantom, or as a figure returning from the world of the dead. As we will see, Bassani positions himself in the most classical coordinates of the poet in mourning, playing with the antecedents of Orpheus and Dante.

2. Bassani's lyrical persona in *Epitaffio* and *In gran segreto*

One of the most famous poems by Bassani, 'Gli ex fascistoni di Ferrara' [Former Fascist enthusiasts from Ferrara], describes a journey back to Ferrara after the war. Those among the citizens who used to be sympathisers of the Fascist government in the past, and who in the 1930s had rejected the poet ('alcuni | di quelli che nel '39 | mostravano di non più ravvisarmi' [some | of those who in 1939 | had stopped recognising me]) (ll. 3–5), now, hypocritically, show affection and compassion for him as a member of the Jewish community: 'eh voi' [ah, you] (l. 9). But, while exhibiting fraudulent benevolence, the Ferrarese betray their falsity by firstly minimising the importance of the poet's own survival, implicitly deeming him a phantom and inviting him to 'forget it':

> Hanno l'aria di insinuare
> nel mentre dài piantala
> non lo vedi che sei tu quoque
> mezzo morto?
> (ll. 25–27)

> [It's as though they're suggesting
> in the meantime come on drop it
> can't you see you are *tu quoque*
> half-dead?][54]

Secondly they suggest that before the war they had been helpful and generous towards the victims ('in che altro modo senza di | noi | avresti potuto metterle insieme | le tue balle con relativo | appoggio di grana eccetera?' (ll. 33–37) [how else, without | us | could you have put together | your lies with the related | load of cash etcetera?]).[55] Their generosity should be rewarded, they seem to imply, by eliminating the boundary between Jewish and non-Jewish Ferrarese citizens, and building a friendly extended family:

> Corrazziali? Voi quoque? Dei quasi
> mezzi cugini? No, piano[56]
> (ll. 41–42)

> [Distant reative? You *quoque*? Like some
> sort of half-cousin? No, wait]

The poet refuses energetically: the repetition of 'tu quoque' / 'voi quoque', linked to the memory of Julius Caesar's death, might aim to reinforce his sense of betrayal. There cannot be a reconciliation between the survivor and the *ex fascistoni*, because the latter lack the direct experience of death that the Jews have endured:

> Prima
> cari
> moriamo[57]
> (ll. 45–47)

> [Before this
> my dear
> let's die]

The survivor, Bassani seems to imply, is 'dead', as his community is shredded, and his home town is unrecognisable. Without this metaphorical death, there is no 'us', no community, no solidarity; even communication is almost impossible. Bassani therefore exposes the sense of guilt attached to his fellow citizens, and rejects any possible identification with them. So, in one of the first of his post-war poetry books, the poet portrays himself as 'mezzo morto' [half dead], even though he does so through the hypocritical gaze of the former Fascist supporters. This is one of Bassani's most outstanding poems because of its immediate connection with the Ferrarese environment evoked in the novels, which makes this poem easy to contextualise and understand. The image of the I as living dead/half dead/ghost recurs throughout this collection and also in the following, *In gran segreto*.

As Bassani himself stated, poetry and essay writing are essential complements to his novelistic production (see above). As 'Le leggi razziali' shows, Bassani often looks back to Ferrara as a home town and as the backdrop to the horrific show of Fascist and Nazi persecution being played out. This perennial backward gaze, that keeps Bassani trapped in his past, is represented in several poems. In the following one, dedicated to Fortini, the poet explicitly portrays himself and his friend as ghosts. Firstly, Bassani observes Fortini as almost metamorphosed in a monument: his face, Bassani says, resembles that of a Swiss Nobel prize. This monumentalisation of the poet is, however, conquered through exceptional effort ('a forza'), and serves only to hide his fragility:

> Che fatica lo so
> anche io per esperienza
> che fatica e che noia per dei fantasmi
> dei semivivi del tuo e mio stampo
> sentirsi sempre obbligati a far lavorare il
> muscolo
> a sfidare la vetta
> essere quelli che siamo
> e passare per dei Bassani e dei
> Fortini[58]
> (ll. 14–23)

> [How exhausting I know
> me too from experience
> how exhausting and how boring for ghosts
> remnants like me and you
> feeling forever obliged to work the
> muscle
> to tackle the summit

> to be what we are
> and still pass for Bassanis and
> Fortinis]

Both Bassani and Fortini might be ghosts or half-dead because of their direct involvement with the racial persecution; we do not know, as the poet provides no clarification. There is a silent nod from Bassani's side, a hint to something shared and unsaid which results in their ghostly wandering. This evanescent existence is made evident in their meeting through their vain conversation about Fortini's purchase of a villa at the seaside, the 'villetta del weekend e delle grandi | vacanze' [a small villa for weekends and long | holidays] (ll. 5–6). Such a bourgeois symbol of wealth and normality, of routine, evidences the ways in which both Fortini and Bassani feel unfit to lead normal, anonymous lives. Why Bassani and Fortini are connected in living a non-life is not said. Yet it is worth remembering that the two, both Jews, shared similar experiences during the war, hiding and living incognito. Fortini, as is well known, had to change his surname in 1940 (from the more openly Jewish surname Lattes to his mother's maiden name Fortini), and Bassani published his first writings in the early 1940s using the pseudonym of Giacomo Marchi. To borrow an idea from Eng and Kazanjian's work on loss and mourning, it is possible to say that, in Bassani's view, their experience had compromised their bodies, dematerialised them, making them paradoxically like those who lost their lives, and their bodies, during the Shoah.[59]

This poem is also a good example of the importance of context in Bassani's poetry. As he reclaims, he is sometimes extremely careful in providing dates, places, and other contextual information in his poem. For example, the very first poem from *Epitaffio* is entitled 'Foro Italico, giugno '72' [Italic Forum, June '72].[60] In this case we have a place, clearly indicated (near Monte Marcello, in Liguria), a means of transport (a bike), and a vague indication of time (years ago): the relevance of the addressee/dedicatee of the poem, stated by the title, makes this poem an event, situated in a here and then. The pagination of the poem is also relevant, since by its layout the poets' surnames, particularly that of Fortini, receive special prominence. Laid out at the centre of the page, alone, it is as noticeable as a name carved in an epigraph or a gravestone. The effect obtained by Bassani is that of giving Fortini's name a sepulchral and solemn echo, which gives substance to the representation of the two poets as ghosts, but at the same time thickens their presence: an epigraph, unlike a phantom, is destined to eternity and endurance.

The half-dead condition of the poet affects also his writing:

> simile anch'io a certi pittori di soffitti
> [...]
> costretti a lavorare al chiuso
> per mesi e mesi magari per
> anni
> [...]
> non mai dimessi prima che fosse ben
> notte
> e nel frattempo soltanto a sognarsela

la trepida la cangiante l'instabile
luce di fuori
inventandosela
ricordandosene e
basta[61]
(ll. 4; 9–10; 17–24)

me too like some ceiling painters
[...]
forced to work inside
for months and months and maybe for
years
[...]
never let off before the dead
of night,
and in the meantime, only dreaming of it
the trepid, shifting, unstable
light outside
inventing recalling it,
and nothing more]

Here the poet portrays himself as a ceiling painter, working for months 'dreaming', 'inventing' and 'remembering' the light of outside in the dark, badly fed, and paid by an impatient patron: a clear image of burial. The poet is in a small, closed and dark place and keeps on remembering and painting the light, which is 'trepid', 'shifting', and 'unstable' just as much as his place is still and static. The poet portrays himself as inhabiting a place which is between life and death, and acts like an intermediary figure, representing the external world through invention and memory. The representation becomes a link between the inaccessible external world and the darkness within which the poet is confined. This is an explicit portrayal of Bassani's activity as a writer of novels ('i miei libri | in prosa' [my books | in prose]), which, as he clearly stated on several occasions, are made up of both memory, history, and invention. These are the two techniques that, like a painting, maintain access to the external world, which is, once again, the lost world of Ferrara, the 'matter' of Bassani's testimony.[62]

As discussed above, Bassani's poetry can be seen as retrospective, always looking backwards. Paola Frandini has suggested a direct inspiration from Benjamin's 'angel of history'.[63] This might be confirmed by this striking passage from 'Muore un'epoca' [An era dies]: 'anche questa [epoca] lo so non la | potrò vivere che girato | perennemente all'indietro a guardare | verso quella testé | finita a tutto indifferente tranne a che | cosa davvero fosse la | mia vita di prima | chi sia io mai | stato' (ll. 4–13) [but again I know the only way | I am able to live this one [era] is facing | perennially backwards looking | at what has just | finished indifferent to everything except to what | was my life of before | who I ever | was].[64] Bassani also plays with this by opening the last section of *In gran segreto* with a toast to his future poetry:

da oggi in poi le mie poesie voglio farle
giuro

sulla prima cosa che mi verrà in
mente sul
niente
di tutti i minuti d'ogni mia
ora d'adesso sul nulla
del mio
futuro[65]

[From now I want to write my poems
I swear
about the first thing that comes into
my mind, about
nothing
of all the minutes of each of my
hours now on the nothingness
of my
future]

As *In gran segreto* is the last collection of Bassani's poems, he is ironically pointing at poetry he will never write.

3. The infernal paradigm

Grazie diamine grazie d'aver citato recensendo Epitaffio Catullo
grazie tante

Ma
e
Dante?[66]

[Thanks, a goddamn bunch for mentioning in your review of Epitaffio
Catullus
thank you very much

But
what about
Dante?]

Not only does Bassani explicitly point out his Dantean model, he also protests that it has gone unrecognised. Certainly, the model of Dante is evident in *Epitaffio*. Not only is the poet directly evoked in one of the first poems, 'Ormai lo so' (l. 8) [Now I Know],[67] but on more than one occasion the poet describes himself as someone coming back from hell. We have already seen in 'L'ho già detto' how the poet locates himself in a dark and enclosed place, similar to that of a tomb. However, a Dantean paradigm emerges with peaks of extreme transparency like the poem that follows:

Davvero cari non saprei dirvelo
attraverso quali
strade così di lontano
io sia riuscito dopo talmente
tanto tempo a tornare

> Vi dirò soltanto che mi lasciai
> pilotare nel buio
> da qualcheduno che m'aveva
> preso in silenzio per la
> mano[68]

> [I really couldn't say, friends,
> along which
> road from so far away
> I managed after such a
> long time to come back.

> I will only tell you that I let
> myself be led in the darkness
> by someone who had taken
> me, silently, by the
> hand]

Here, the poet refers to a dark place where he was lost for a long time; he only managed to 'come back' by letting a mysterious figure lead him silently out of darkness. A reference to the first cantos of the *Divine Comedy* is likely: the poet embodies the wandering Dante and the silent figure Virgil, the leader, teacher, and authority. The use of the verb 'pilotare' is interesting, not only because it reinforces the poet's passivity and the leader's authoritative role, but also as it usually refers to boats or ships, or in any case anything that features a driving wheel (*pedon* in Byzantine Greek). This verb recurs in another poem from *Epitaffio*, when the poet is forced to run home to assist his mother who is sick. His cousin, who is a physician, leads him to her bedside:

> Insiste frattanto a guidarmi di stradetta in stradetta
> nel buio con la dolcezza un tantino beffarda
> del cittadino trovatosi a pilotare per caso l'illustre
> ospite forestiero
> la dolcezza anche del vecchio che accoglie il quasi
> vecchio altrettanto
> o magari di chi defunto da assai più lungo
> tempo l'appena[69]
> (ll. 25–32)

> [He insists in the meantime to guide me from street to street
> in the dark with that slightly amused sweetness
> of the citizen who finds himself by chance to guide the noble
> foreigner guest
> the sweetness also of the old man greeting someone almost
> as old as him
> or even of those who died a long time
> ago greeting the one who just died]

Again, the poet is described as being led in the darkness by a friendly figure: this situation is metaphorised three times, framing the relationship between the leader and the led as that of 1) a local with a foreigner, 2) an old man with a slightly younger man, and 3) a dead soul who has been dead for a long time with the soul of a man who has just passed away. The last comparison also has a subtle Dantean taste: in *Inferno* X (ll. 58–60), through the example of Cavalcante Cavalcanti expecting to meet his son Guido in hell, Dante introduces us to the different temporalities of the afterlife and suggests that the recently deceased can meet and welcome those who died a long time prior. The second comparison, instead, gives an almost Homeric nobility to the relationship between the 'citizen' and the 'foreigner' with a reference to the sacred value of hospitality in the ancient world. A possible archetype for this scene might be the awakening of Odysseus in Phaeacia after his shipwreck, who is welcomed by the princess Nausicaä. This passage from the *Odyssey* has already been proposed as a model for the first encounter between the narrator and Micòl in *Il giardino*.[70] The idea of the poet as a foreigner recalls a similar image in 'Davvero cari non saprei dirvelo' (above), where the poet declares that he has come back from far away ('così [...] lontano') (l. 3).[71] This idea is amplified by the figures of the old and the dead, recalling the idea that the poet's *nostos* from darkness has taken a long time, so much so that he has become old. The poet describes himself again as alienated: a foreigner, an old or dead man, but not old enough, or dead long enough, that he has acquired sufficient experience of his new place.

Bassani portrays himself as accompanied by figures which might sometimes take on Virgil's, sometimes Charon's leading role. In 'Rolls Royce' [Rolls Royce], Bassani dreams of coming back to Ferrara after his death ('Subito dopo aver chiuso gli occhi per sempre', l.1). The afterlife journey is imagined as a car journey, where Bassani is the passenger of a dark metal limousine led by a silent 'stiff' chauffeur seated 'a dritta' [on the starboard side] (l. 12), another borrowing from naval vocabulary that might recall the infernal ferryman.[72] Images of places of Ferrara flow through the concave rectangle of the windscreen, places that have a memorial significance for the poet, and he is anxious and excited to recognise and 'travel through again' the familiar places (churches, bakeries, roads, houses once inhabited by family friends).[73] Through the car windows he has a vision of himself as a child on his way to school. At this point he is tempted to ask the chauffeur to stop and get out of the car, but it is too late: the Rolls Royce is already travelling along large, deserted, unknown roads. In another poem, 'Isola Bisentina' [Bisentina Island], the poet is portrayed with a friend on board a small boat sailing across Lake Bolsena, in Central Italy, towards a small island. While landing, the poet reflects on death: 'Come è bella la vita e che peccato | dover lasciarla' (ll. 1–2) [How beautiful is life and what a pity | we have to leave it].[74] Although it is unclear who the leader of the boat is, this representation immediately reminds the reader of the crossing of the infernal river Acheron. The poet's friend chides him for his mournful thoughts, menacing him (ll. 8–9), perhaps reproducing Charon's shouts (*Inf.* III). But he finally agrees with the poet: 'sì | è vero benché a morire | in fondo c'è sempre tempo'(ll. 10–12) [yes | it's true however to die | after all there is always time].[75]

The image of the writer as somebody who comes back from a very distant place — sometimes explicitly described as the world of the dead — which characterises *Epitaffio*, will be reiterated in *In gran segreto*:

anch'io cosa credi ho sempre nel cuore i poveri

morti
con questo di diverso però ricòrdati che io stesso vengo
proprio di là cioè da quei luoghi
donde — e so bene che lo
sai —
per solito non si ritorna respirando anzi mai e
poi mai[76]
(ll. 8–15)

[me too I have always in my heart the poor
dead
but with this difference remember that I myself come?
precisely from there, from those places
from where — and I know that
you know —
usually one doesn't come back still breathing or rather never
ever does]

And again:

Ero molto lontano non sai
quanto

ti ho stretto forte la mano per restarti
accanto
per non tornarci mai più
là[77]

[I was so distant away you can't imagine
how far

I gripped your hand to stay
beside you
to never return ever
there]

Interestingly, the same semantic field is used to describe Geo Josz, the Nazi concentration camp survivor, in 'Una lapide in via Mazzini':

> Così dunque, come se pallido e gonfio emergesse da profondità sottomarine [...] Geo Josz ricomparve a Ferrara, fra noi. *Veniva da moto lontano, da assai più lontano di quanto non venisse realmente.* Tornato quando nessuno più l'aspettava, che cosa voleva adesso?[78]

> [Thus, then, as if, pallid and swollen, he had emerged from the depths of the sea [...], Geo Josz reappeared in Ferrara, among us. *He came from far away from much further away than he had actually come.* Returned when no one expected him; what was it he wanted now?]

Despite the fact that Bassani was never deported, the character of Geo bears some similarities with the lyrical I as it is portrayed by the poem 'Gli ex fascistoni di Ferrara', discussed above. Like Geo, the lyrical I also scandalises the Ferrarese conformists that had supported the Fascist laws and brings their sense of guilt to the surface. Like Geo, the lyric I also claims to have come back from a dark place which is far away, further than Auschwitz or Buchenwald, and to have 'died' a little from the pain experienced. Bassani himself will make the comparison between Geo and an archetypical poet explicit in an interview:

> Se i poeti non parlano sempre, o quasi sempre, di vicende che è quasi impossibile raccontare, non sono dei poeti. [...] Geo Josz, per esempio, [...] torna dal regno dei morti in una città dopo tutto normale. Ma anche i poeti, se sono veramente tali, tornano sempre dal regno dei morti'.[79]

> [If poets do not always, or almost always, tell things that are almost impossible to tell, they are not poets. Geo Josz, for example, comes back from the realm of the dead in a more or less normal town. But also poets, if they really are poets, always come back from the realm of the dead.]

Challenging the ineffable, therefore, is to Bassani the nature of poetry itself. A response is offered to the frustrating experience of survivors, who are often incapable of reducing their experience to words.[80]

The image of the poet as coming back from hell might also evoke the archetype of Orpheus. Anna Dolfi describes Bassani authorial persona as that of a 'psicopompo', or leader of the souls in the afterlife: in ancient mythologies ψυχοπομπός is the attribute of a god entrusted with the responsibility of accompanying dead souls in their passage to the afterlife, examples including Hermes for the Greeks, or Osiris for the Egyptians. Dolfi argues that Bassani leads the reader through a world of the dead: his narrative universe is a world crystallised in time, in a temporality set 'before' the acceleration of events leading to the catastrophe of the war and the extermination.[81] If not dead, his characters live as ghosts, zombies, or the living dead, as is the case of Geo in 'Una lapide in via Mazzini' or of Limentani in L'airone. These are characters who have experienced trauma to such a degree during the war, their identities taken from them, that they cannot go back to live a 'normal' life.

If taken from the perspective of the external reader, who is led by Bassani through a world of the dead, Dolfi's interpretation is certainly valid. Yet, as we have already seen, Bassani describes himself often as *led* rather than as *leading*. Specifically, he clearly states that his return from darkness could not have happened without being led by the hand. Orpheus, instead, penetrates hell alone in an attempt to *lead* Eurydice out of it. This allows us to suggest that in the case of Bassani the model of Dante is more appropriate than that of Orpheus. Indeed, Dante's is the only model that Bassani reclaimed for himself, as discussed above.

An archetypal scene framing the author as *led* is at the beginning of *Il giardino*, when the narrator, *alter ego* of the author, describes one of his first encounters with Micòl: when she leads him into the dungeons of the family house to park his bike, she is clearly leading him into a dark world of the dead. In this sense, Claudio Cazzola and Gianni Venturi have already suggested the interpretation of the main character in *Il giardino*, the young Micòl, as a Kore. Canonised in Greek mythology as Persephone, a Kore is a mythical figure, who lives a double life between the world of the dead and that of the living, and who is the go-between between two opposite and yet complementary universes. It is likely that the description of the poet as a lost wanderer in a waste land, accompanied by an almost invisible figure, is linked to the description of the narrator in *Il giardino* as a figure *led* by Micòl. As Cazzola has explained, Micòl appears in the novel at a young age, leading the poet into the enclosed house of the Finzi-Contini (a necropolis, a space of the dead) by first expertly explaining to him how to climb the external wall of the garden, then descending the wall to lead the narrator, finally accompanying him when he leaves his bike in a dark grotto in the proximity of the Finzi-Contini house: a scene that has correctly been interpreted as a *catabasis*, that characterises the narrator as a wandering soul, and Micòl as a figure capable of blurring the boundaries between earthly life and afterlife.[82] It is also likely that this initial scene can be interpreted as a metaphor not only of the writing of *Il giardino*, but of Bassani's *oeuvre* in its entirety.

It is therefore not a surprise that a similar representation of the self as *led* also penetrates Bassani's poetry and calls for a direct comparison with the illustrious antecedent of Dante. As Bassani himself will clarify:

> Geo Josz è morto, è andato là dove non si torna, ha visto un mondo che soltanto un morto può aver visto. Miracolosamente torna, però, torna di qua. E i poeti, loro, che cosa fanno se non morire, e tornare di qua per parlare? Cosa ha fatto Dante Alighieri se non morire per dire tutta la verità sul tempo suo? È stato di là: nell'Inferno, nel Purgatorio, nel Paradiso, per poi tornare di qua.[83]

> [Geo Josz has died, he has been in a place from where you can't come back, he has seen a world that only a dead man can see. Miraculously, though, he returns, he comes back here. And poets, what do they do, if they do not die and then come back here to talk? What did Dante Alighieri do, if he did not die and then reveal all the truths of his time? He was down there: in Hell, in Purgatory, in Paradise, in order to come back here.]

As Piero Pieri has highlighted, this passage, read beside Bassani's self-identification with his own character Geo Josz (in 'Gli ex fascistoni di Ferrara', l. 7), and of Geo with Dante, shows that Bassani thinks of himself as a poet-witness and reclaims his testimonial role.[84]

To conclude, I would like to propose that *Epitaffio* and *In gran segreto*, reunited in the section 'Senza [rima]' of Bassani's canzoniere, can be read as the 'in morte' section of Bassani's lifetime poetry book. Unlike the novels, Bassani's late poetry embraces and cherishes ephemerality as a signifier of the frailty, but also the lightness, of earthly life. In this sense it provides an apt counterpart of the monumentality of *Il romanzo di Ferrara*, dedicated, as discussed above, to counteract the erosion of time and to preserve the memory of the dead, especially those who did not even have 'a grave of any kind': 'una sepoltura qualsiasi'.[85] Anna Dolfi has already connected *Epitaffio* and *In gran segreto* to a related lineage of Italian poetry: poetry of loss, quintessentially retrospective, contemplating its objects through the lens of posterity.[86] According to Dolfi, such a lyrical genealogy starts with Leopardi: she builds on Pietro Bigongiari's consideration of Leopardi's *Canti* [Songs] as divided in sections 'in vita' and 'in morte dell'io', separated by the poem *Il risorgimento* [Resurrection]. However, Dolfi does not conclude that the fracture dividing Bassani's book in two parts calls for a direct comparison with the models of Dante's *Vita nova* and Petrarch's *Rerum vulgarium fragmenta*.

Bassani's late poetry, as we have seen, mourns the loss of his youth, and visualises his own decay; it also mourns Ferrara as the chronotope of Bassani's irenic youth, wiped away by the violence of the isolation, the racial laws, and the persecution. Most importantly, Bassani's late poetry celebrates Bassani's own metaphorical 'death', that is to say his visit to hell from where he miraculously returned with a renewed lyrical *langue* to speak for those who can no longer speak. Bassani's incorporation of the model of Dante's infernal journey is particularly important: through his embodiment of the Dantean model, Bassani is, I believe, reclaiming not only his place in an illustrious genealogy of Italian poetry, but also constructing his own role of witness and survivor of Nazi-Fascist persecution. Indeed he explicitly *asks* the reader to believe that he has returned from hell with a powerful story to tell the living. However, a small part of him has been lost in the process. The poet is therefore forced to live a half-life, the life of one both alive and dead, at least until he has completed his memorial duty: after that, that is to say, after the final stone of the oeuvre-monument *Il romanzo di Ferrara* is set down, he will remain forever silent.[87]

Bibliography

AGAMBEN, GIORGIO, *Remnants of Auschwitz: The Witness and the Archive* (New York: Zone Books, 1999)

ASTBURY, KATHERINE, *Narrative Responses to the Trauma of the French Revolution* (Oxford: Legenda, 2012)

[BASSANI, GIORGIO], 'Intervista a Giorgio Bassani', by Stelio Cro, in *Canadian Journal of Italian Studies*, 1 (1977), 37–45, now in *Lezioni americane di Giorgio Bassani*, ed. by Valerio Cappozzo (Ravenna: Giorgio Pozzi, 2016), pp. 125–34

BASSANI, GIORGIO, *Opere*, ed. by Roberto Cotroneo (Milan: Mondadori, 1998)

—— *Rolls Royce and Other Poems*, trans. by Francesca Valente (Toronto: Aya Press, 1982)

—— *The Novel of Ferrara*, trans. by Jamie McKendrick (London: Penguin, 2018)

BASSANI, PAOLA, *Se avessi una piccola casa mia. Giorgio Bassani, il racconto di una figlia*, ed. by Massimo Raffaeli (Milan: La nave di Teseo, 2016)

BENJAMIN, WALTER, 'Der Erzähler. Betrachtungen zum Werk Nikolai Lesskows' [1936/37], in *Schriften*, ed. by Theodor e Gretel Adorno (Frankfurt: Surkamp, 1955), trans. by Harry Zohn, 'The Story-Teller: Reflections on the Works of Nicolai Leskov', *Chicago Review*, 16:1 (1963), 80–101

CAMILLETTI, FABIO, *Classicism and Romanticism in Italian Culture: Leopardi's Discourse on Romantic Poetry* (London: Pickering and Chatto, 2013)

CAMPEGGIANI, IDA, 'Proust nell'opera di Bassani', in *Chroniques italiennes*, 23 (2012), 1–29

CARUTH, CATHY, *Unclaimed Experience: Trauma, Narrative and History* (Baltimore: Johns Hopkins University Press, 1996)

—— ED., *Trauma: Explorations in Memory* (Baltimore: Johns Hopkins University Press, 1995)

—— ED., *Trauma: Conversations with Leaders in the Theory and Treatment of Catastrophic Experience* (Baltimore: Johns Hopkins University Press 2014)

CAZZOLA, CARLO, 'Kore l'oscura: (In)seguendo Micòl', in *Poscritto a Giorgio Bassani: Saggi in memoria del decimo anniversario della morte*, ed. by Roberta Antognini and Rodica Diaconescu Blumenfeld (Milan: LED, 2012), pp. 271–99

CULLER, JONATHAN, *Theory of the Lyric* (Cambridge, MA: Harvard University Press, 2015)

Dolfi, Anna, 'Après la mort du moi: da Leopardi a Bassani', in Studi di letteratura italiana per Vitilio Masiello, ed. by Pasquale Guaragnella and Marco Santagata (Bari: Laterza, 2006, p. 557–71), now in Dopo la morte dell'io: percorsi bassaniani "di là dal cuore" (Florence: Firenze University Press, 2017), pp. 15–26

Ferroni, Giulio, 'Il tempo di Bassani e il nostro tempo', in Giorgio Bassani critico, redattore, editore, ed. by Massimiliano Tortora (Rome: Edizioni di Storia e Letteratura, 2012), pp. 3–11

Fortini, Franco, Saggi italiani, Milano, Garzanti, 1987

Frandini, Paola, Giorgio Bassani e il fantasma di Ferrara (San Cesario di Lecce: Manni, 2004)

Gialdroni, Michele, Giorgio Bassani, poeta di se stesso: un commento al testo di Epitaffio (1974) (Frankfurt: Peter Lang, 1996)

Giusti, Francesco, Canzonieri in morte: Per un'etica poetica del lutto (L'Aquila: Textus, 2015)

Lenzini, Luca, Interazioni: Tra poesia e romanzo: Gozzano, Giudici, Sereni, Bassani, Bertolucci (Trento: Tipolitografia editrice, 1998)

Leopardi, Giacomo, Zibaldone, crit. edn by Giuseppe Pacella (Milan: Garzanti, 1991)

—— Zibaldone, Eng. trans. ed. by Michael Caesar and Franco D'Intino (London: Penguin, 2013)

Leys, Ruth, Trauma: A Genealogy (Chicago: Chicago University Press, 2000)

—— From Guilt to Shame: Auschwitz and After (Princeton: Princeton University Press, 2007)

Nemerow Ulman, Linda, 'Visual Memory and The Nature of The Epitaph: Bassani's "Epitaffio"', in Italian Quarterly, 27:106 (1986), 33–44, now in Lezioni americane di Giorgio Bassani, ed. by Valerio Cappozzo (Ravenna, Giorgio Pozzi, 2016), pp. 135–45

Pasolini, Pier Paolo, Descrizioni di descrizioni (Milan: Garzanti, 2014)

Pieri, Piero, 'Poesia e verità in Giorgio Bassani', in Giorgio Bassani: La poesia del romanzo, il romanzo del poeta (Ravenna: Giorgio Pozzi, 2011), pp. 17–31

Pogue Harrison, Robert, The Dominion of the Dead (Chicago, University of Chicago Press, 2003)

Prebys, Portia, 'Giorgio Bassani tra verità e realtà', in Ritorno al "Giardino": Una giornata di studi per Giorgio Bassani, ed. by Anna Dolfi and Gianni Venturi (Rome: Bulzoni, 2006), pp. 253–59

Rae, Patricia, ed., Modernism and Mourning, ed. by Patricia Rae (Lewisburg: Bucknell University Press, 2007), pp. 13–49

Ramazani, Jahan, Poetry of mourning: The Modern Elegy from Hardy to Heaney (Chicago: University of Chicago Press, 1994)

Rueff, Martin, '"Alas, poor Emily!": Bassani poeta', in Poscritto a Giorgio Bassani: Saggi in memoria del decimo anniversario della morte, ed. by Roberta Antognini and Rodica Diaconescu Blumenfeld (Milan: LED, 2012), pp. 387–428

Venturi, Gianni, 'Dimenticare Euridice: il destino infero di Micòl Finzi-Contini', in Ritorno al "Giardino": Una giornata di studi per Giorgio Bassani, ed. by Anna Dolfi and Gianni Venturi (Rome: Bulzoni, 2006), pp. 91–102

Notes to Chapter 4

1. Giorgio Bassani, 'Di là dal cuore' [Beyond the Heart], in Opere, ed. by Roberto Cotroneo (Milan: Mondadori, 1998) [henceforth Opere], pp. 947–1339 (p. 1325). Unless otherwise indicated, all translations into English are my own; I am grateful to Georgia Wall for her indispensable generous collaboration in revising them.

2. 'Di là dal cuore', in Opere, p. 1326.

3. Cathy Caruth, Unclaimed Experience: Trauma, Narrative and History (Baltimore: Johns Hopkins University Press, 1996), Trauma: Explorations in Memory (Baltimore: Johns Hopkins University Press, 1995), and Trauma: Conversations with Leaders in the Theory and Treatment of Catastrophic

Experience (Baltimore: Johns Hopkins University Press 2014); Ruth Leys, *Trauma: A Genealogy* (Chicago: Chicago University Press, 2000) and *From Guilt to Shame: Auschwitz and After* (Princeton: Princeton University Press, 2007).

4. Fabio Camilletti, *Classicism and Romanticism in Italian Culture: Leopardi's Discourse on Romantic Poetry* (London: Pickering and Chatto, 2013), Katherine Astbury, *Narrative Responses to the Trauma of the French Revolution* (Oxford, Legenda, 2012).

5. See Franco Fortini, 'Tre come noi', in *Saggi italiani* (Milan: Garzanti, 1987), pp. 200–02.

6. Luca Lenzini, *Interazioni: Tra poesia e romanzo: Gozzano, Giudici, Sereni, Bassani, Bertolucci* (Trento: Tipolitografia editrice, 1998), p. 172.

7. Portia Prebys, 'Giorgio Bassani tra verità e realtà', in *Ritorno al "Giardino": Una giornata di studi per Giorgio Bassani*, ed. by Anna Dolfi and Gianni Venturi (Rome: Bulzoni, 2006), pp. 253–59.

8. Martin Rueff, ' "Alas, poor Emily!": Bassani poeta', in *Poscritto a Giorgio Bassani: Saggi in memoria del decimo anniversario della morte*, ed. by Roberta Antognini and Rodica Diaconescu Blumenfeld (Milan: LED, 2012), pp. 387–428.

9. Lenzini, *Interazioni*, pp. 159–64. When discussing the semantic potential of the spatial distribution of the text in the page, Lenzini also significantly connects Bassani's use of epigraph with that of Leopardi's *Filippo Ottonieri*, written as to mock an epitaph.

10. Lenzini, *Interazioni*, p. 159. Interestingly, the only partial translation into English of Bassani's poems does not respect the original layout and lines up the poems on the left side of the page; the translation was however produced under Bassani's supervision so the choice might be the author's: Giorgio Bassani, *Rolls Royce and Other Poems*, trans. by Francesca Valente (Toronto: Aya Press, 1982).

11. About the opposition between *opsis* and *melos* in lyric poetry, see Jonathan Culler, *Theory of the Lyric* (Cambridge, MA: Harvard University Press, 2015), pp. 252–58.

12. Jahan Ramazani, *Poetry of Mourning. The Modern Elegy from hardy to Heaney* (Chicago: The University of Chicago Press, 1994), p. 3.

13. From Bassani, 'Epitaffio', in *Opere*, pp. 1413–65 (p. 1450). See Prebys, *Giorgio Bassani*, p. 257.

14. Culler, *Theory of the Lyric*, pp. 258–63.

15. Patricia Rae, 'Introduction: Modernist Mourning', in *Modernism and Mourning*, ed. by Patricia Rae (Lewisburg: Bucknell University Press, 2007), pp. 13–49.

16. Giorgio Bassani, 'Una lapide in via Mazzini', in *Opere*, pp. 85–87. In real life too Bassani showed a persistent interest in cemeteries, epitaphs, and sepulchers. See his daughter's memories in Paola Bassani, *Se avessi una piccola casa mia: Giorgio Bassani, il racconto di una figlia*, ed. by Massimo Raffaeli (Milan: La nave di Teseo, 2016), pp. 21–22.

17. See Pier Paolo Pasolini, *Descrizioni di descrizioni* (Milan: Garzanti, 2014), p. 66.

18. Giacomo Leopardi, *Zibaldone*, crit. edn by Giuseppe Pacella (Milan: Garzanti, 1991); *Zibaldone*, ed. by Michael Caesar and Franco D'Intino, trans. by Kathleen Baldwin et al. (London: Penguin, 2013) indicated as *Zib.* and followed by the page number in the manuscript.

19. Giorgio Bassani, 'Di là dal cuore', in *Opere*, p. 1344.

20. 'In fondo io non cambio mai penna. Non ho una penna per la prosa, una penna per la poesia, una penna per i saggi critici, una penna per le lettere. Sono sempre io' [After all, I never change my pen. I don't have a pen for prose, a pen for poetry, a pen for critical essays, a pen for letters. It's just me, always], from Stelio Cro, 'Intervista a Giorgio Bassani' [1971], in *Lezioni americane di Giorgio Bassani*, ed. by Valerio Cappozzo (Ravenna: Giorgio Pozzi, 2016), pp. 125–34 (p. 126).

21. Francesco Giusti, *Canzonieri in morte: Per un'etica poetica del lutto* (L'Aquila: Textus, 2015).

22. Roberto Cotroneo, 'La ferita indicibile', in Giorgio Bassani, *Opere*, pp. ix–lvii (p. xi).

23. Giulio, Ferroni, 'Il tempo di Bassani e il nostro tempo', in *Giorgio Bassani critico, redattore, editore*, ed. by Massimiliano Tortora (Rome: Edizioni di Storia e Letteratura, 2012), pp. 3–11 (p. 3).

24. Details in Lenzini, *Interazioni*, p. 159.

25. *Cinque storie ferraresi*, 1956, later revised and reprinted as *Dentro le mura* [Within the Walls], 1973; *Gli occhiali d'oro* [The Gold-Rimmed Spectacles], 1958; *Il giardino dei Finzi-Contini*, 1962; *Dietro la porta* [Behind the Door], 1964, *L'airone* [The Heron], 1968, *L'odore del fieno* [The Smell of Hay], 1972.

26. Harrison, *The Dominion of the Dead*, p. 56.

27. Harrison, *The Dominion of the Dead*, p. 69–70, emphasis added.

28. Bassani, 'Di là dal cuore', p. 1264.

29. Bassani, 'Di là dal cuore', p. 1350.

30. The idea of modern elegy as the archive of the dead is mentioned by Giusti, *Canzonieri in morte*, pp. 100–04. However, the notion of archive is common also in classic studies on post-Auschwitz testimony, such as Giorgio Agamben, *Remnants of Auschwitz. The Witness and the Archive* (New York: Zone Books, 1999), especially ch. 4 (pp. 137–71).

31. Bassani, 'Epitaffio', pp. 1428–29.

32. Bassani, 'Epitaffio', p. 1430. Bassani, *Rolls Royce and Other Poems*, p. 17.

33. Bassani, 'Epitaffio', pp. 1438–39. Bassani, *Rolls Royce and Other Poems*, p. 19.

34. Bassani, 'Epitaffio', p. 1459.

35. Bassani, 'Epitaffio', p. 1468.

36. Bassani, 'Dove vivi?' [Where to you live?], in 'In gran segreto', in *Opere*, pp. 1469–1517 (p. 1483).

37. Harrison, *The Dominion of the Dead*, p. 38.

38. Franco Fortini, 'Di Bassani: Il Giardino dei Finzi-Contini' (1962), in *Saggi italiani*, pp. 233–41 (p. 238); emphasis added.

39. The translation from Franco Fortini's text is mine; the two sentences from *Il giardino dei Finzi Contini* are taken from Jamie McKendrick's translation. The numbers of pages refer to the first Italian edition that Fortini was reading (Turin: Einaudi, 1962).

40. Bassani, 'L'airone', in *Opere*, pp. 701–851 (pp. 833–34); emphasis added.

41. Bassani, 'The Heron', in *The Novel of Ferrara*, trans. by Jamie McKendrick (London: Penguin, 2018), p. 111; emphasis added.

42. Bassani, 'Il giardino dei Finzi-Contini', in *Opere*, pp. 315–575 (p. 321).

43. Bassani, 'Parafrasando Engels', in 'Epitaffio', p. 1468.

44. Walter Benjamin, 'Der Erzähler. Betrachtungen zum Werk Michail Lesskows' [1936/37], in *Schriften*, ed. by Theodor and Gretel Adorno (Frankfurt: Surkamp, 1955); trans. by Harry Zohn, 'The Story-Teller: Reflections on the Works of Nicolai Leskov', *Chicago Review*, 16:1 (1963), 80–101 (pp. 91–92).

45. Bassani, 'Epitaffio', pp. 1419–20.

46. Bassani, 'Gli spettri (frammento), in 'In gran segreto', pp. 1514–17 (p. 1515).

47. See Paola Bassani's memoir, in *Se avessi una piccola casa mia*, p. 114.

48. Bassani, 'Epitaffio', pp. 1448–49.

49. Bassani, 'Il giardino dei Finzi-Contini', p. 479. On this passage, and in general on the inauspicious role of the monument in Bassani, see Ida Campeggiani, 'Proust nel'opera di Bassani', in *Chroniques italiennes*, 23 (2012) (p. 21).

50. Bassani, *The Novel of Ferrara*, p. 99.

51. Bassani, 'Epitaffio', p. 1453.

52. Bassani, 'Passo veloce come il vento', in 'Epitaffio', p. 1453.

53. Bassani, 'Valzer', in 'Epitaffio', p. 1460.

54. Bassani, 'Gli ex fascistoni di Ferrara', in 'Epitaffio', pp. 1417–18.

55. Ibid.

56. Ibid.

57. Ibid.

58. Bassani, 'A Franco Fortini' [To Franco Fortini], in 'Epitaffio', p. 1423.

59. David L. Eng and David Kazanjian 'Introduction' to *Loss: The Politics of Mourning*, ed. by David L. Eng and David Kazanjian (Berkeley: University of California Press, 2003), pp. 1–25 (p. 8).

60. 'Credo proprio di essere uno dei pochi scrittori odierni, dei pochissimi, che usa mettere le date dentro il contesto di ciò che scrive, racconti o poesie che siano. Come narratore, la mia ambizione suprema è sempre stata quella di risultare attendibile, credibile, insomma di garantire al lettore che la Ferrara di cui gli riferisco è una città vera, certamente esistita.' [I believe I am one of the few, of the very few, living writers, to be used to putting dates in the context of what I write. As a narrator, my great ambition was that of proving myself credible, to guarantee to the reader that the Ferrara I talk about is a real city, which really existed], Bassani, 'Di là dal cuore', p. 1322.

61. Bassani, 'L'ho già detto' [I've Already Said It], in 'Epitaffio', p. 1427.

62. The notion of 'matter of testimony' is borrowed from Leys, *From Guilt to Shame*, p. 165.
63. Paola Frandini, *Giorgio Bassani e il fantasma di Ferrara* (San Cesario di Lecce: Manni, 2004), p. 23.
64. Bassani, 'Muore un'epoca' [An era dies], in 'In gran segreto', pp. 1477–78.
65. Bassani, 'Brindisi per l'anno nuovo' [Toast to the New Year], in 'In gran segreto', p. 1511.
66. Bassani, 'Al critico di un rotocalco' [To a Critic in a Magazine], in 'In gran segreto', p. 1482.
67. Bassani, 'Epitaffio', p. 1416.
68. Bassani, 'Davvero cari non saprei dirvelo' [I Really Couldn't Say, Friends], in 'Epitaffio', p. 1445.
69. Bassani, 'Arrivo mia madre non sta bene' [Coming, My Mother is Unwell], in 'Epitaffio', pp. 1441–42.
70. Claudio Cazzola, 'Kore l'oscura: (In)seguendo Micòl', in *Poscritto a Giorgio Bassani*, pp. 271–99 (p. 280).
71. Bassani, 'Epitaffio', p. 1445.
72. According to Francesco Giusti, the dream is an established trope in the tradition of poetry of mourning, which allows the living poet to get in touch with the dead: *Canzonieri in morte*, pp. 364–65.
73. Bassani, 'Epitaffio', pp. 1430–31, ll. 12–29. 'Immediately after having closed my eyes forever, | here I am once again, who knows how, recrossing Ferrara by car [...]. His neck long and stiff the chauffeur, seated in front on the right, | certainly knew very well which way to go', Bassani, *Rolls Royce and other poems*, p. 11, ll. 11–26. See also the reading by Michele Gialdroni, *Giorgio Bassani poeta di sé stesso: Un commento al testo di Epitaffio (1974)*, (Frankfurt: Peter Lang, 1996), pp. 143–44, and Linda Nemerow Ullman, 'Visual Memory and The Nature of The Epitaph: Bassani's "Epitaffio"', in *Italian Quarterly*, 27:106 (1986), 33–44, now in *Lezioni americane di Giorgio Bassani*, pp. 135–45.
74. Bassani, 'Epitaffio', p. 1447.
75. Ibid..
76. Bassani, 'Alla stessa (Natalia Ginzburg)' [To the Same, Natalia Ginzburg], in 'In gran segreto', p. 1476.
77. Bassani, 'In un orecchio' [In the Ear], in 'In gran segreto', p. 1493.
78. Bassani, 'Una lapide in Via Mazzini', p. 89, emphasis added.
79. Bassani, 'Di là dal cuore', p. 1323.
80. See Leys, *From Guilt to Shame*, p. 48.
81. Anna Dolfi, 'Bassani, 'La storia, il testo e l'"effet de réel"', in *Poscritto a Giorgio Bassani*, pp. 103–24, now in *Dopo la morte dell'io: Percorsi bassaniani 'di là dal cuore'* (Florence: Firenze University Press, 2017), pp. 89–108 (p. 98).
82. Cazzola, 'Kore l'oscura: (In)seguendo Micòl', p. 278. See also Venturi, 'Dimenticare Euridice'.
83. Bassani, 'Un'intervista inedita' [An unpublished interview], in *Opere*, pp. 1341–50 (p. 1344). See also Rueff, '"Alas, poor Emily!"', p. 407.
84. Piero Pieri, 'Poesia e verità in Giorgio Bassani', in *Giorgio Bassani: La poesia del romanzo, il romanzo del poeta* (Ravenna: Giorgio Pozzi, 2011), pp. 17–31 (p. 18).
85. Bassani, 'Il giardino dei Finzi-Contini', p. 322.
86. Anna Dolfi, '*Après la mort du moi*: da Leopardi a Bassani', in *Studi di letteratura italiana per Vitilio Masiello*, ed. by Pasquale Guaragnella and Marco Santagata (Bari: Laterza, 2006), pp. 557–71, now in *Dopo la morte dell'io*, pp. 15–26.
87. The essay is dedicated to the memory of Tommaso Marcosignori (1984–2018).

CHAPTER 5

❖

The Space of Mourning:
Elettra's *mise en abyme*

Marzia D'Amico

1. Introduction

In order to understand the difficult and ambivalent relationship between women and the lyric genre in the Italian literary tradition, it is necessary to first problematise the value-system created and perpetuated by men to reward each other. The literary canon, and the lyric one in particular, developed from male authors' contributions to a heteronormative dynamic.[1] As a consequence, the recurrence of the love theme only evolved with a male subject voicing his desire towards a female object. Although the lyric genre supposedly has per subject a beloved person and usually a woman, women's presence was reinforced as silent. In this male-built poetic system, women were inspiration for songs and yet never allowed to sing; this inevitably affected the silencing of women and contributed to their misrepresentation. The literary convention influenced and, at the same time, was influenced by the features of the masculine and feminine categories also in social and cultural terms. Considering the structural terms in which women developed personal and collective poetics, in order to 'identify, remember, and reassert the female voices within Italian poetry, it is important that these voices be "heard" in a way that honors rather than questions the agency and intent of both the modern and historical woman'.[2]

How do women interact with the above-described pre-existing dynamic? And to what extent can the author and the poetic subject be considered as free, considering the rigid tradition of roles? In which ways can a woman perform an authentic subjectivity inscribing her authorial experience in this tradition? And how can this poetic subject reclaim its performative actions while considering the function? Regarding the case of Amelia Rosselli, as investigated in detail by Emanuela Tandello, the author's intent is to expose the underlying falsification of women in lyric.[3] Whilst traditional lyric sublimation of women occurs as a rhetorical strategy that detaches their description from reality, serving men's gaze and intents and confining women to subordinate roles, Rosselli reverses the trope, performing longing for a male figure (see *La Libellula*, 1985) and dislocating her lyric subject into a process of fragmentation and of dialogue with the female classic and modern pantheon.[4]

This chapter will analyse the ways in which Rosselli acts on the rewriting of women in literary collective consciousness, whilst also redefining the authorial state of women writers. It will address the poem that presents the figure of Electra as representative of the eternally mourning *fanciulla* [maiden], whom Rosselli is prone to identify with, and be identified with, because of the traumatic similitudes with her own life, particularly regarding the loss of her father, a national martyr for the anti-fascist cause.

> Con un padre assassinato, per me sarebbe stato facile farne un tema, un'ossessione. Ma la nevrosi non si può dilagare in forma di libro da far comprare. È inutile esprimerla come sostanza della poesia. Per questo tendo all'eliminazione dell'io. L'io non è più al centro espressivo, va messo in ombra o da parte. Credo che solo così si raggiungono risposte poetiche e morali valide, valori utili anche alla società. Ma bisogna evitare il tran-tran montaliano: non parlare né dell'io né del tu.[5]

> [With a murdered father, it would have been easy for me to make it a theme, an obsession. But neurosis cannot be spread in the form of a book aimed to be bought. It is useless to express it as the substance of poetry. This is why I tend to eliminate the self. The self is no longer at the expressive centre, it must be overshadowed or set aside. I believe that this is the only way to achieve valid poetic and moral answers, values that are also useful to society. But it is necessary to avoid the Montalean routine: to speak neither of the self nor of you.][6]

However, Rosselli's intention is not limited to liberating her self, both personal and poetic, from the accusation of intimism and biographical adherence in poetry. She also develops a rhetoric of emancipation from private trauma as performative, obtained through the abnegation of a one and only self, and by opening up to relocation and fragmentation of such a self in many experiences and possibilities. Contributing to the investigation by Tandello, Carpita accurately demonstrates that:

> [g]li interpreti hanno notato in più occasioni come la poesia rosselliana metta in scena un dialogo fittizio io-tu, dove la presenza fantasmatica del tu, più che riferirsi a una persona reale, è da interpretarsi come l'interiorizzazione della presenza inquietante dei morti oppure come dialogo mistico. Credo che il processo di moltiplicazione dell'io poetico debba essere letto come riproduzione nello spazio letterario del disorientamento dell'io reale nello spazio e nel tempo causato dal trauma.[7]

> [Critics have noted on several occasions how the poetry of Rosselli staged a fictitious dialogue *me-you*, where the phantasmatic presence of the 'you', rather than referring to a real person, is to be interpreted as the internalisation of the disturbing presence of the dead or as mystical dialogue. I believe that the process of multiplication of the poetic self must be considered a reproduction in the literary space of the disorientation of the real self in space and time caused by the trauma.]

This complicated relationship with time and space becomes particularly evident in the mise en abyme performed in the *elegia paterna* [an elegy for a father], exemplary of the infinite repetition imposed on Electra and here presented as both a temporal and spatial recurrent movement.[8] Through the rewriting of the figure of Electra, it is possible to identify the liberation of the symbolic female *persona* to whom Rosselli is synthesised. By distancing herself from the assigned category of 'ideal mourning daughter', she regains her personal identity; and by performing a self-elegy of her established role, she declares her poetic self as autonomous. On the basis of this study, I argue that Rosselli not only unmasks this lyric strategy in order to liberate the poetic-woman and the social-woman from the role of object; she also redesigns women's presence in poetry, both as poetic subjects and as authors of poetry. This is done, most importantly, with the clear intention of formally recreating the lyric, whilst simultaneously enacting a detachment from the same.

2. The history of the *addii*: farewells

Rosselli was born in 1930 in Paris, where her family was fleeing from the Fascist regime's persecution under the guaranteed status of political refugees. Her mother was Marion Cave, an English-born feminist and anti-fascist activist who was arrested in 1929 when two-months pregnant with Amelia, and released by the end of the month thanks to an outstanding campaign in England by feminist and anti-fascist groups. Marion's contribution to the transnational anti-fascist cause surely defines her persona and her experience, up to the point of being described as follows:

> A fanatic who even before her marriage had expressed her antifascist sentiments in sensational fashion by travelling on purpose from Florence to Rome to lay a wreath on the very spot where (the opposition MP) Giacomo Matteotti had been abducted.[9]

At the time of Marion's arrest, Carlo Rosselli (Amelia's father) was sentenced to ten months in Lipari — the so-called Fascist 'Devil's Island' — the place where all opponents to the regime were interned. During this detention he wrote *Socialismo Liberale*,[10] and in that same year managed to escape the island together with Francesco Fausto Nitti and Emilio Lussu.[11] Once in France, he published the book and founded the 'Giustizia e Libertà' movement with other exiles (such as Gaetano Salvemini).[12]

On 9 June 1936, Carlo and his brother Nello were murdered by members of La Cagoule. This far-right clandestine French paramilitary group was sanctioned by the Italian Fascist government in exchange for 'one hundred semi-automatic Berretta rifles':[13]

> Amelia Rosselli's childhood and youth were scarred by this traumatic event [...] in 1940 her English mother led the family to the relative safety of England and then on to the United States for the duration of the war. It was not until 1946 that she first came to Italy, where she eventually settled (in Rome) in 1948.[14]

In addition to the political antagonism of the regime that resulted in the heinous homicide of her father, Italian Jews such as the Rossellis had to face the repercussions of a growing profound antisemitism:

> I am a Jew who doesn't go to temple on the Sabbath, who doesn't speak
> Hebrew, who is completely unobservant. And yet I am attached to my Jewish
> identity, and I want to defend it against any kind of deviation that may be a
> broadening or a reduction of itself.[15]

The national and patriotic Italian identity of all the members of Rosselli's family
had always happily coincided with a pro-assimilation stance, and as explained by
Nello Rosselli, this did not ever feel like a renunciation of the Jewish identity. When
religious persecution was institutionalised by the Fascist party in 1938, the infamous
'Racial Laws' — promoted through a pseudo-scientific race-based 'Manifesto della
Razza'[16] — excluded Jews from the Italian race. Italian Jews endured economic,
political, and social restrictions, and were deprived of their citizenship.

Years after these traumatic events, Amelia suffered greatly at Marion's loss, which
happened in 1949, though the relationship with her mother is frequently described
as uncaring and unaffectionate. At the time, Amelia was in Florence, her mother
in London, so it was once again the geographical distance which interfered with
her mourning, and the power of this all-consuming grief was explored as part of
her own identity. She would start calling herself Marion,[17] therefore somehow
absorbing into her own adulthood the woman who forsook her role as caring
mother but surely never failed to be exemplary. As for the news of the assassination
of her father, when, in Amelia's memories of the day the bodies of Carlo and Nello
were found, Marion Cave approached her own children and calmly asked them if
they were familiar with the word 'assassination' and later insisted that they see the
corpses.[18] This strongly political attitude of Marion, then, also intruded on the most
intimate aspects of Amelia's life, linking her own process of mourning with the
public sphere from the beginning.

The constant dislocation under the political circumstances outlined above turns
Amelia Rosselli into an *apolide* [stateless person], as she herself defined her status
in opposition to the term *cosmopolita* [cosmopolite]. The word 'cosmopolite' derives
originally from a note by Pier Pasolini which accompanied the first significant
publication of Amelia Rosselli, a corpus of twenty-four poems was published in
the literary journal *il Menabò* in 1963. The following year, thanks again to Pasolini
who put her in touch with his own editor, Rosselli published her fierce first poetry
collection (*Variazioni Belliche*, 1964). *War Variations* was followed by *Serie Ospedaliera*
(1969) (*Hospital Series*), *Documento* (1976), *Primi Scritti* (1980), *Appunti sparsi e persi*
(1983), *Impromptu* (1981), *La Libellula* (1985) (*The Dragonfly*), and her English poems
collected in *Sleep* (1992). She established herself as an author also through creative
prose (*Prime prose italiane* (1954) and *Diario Ottuso* (1968) [*Obtuse Diary*]), critical
writings (*Spazi Metrici* (1964)), translations of Sylvia Plath, Paul Evans, and Emily
Dickinson among others, and self-translations.[19]

Rosselli's trilingual existence and her formal studies in music (until the age of
29) profoundly influenced her writing. The combination of those elements were
carefully adopted, as much as a methodology of constant research as of authorial
self-assertion in her poetry. At the time of her first publication in *il Menabò*, Pasolini
commented on her discordant syntactical and grammatical choices and on her

intentional playful clash of languages as *lapsus intraverbale* [intraverbal slip], leaving room for a reading of her research as a natural and informal style of expression.[20] Again, in 1978 Pier Vincenzo Mengaldo included her in the anthology *Poeti italiani del novecento* [Anthology of Italian twentieth-century poetry] as the only woman poet. Once again, the focus on her linguistic practice led to a non-mediated consideration of her conversely highly structured experimentalism.[21]

The mischaracterisation of Rosselli as a 'confessional poet' led to a superficial reading of her 'poetica della ricerca' [research poetics], which was, on the contrary, particularly innovative in the Italian landscape.[22] From her first publication in 1964, Rosselli demonstrated a meticulous attention to the multiple levels of meanings. The careful lexical choices which always mark Rosselli's poetic practice are key in indicating relevance to prove her methodology from the very title. In presenting the poems as a series of 'war variations', Rosselli is anticipating the dualistic development and embedded possible readings of the book.

Variazioni Belliche is doubtless a collection which reflects on the post-war state of the world, and speaks to and speaks for a traumatised collectivity about the horror of World War II. Nonetheless, it refers at the same time to the inner struggles of her tormented mind and self: the two aspects are indeed combined, and coexisting. This coexistence is possible because of the conscious identification of personal with political, an ethical and poetical methodology adopted in life and writing in order to protect what is, instead, intimate, and to share a personal experience with which the community can relate as a political act of presence and of remembrance. The *belligeranza* [belligerency] expressed in the title is also evocative of the conflicting relationship between the poetic-self and the lyrical 'you' — usually a male addressee — that creates a constant movement throughout the whole collection.

The choice of referring to these experiments as variations also assumes a plural potentiality of meaning. The most immediate and consistent reading is the one which moves towards musicality,[23] in which a variation is the recurrence of the same material but in altered form; similarly, the book is structurally composed by repetitions, with the themes of circularity and return being frequent. Another relevant use of variation is given by the linguistic reading, obtained through a conscious manipulation of her polyglot background to reach a more universal speaking that re-signifies the semantic traits into an accessible sonority. And ultimately, the variation on the theme of the myth works as an experiment whereby Rosselli challenges the traditional depiction of the archetypical female pantheon and the tragic destiny to which femininity is tied. The re-appropriation of this pantheon — Antigone, Cassandra, and Electra in particular — by a female author is a distinctive trait of rewriting. Rosselli's intent is to regain authority over the archetypical images offered to women for identification.

3. Rewriting the tragic destiny by re-signifying the myth

As argued by Bronislaw Malinowski, myths are both the product of human narratives and, by setting examples, are the producer themselves of consequent human behaviours:[24]

> The process of *semeiosis*, the use of signs and symbols, operates within the whole sphere of living organisms and was evidently invented long before the advent of man. This does not mean that genes prescribe culture — clearly, they do not. But it could be said that they give recommendations that become manifest in the repetition of like patterns, 'the kinds of memories most easily recalled, the emotions they are most likely to evoke.'[25]

Nonetheless, since early civilisation, myths have been adopted as vehicles for ideology in a growing cultural situation mostly interested in preserving the status quo, and therefore rewriting these myths is a powerful and effective tool for setting a (new) cultural structure. Cultural evolution has taken off precisely because of this unique human ability to extract information from one context and manipulate it in another, which brings with it the possibility of new species emerging from the convergence of old ones. We can see this in the evolution of languages, of genres in literature and music, and in any other cultural area you care to mention.[26]

'Building on Lucia Re's theoretical notion of mythic revisionism, according to which female poets are engaged in the rewriting of foundational myths with the aim of resisting and subverting the patriarchal symbolic order',[27] the rewriting of myth promoted by authors that belong to a silenced minority is particularly relevant in the historical framework of post-World War II, and most of all in the case of Rosselli — a Jewish woman whose existence was marked by her older relatives' choices before she could make her own. What is the culture that implicates the next generation? What is the history we want to pass on? It is necessary to expand traditions and include a different vision of the world. To expand the world to minorities; to include those excluded; to listen to the persecuted; to value their perspective on reality that has not been brought forward by traditional views. It has been obscured, silenced, and as we will see, it has been regulated by the traditional narrative, a narrative to which resistance is necessary.

Re-vision — the act of looking back, of seeing with fresh eyes, of entering an old text from a new critical direction — is for us more than a chapter in cultural history: it is an act of survival.[28]

The aim of Amelia Rosselli is, then, to return to those consecrated and fixed behaviours established in a patriarchal society that linked femininity with dramatic destinies. The category of feminine, as intended in philosophy and literature before the practice of revision, is defined by tragedy and non-agency:

> The women in dramas who take the initiative, Clytemnestra, Medea, even Antigone, end badly regardless of their motives. The plots of tragedies so often concern the fortunes of females because women were considered powerless by nature, and tragedy is the genre that celebrates man's inability to triumph over forces beyond his control. Choruses are frequently composed of women because by convention a chorus can never act to prevent the disasters it must witness.[29]

Since antiquity, female characters have been presented as helpful tools of the narration, but never actually considered as active *personae*:

> Each deception or description of a female in the Odyssey is aimed either at the external audience of the poem or at some internal audience of one or more characters as well as the external audience. Each appeals to, or plays against, audiences' conceptions of females generally as well as the expectations shaped by representations of particular females in the mythical and oral poetic tradition behind the poem. None of these descriptions or representations within the Odyssey are totally authoritative; taken together, they contribute greatly to the poem's narratological, dramatic, and moral complexity. In particular, the multiplicity and complexity of females represented as making decisions, taking actions, and telling stories challenge listeners and readers to shape views of Odysseus' distinctive heroic identity, evaluate his authority as a narrator, and consider how his interactions with females help constitute both his identity and his authority, even while these representations render problematic any particular interpretation of the hero, the females, and the poem.[30]

The myths regarding stories of women remain, then, mostly untold, as in the case of Penelope;[31] and when told, we predominantly look at stories produced by men, in a men-focused society to which women are only welcome to participate when functional. The relevance of female subjectivity is therefore excluded by default in many forms of storytelling, and their existence confined to the margins of history. In ancient Greek literature, the margins have frequently been identified with walls, originating the narrative strategy of *teichoscopy*. Although referring to both genders, the narrative practice of *teichoscopy* originates with Helen (*Iliad* 3) and in many occasions reinforces how the female gaze has been considered and represented as 'subjective, fallible, ineffective, passive'.[32]

That same powerless gaze is the one which female characters are forced to emulate when they are abandoned by their (male) heroes. Looking either 'at the departing hero [...] from the walls or from the shore (both marginal locations)',[33] they are watching someone questing for glory whilst they are left behind; in the immediate juxtaposition with men's mobility, the women's duty to stay still — physically and metaphorically — becomes even clearer. The female characters, in fact, are proven once again to be only developing, when it happens, by the function of the male hero and his narrative. Some rare examples excepted, females cannot take part in the action but can still be tellers of the horror. In this perspective, the heroes embracing their destinies become then both the object of desire and lament, and women's functional priorities become the one defining them.

Lament, indeed, is usually a space where female characters find a suitable place. Mourning time is a moment of mediation between the horror of the battles and their consequences. Women have usually been assigned this role because of their *nature*, long considered as only sentimental. At the same time, because of the impossibility of taking part in the action, women in literature had to renounce the viewing of the bodies of their heroes; this privation might be considered the cause of the natural reaction of necessity of seeing the body for mourning.

The action of lament requires an emotional and physical unveiling that shows female characters in their humanity. Because of the association of femininity with sentimentality, women's beings were vehicles of feelings for the whole community. This is investigated in detail by Nicole Loraux, who focuses her investigation on the female lament as the cathartic moment of mourning for the collective group. Once again though, women's subjectivity is reduced to a bare minimum since it is only manifested in public for fulfilling a function. Women and grief are tied together in the expression of mourning for the sake of the accomplishment of the ritual, and very little autonomy in processing such emotions is given to them. It was in fact a prerogative of the state to legislate the exact terms under which grieving was to be manifested by women and when it should come to an end, before risking the loss of dignity. In both Roman and Greek antiquity, public grief was regulated by strict laws. To summarise Loraux, there was a tendency to refuse passions in ancient Greek society and a consequent necessity to legislate the space and time dedicated to *pathos*, 'thus the city, as a well-organised collectivity, enacts a series of laws and regulations against the danger of unbridled passion'.[34]

The symbolic use of myth has long stood as the perfect *escamotage* for the representation of pain for the dead in society: 'the unmanageable remnant flows back to the theater, *intra muros*, but is kept away from the civic self.'[35] The representation of grief was, therefore, usually symbolised and exorcised with the help of drama and, in particular, the use of female characters as representatives of the whole community. The abandonment of crying and lamenting was a ritual related and circumscribed to female entities, both in the city and in theatre. Loraux's study focuses on the emblematic figure of the mother (of a male hero), and highlights that, for example, in the case of the *History of the Peloponnesian War* by Thucydides, women would not walk the bodies down the streets of the city of Athens but rather would 'appear later, at the cemetery, the only place where their lamentations are allowed, albeit in a codified form'.[36] The city is not a place for lament and therefore it is not a place for women. Moreover, Loraux notices how not women in general but 'more exactly, some women, the relatives, are there (*gynàikes pàreisin, hai prosèkousai*)'. This is a rather restricted group, then, in which mothers are tacitly included without deserving any special mention'.[37] Although burdened with the collective grief, Loraux's analysis shows how no distinction is made among the women grieving the loss of heroes. This happens because what the (male-structured) community requires is a symbolic representation of grief; from this perspective, it is meaningless to discuss the role of a single female relative — even the closest one, the mother — since her only reason for existence is figurative. Women are sequestered in the category of 'representing something' rather than, ever, 'being someone'.

The classical masculine elaboration of grief is therefore mediated by a generic (and usually collective) feminine *medium* and has no need and, more importantly, no right to be exposed by crying or lament. If a man should act similarly, that would make him a woman. As perfectly indicated by Plutarch and quoted by Loraux in her argumentation:

> le colpevoli manifestazioni di dolore alle quali si abbandonano durante i funerali sono indegne di un uomo e effeminate (*hos anàndrois kài gynaikòdesi tòis però ta pènthe pàthesi kài hamartèmasin enechomènous*).[38]

[the guilty manifestations of pain to which they abandon themselves during funerals are unworthy of a man and effeminate (*hos anàndrois kài gynaikòdesi tòis perì ta pènthe pàthesi kài hamartèmasin enechomènous*).]

Does the expression of his own grief through tears and lament necessarily make a woman of a man? According to what Loraux states in the quotation above and more widely in several of her publications, it certainly does.

The recurrence of assimilation between females and grief is a constant that can be traced through centuries. A very recognisable example is given by Shakespeare, in *Hamlet*. When Laertes is informed of the death of his sister, Ophelia, he is tempted to abandon himself to a crying lament; only when his crying is done, his *acting like a woman* will also be over.

> Too much water hast thou, poor Ophelia,
> And therefore I forbid my tears. But yet
> It is our trick. Nature her custom holds,
> let shame say what it will. *When these are gone,*
> *the woman will be out* [...][39]

The role of women was therefore the one of the exhibitions of pain, and the consolatory element of expression of pain. Grieving the dead, then, has always been considered a feminine quality and duty, in life and in literature. Rosselli's grieving is mediated by the consciousness of what is symbolically expected from her as a woman, the request of being functional to the community in mourning her father — a martyr, a hero. She nonetheless plays with this role, exploring what she is willing to perform as an author. Moreover, her political lucidity played a major role in her decision to portray through art her grief for her father: heroes need monuments to be remembered, and for their behaviours to become an example. As 'Virgil claims for poetry the same power to immortalise as physical monuments',[40] Rosselli voluntarily represents mourning for her father in a celebratory way, and yet manages to create a space in between her public existence of dutiful *medium* and the private grief of a daughter who exists beyond her function. The mourning experience is political in a profoundly gendered way, in its combination of public and personal that overlaps inevitably but, also, strategically. The self-positioning of Rosselli as author and as poetic subject in both social and literary environments is the result of a practice of self-awareness of the perception of her self, and of her writing as a woman in a gender-biased context.

This conflict already expressed in the title of the collection is shaped in many different ways and addressed very openly on different occasions in *Variazioni Belliche*.[41] Particularly relevant to this enquiry is the struggle of female personal identity in relation to a female archetypal figure (for example, Antigone, Cassandra, or — as for the case soon to be analysed — Electra). In the attempt to liberate one's individuality while also maintaining a direct connection with tradition, Amelia Rosselli explores the controversial aspect of the private and public overlap experienced by women.

4. In the name of the Father

As observed by Jahan Ramazani in his investigation on transnational poetics, 'grief is often conceived as *privatizing* and *depoliticizing*'.[42] However, Judith Butler writes:

> [grief] furnishes a sense of political community of a complex order, and it does this first of all by bringing to the fore the relational ties that have implications for theorizing fundamental dependency and ethical responsibility. If my fate is not originally or finally separable from yours, then the 'we' is traversed by a relationality that we cannot easily argue against; or, rather, we can argue against it, but we would be denying something fundamental about the social conditions of our very formation.[43]

This analysis offered by Butler is particularly fitting for the case of Carlo Rosselli, since the ethical responsibilities of Amelia as the daughter of the anti-fascist martyr are enacted as exemplary in the chosen poem. Despite focusing only on the character of Electra, the established reading of her *persona* as grieving daughter makes the father — although not named — an absent referent with an unwieldy presence. Sophocles' Electra makes the conscious choice of not letting go of the mourning for her assassinated father, and decides to define her own self not in relation to that grief but rather by embodying this same grief. Electra becomes a personified *threnos*:

> Well before Clytemnestra's words are spoken, the chorus has already put Electra on her guard: 'you are not the only mortal, child, who has seen suffering' (Sophocles, *Electra*, 154).[44]

On the contrary, Rosselli is highly aware of her not being the only mortal and that her loss is part of a broader suffering. Both Carlo and Nello were outspoken in their antagonism towards the fascist regime. With Carlo more prominently active in his praxis, through their moral and ethical resistance to Mussolini they encouraged many to refuse to be silenced by the dictatorship (e.g. rallying people to work on their magazine *Non mollare!* — *Do not give up!*). Unsurprisingly, the city of Paris being at the time a destination for exiled intellectuals and activists, a very high number of people crowded the streets for the Rosselli brothers' funeral. As recounted in an article written by Stanislao Pugliese:

> [n]ews of the double assassination shocked and stunned the anti-fascist community. A crowd estimated at between 100,000 and 200,000 people attended the funeral services in Paris and the cortege made its way to the Père Lachaise cemetery accompanied by the music of Beethoven's *Eroica* symphony.[45]

It would be impossible for Rosselli not to acknowledge the loss of her father as a traumatic experience on both a personal and communal level. The political nature of the assassination and the collective recognition of the cause embodied by Carlo required the whole family to mourn publicly. The responsibility of mourning a father who was a national martyr creates inevitable links with a mourning community; the experience of the loss of the community is projected on to Amelia, overlapping with her own personal negotiation with such loss. Far from being privatising and de-politicising:

[w]hat grief displays, in contrast, is the thrall in which our relations with others hold us, in ways that we cannot always recount or explain, in ways that often interrupt the self-conscious account of ourselves that we might try to provide, in ways that challenge the very notion of ourselves as autonomous and in control.[46]

To process grief both on a private and on a public level, Rosselli acknowledges a limited autonomy deriving from the loss but also refuses to monumentalise the grief in her own person and her *persona*. After having at first escaped this overshadowing figure, the poetic subject engages in an identification with Electra; however, the subject later actively detaches from Electra's self-condemnation and abandons the permanent state of mourning. Rosselli refuses to reduce herself and her poetic subject to a *threnos* and faces instead the impossibility of autonomy from the experience of loss by making it topical in her writing.

> l'evocazione di Elettra è l'espediente poetico scelto da Amelia Rosselli per materializzare la propria tragica e infelice esistenza: Amelia condivide con (e contro) Elettra la sua infanzia spezzata, un'ideale di vita spentosi ancor prima di essere formulato, una vita, per di più, che anziché essere vissuta, sembra scorrerle di fronte agli occhi [...][47]

> [the evocation of Electra is the poetic expedient chosen by Amelia Rosselli to materialise her own tragic and unhappy existence: Amelia shares with (and against) Electra her broken childhood, an ideal of life extinguished even before being formulated; a life, moreover, that instead of being lived, seems to flow in front of her eyes [...]]

It is in fact appropriate to observe Rosselli presenting her poetic self as a self in between life and death, as once again sharply defined by Tandello's aforementioned enquiry. The poetic subject of Rosselli, frequently identified as a young woman — a *fanciulla* — is an everlasting mother's daughter, just like Persephone.[48] Alive in the realm of the dead, this Persephonean subject inherits the ambiguity of her archetype's willingness and duties from the myth. Persephone, abducted and deceived into being confined to the Underworld, adjusts to the circumstance of her being in between worlds by fitting in nowhere in particular but serving both at her best. She embodies the bridge in between these worlds, something towards which the poetic subject of Rosselli also seems to aspire. Rosselli, in fact, articulates a relational poetics with the dead, to the point of establishing a literally named 'Dialogo con i Morti' (Dialogue with the Dead) in which the poetic subject is, once again, a *daughter*. In this poem, the poetic subject invites a plural 'you' (in Italian, explicitly 'voi') to descend and reach for her with open arms: 'scendete voi, abbracciate questa vostra | figlia che annaspa' — 'come down, of you, embrace this daughter | of yours'.[49]

In the same way as Persephone spending time in the Underworld and cyclically reuniting with her mother on Earth, this continuous self-placement in and outside the realm of the dead (or somehow on the edge of both, with a relational energy equally expanding towards each realm) of the poetic subject is a torturous re-enacting of *addii*. The poetic subject is continuously connecting to others only as part of a preparation for another announced farewell. Persephone veers between her role as a spouse and her role as a daughter in between worlds, and in so doing she also detaches from her own self each time: a similar detachment is performed and exposed by Rosselli in her writing.

> Allora nel teatro letterario rosselliano verrebbe spontaneo parlare di *addii*, delle cerimonie e dei rituali ove si consuma l'addio, o meglio ancora: dell'atto ove si dice 'addio' all'addio, ove *ci si* dice addio abbandonandosi. Abbandono da sé e *dal sé*, dalla presenza. Ma questo abbandono della presenza viene comunque ostentato e presentato, si rende presente, diviene addirittura *un presente*, anche nel seno di regalo, dono.[50]

> [In the literary theatre of Rosselli, then, it would be natural to talk of *farewells*, ceremonies and rituals where farewell is consummated, or better yet: the act where one says 'farewell' to farewell, where one says goodbye, abandoning oneself. Abandonment by oneself and *from oneself*, from presence. But this abandonment from presence is nevertheless displayed and presented; it becomes present, it actually becomes *a present*, even in the sense of a *gift*.]

Rosselli 'non rivela, protegge, e se rivela universalizza, o, meglio, converte il disagio privato in anonimità'[51] — 'does not reveal, she protects, and there where she reveals she universalises or, better, converts private distress into anonymity' — or, in this case, she names the archetype: Electra.

> Perché il cielo divinasse la tua ansia di morire
> sepolto da una frana di sentimenti, io mi appartai
> alla rincorsa d'un nuovo cielo. L'eletta compagnia
> sepolse Elettra, essa cinse il suo fronte di allori
> imbiancati di polvere e di lacrime: il rosa e il sale,
> la pietà e il gridare agli attenti! Sinonima della
> paura, iena della valle umanissima — lei, io ed
> essa cangiammo ogni pietà ricoprimmo la più piccola
> cicatrice di erbe flessibili bianche e gialle, rosse
> di vendetta e il sorriso sulle labbra. Impiastrata
> si separò, divorata si levò l'anello di congiunzione
> dal collo magro. Adibita ad una fiera di ruoli
> secondarii — si levò l'anello, tolse l'allori, sparì
> per un breve viaggio impossibile, tornò disfatta
> e disparita, secondaria d'importanza e primaria
> nella sua vittoria.

> (Elettra! Le tue terribili università! Le esperienze
> del peccato arrotondano il tuo misero stipendio)

> [So that the heavens might divine your urge to die
> Buried by a landslide of feelings, I stood apart
> Running after a new heaven. The elect company
> Buried Electra, it crowned her forehead with laurel
> bleached by dust by tears; the pink and the salt,
> The pity and the call to attention! Synonym of
> fear, hyena of the most human valley — she, I and
> she switched every mercy we covered the smallest

scar with supple white and yellow grasses, red
with revenge and the smile on the lips. Smeared
she cut herself off, devoured she took the conjugal ring
from her skinny neck. Used in a host of secondary
roles–she took off the ring, removed the laurels, vanished
from a brief impossible journey, came back undone and
faded, secondary in importance and primary
in her victory.

(Electra! Your terrible universities! The experience
of sin fills out your miserable salary.)][52]

5. Elettra: on stage

The structure of the poem is fixed and traditional; its visual representation is
somehow monolithic as requested by Rosselli herself for the most accurate printed
version of the book. The visual and spatial dimension is a fundamental aspect of
the research conducted by Rosselli throughout her whole poetic activity, and it is
particularly true for the case of *Variazioni Belliche* that is also the starting point for
a written elaboration of her poetics which is based on the constant interaction of
spatial and acoustic aspects.[53] The whole book is characterised by a frequent use
of repetition, a syntactic parallel with the recurrence of violence and trauma as
part of human history; in what, in terms of the structure adopted, seems cyclically
always to repeat itself, Rosselli does impose a radical variation: the linguistic one.
Her trilingual education results in frequent neologisms and wordplays consciously
adopted to bring to the surface that internal conflict; to enact such conflict liberates
a variety of relatable experiences of struggle for the formation of one's identity.
The rigid form in which the phonetic and semantic variations take place is a self-
imposed limitation necessary to confront oneself with reality, and thus discover the
possibilities for the self in this same structure.

The staging of a modern Electra in relation to the archetypical one is probably
one of the most overtly revelatory examples of a successful revision, reached in this
poem through a *mise en abyme*. Although the poem is presented very much as such,
the tendency for Rosselli is to blend literary categories through genre hybridisation.
For this specific case, as already argued in detail by Tandello, the larger frame
reminds the reader of a theatrical *mise en scene* of a tragedy. Electra is indeed a
character traditionally portrayed in drama, and that is the textuality — with its
intrinsic performative power — to which one must inevitably refer for the revision,
by Rosselli, and for the critical reading. The most evident literary experiment is to
inscribe the spatial and performative dimension of theatre into poetic form whilst
also opening the space-time of the myth. Both myth and drama, which have always
been applied to read the *persona* of Electra, are regulated in the poetic structure
adopted by Rosselli.

> Perché il cielo divinasse la tua ansia di morire
> sepolto da una frana di sentimenti, io mi appartai
> alla rincorsa d'un nuovo cielo. L'eletta compagnia

> sepolse Elettra, essa cinse il suo fronte di allori
> imbiancati di polvere e di lacrime; il rosa e il sale,
> la pietà e il gridare agli attenti! [...] (ll. 1–6)

From the very first line, the mythical setting in which the poetic 'I' and 'you' relate to each other is determined through key words: '*divinasse* e *cielo* stabiliscono già il rapporto tra questo tu e questo io in termini mitici' ['*divining* and *sky* already establish the relationship between the "you" and the "I" in mythical terms'].[54] The time of the event — a loss — is not clarified, but the syntax propels the reader into a mythical time in which the use of the term *appartarsi* recalls the intent both of hiding and of removing oneself from a social and communal experience. In relation to the death of a male-gendered 'you', the poetic subject must emerge from the *cielo*, enacting the very first of a long series of movements. This first action seems to coincide with the ultimate one: the self-removal from the space of the scene and a displacement outside the area of visibility. The negotiation of power is already portrayed in a number of verses which later on will find a better clarification.

Electra has been buried too — yet not physically — by her duty and by her role, which correspond perfectly. 'Sepolta' [buried] by her behaving like a good daughter, like a good model, like a woman, performing the actions that are demanded of her:

> Nel rito funebre, come ha scritto Ernesto De Martino, il cospargersi la testa di polvere equivale a una 'simbolica autoinumazione' ma anche a un 'occultarsi e rendersi irriconoscibile di fronte alla sgomentante estraneità del cadavere'; ammettere l'"impurità in cui il caso luttuoso ha gettato la casa e i sopravvissuti', ma anche ammettere il 'contagio che si collega al cadavere'. È un gesto, insomma, che mima la stessa propria sepoltura (il proprio suicidio), in riconoscimento di un destino che il sopravvissuto vuole, o non può non voler condividere; e insieme lo esorcizza, nascondendo la propria presenza all'alterità predatrice del morto.[55]

> [In the funeral rite, as Ernesto De Martino has described it, to sprinkle the head with dust is equivalent to a 'symbolic self-burial' but also to a 'hiding and becoming unrecognisable in the face of the appalling extraneousness of the corpse'; to admit the 'impurity which the tragic case has projected onto the house and the survivors', but also to admit the 'contagion that connects to the corpse'. In short, it is a gesture that mimics one's own burial (one's own suicide), in recognition of a destiny that the survivor wants, or cannot not want to share; and at the same time exorcises it, hiding its presence from the predatory alterity of the dead.]

The rituality of the mournful event thus can be read as a celebration of Electra's own death, her sacrifice and submission to her role: a mourning to be converted into a hymn of glory for the hero, and the community the male hero represents. Still, she puts around her brow the *alloro*, a typical allusion to the poet laureate. It is in this exact moment that the fictional Electra represented on stage — to continue with a theatrical reading of the actions — overlaps with the poetic self of the author. This subject refused to remain under that uncertain sky and, probably running from that sky, stepped into Electra's section of the stage, causing an intersection of time (moving from her chronological timeline of events to the fixed mythical one) and *personae* (with a Freudian assimilation to the character of Electra).

To clarify the suggestion above, it is useful to describe the hypothetical stage on which Elettra and the subject act. The space of the performance is to be considered as perfectly divided into two: these two parallel sections are respectively occupied one by Electra, the other by the poetic subject. Their functions and their actions are, at the very beginning, autonomous, although when the subject moves *alla rincorsa di un nuovo cielo*, it abandons its position; it invades the scenic area of Electra melding with its mythical counterpart. This distinction is in my opinion fundamental in terms of not reducing the close reading to a mediate autobiography; the positioning of the subject is the cause of such a confusion between the *personae* of the poem. This means that the confusion is a lucid act of poetry, an intended attempt to build a manifold *persona*. In this circumstance the celebration of the hero coincides with the celebration of Electra, who, by miming her own sepulture — as suggested by De Martino — synthesises in herself the heroic aspects of the dead. By crowning her head with laurel, she is proclaiming herself a heroine and at the same time recognising the poetic authority of the subject. While pretending to observe her duties of secondary character, she is offering hints to read her *persona* as a deserving active subject.

If we accept this positive potentiality in the text, it is thus necessary to investigate the relation between the *alloro* and the subject. The laurel that Electra physically uses for herself is to be considered in its metaphorical functionality for the subject; the *nuovo cielo* determined by new possibilities is represented by the space of poetry that Rosselli is creating for herself. Poetry is, according to Rosselli, a continuous exercise of the claim of existence. Thus, the fictional self of Rosselli, here named as subject, is also invested with the *alloro*: Electra tries to use it in order to glorify herself and to turn into an active *persona*; to take a chance to escape her own destiny, by taking on the agency of the poetic self.

> [...] Sinonima della
> paura, iena della valle umanissima — lei, io ed
> essa cangiammo ogni pietà ricoprimmo la più piccola
> cicatrice di erbe flessibili bianche e gialle, rosse
> di vendetta e il sorriso sulle labbra. Impiastrata
> si separò, divorata si levò l'anello di congiunzione
> dal collo magro.

The central position of the poem is occupied by this interesting sequence of three pronouns; *lei, io ed essa*. Up to this stage, the poem has two different subjects: a newly released active Electra who rejects *l'anello di congiunzione*, and the poetic subject that introduces the incipit to the reader speaking in first person. These two subjects influence each other in shape and decision. And yet it is not just the two of them: a third female-gendered element is added to the list and interacts in similar ways with the one described up until now for Electra and the subject. Introduced as *essa*, the grammar indicates an inanimate object: although the flexibility of language is a persistent eventuality in Rosselli's experimentalism, it is possible to suggest an actual adherence to Italian grammar. For this case, it would highlight the relevance of poetry itself as a major component in mourning and in reaching one's autonomy. Poetry is in fact *poesia*, a female noun that would be perfectly in accordance with *essa*.

In this game of 'masquerade' and play, Rosselli participates in this *mise en abyme* that only takes place in actions and intentions.[56] The character of Electra is to an extent already a translation of another tragic feminine figure, whose pain seems to be the only comparable one: the mother.

> Elettra, [per contro] — e in due occasioni — non vede altra figura da accostare al suo dolore che quella dell''uccello che si lamenta "Iti!", sempre "Iti!"' [Procne], al quale aggiunge — sorprendentemente? — l'evocazione di Niobe, l''addoloratissima che, nella sua tomba di roccia, ahimè, piange' [...] *questa figlia violentemente in lutto per suo padre non sembra trovare equivalenti mitici che nei racconti delle madri assassine.*[57]

> [Electra, [on the other hand] — and on two occasions — sees no other figure to embody her pain than that of the 'bird that complains "Iti!", always "Iti!"' [Procne], to which she adds — surprisingly? — the evocation of Niobe, the 'most sorrowful who, in his rock tomb, alas, cries' [...] *this violently grieving daughter for her father does not seem to find mythical equivalents in the stories of murderer mothers.*]

These grieving mothers she actively recalls in her speech are a necessary part of her own masquerade, necessary in order to ascribe her pain to the symbolic order of representation. The character of Electra traditionally develops her features and asserts her presence through words. It is the power of her wording that initiates a series of events of revenge: the true capabilities of her character, which derive from her place in the semi-poetic tradition of lamentation, allow her to construct the other characters' experience of time and space.[58]

On the contrary, in the dimension of the poem by Rosselli, Electra has no words but instead affirms herself in actions. As for the poetic subject, it decides to exile itself from the space in which it would keep coexisting with its male counterpart; having asserted that space in the first lines as a limitation for her own self-discovery, the subject rejects its structure and burden and proactively creates a marginalisation of the self. Although this marginalisation is a typically negative experience of non-active subjectivity for female characters, Rosselli revises it by giving the subject a chance to find a way to define itself in the absence of a male *persona* — in this case, the gendered 'you' of the incipit, as clarified by the masculine concordance of 'sepolto' — similarly to what has been theorised for Penelope by Adriana Cavarero.[59]

In this revised dimension of forbidden words, Electra, who has always been the voiced lament, can finally turn into someone else. More specifically, she can ultimately turn into someone instead of remaining a symbolic medium. Similarly, the poetic subject actively finds its own determination through the experience of 'lei' — Electra and 'essa' — 'poesia' (since both poetry and poem can be ascribed to the term 'poesia', the Italian language reveals itself to be more resourceful). There is no specific dominance of a subject over the others, and they now coexist in strict dependency but also in autonomy from the predetermined social regulation of their existence, unafraid to change ('cangiammo').

Electra was in fact previously described as a synonym for fear, probably referring to that fear of the poetic self to have no other choice but to eternally mourn in rage its own father, just like the mythological character of Electra, and to the fear that her poetry may also remain identical to itself. The unification of the three identities in the space of action ('cangiammo', initiating then the changing as a performative action) might be the moment for changing all their destinies. Nonetheless, this cannot happen.

> [...] Adibita ad una fiera di ruoli
> secondarii — si levò l'anello, tolse l'allori, sparì
> per un breve viaggio impossibile, tornò disfatta
> e disparita, secondaria d'importanza e primaria
> nella sua vittoria.

As suggested by a close reading offered by Tandello in *La fanciulla e l'infinito*, in its brevity of only eighteen lines this poem seems to include a proper play: Electra's play, but the untold one. Always bound to a functional role of representations of collective emotions (revenge, family duty, grief) and never capable of acting for herself, Electra seems finally to find a space for herself in which to dismiss her role and interact with others as a subject. But her destiny is tragic and fixed, the mythical Electra having no way to escape her fate; 'un breve viaggio impossibile' [a brief and impossible journey] is the described attempt to avoid her condemnation. After her return, she will be 'sepolta' each time the story has been told.

> Quello che però non è sancito è il destino del Soggetto — che tenta di allestire e mimare la propria rincorsa di un futuro diverso. Se ci si aspettava una catarsi, i versi rosselliani ce la negano (come la negano alla propria poesia). Il dramma rimane invece irrisolto, la tensione tragica si dissolve, ma in una ambiguità sconcertante, disorientante.[60]

> [What is not sanctioned, however, is the destiny of the Subject — who attempts to set up and imitate her own pursuit of a different future. If we were to expect a catharsis, Rosselli's verses deny it to us (as they deny it to their own poetry). Instead, the drama remains unresolved, the tragic tension dissolves, but in a disconcerting, unsettling ambiguity.]

Although no resolution is offered for the poetic subject or for poetry itself in the space of this *mise en abyme*, there is much to be discovered elsewhere: away from the assigned role of eternal mourner, away from the *cielo* that oppresses the subject with the risk of having her 'sepolta' just like Electra. The Subject not only aspires to a 'nuovo cielo' but also celebrates one of the ways in which to gain it: poetry. Once again, Electra is left alone and the subject observes the compelling stasis of time in tragedy. None of Electra's attempts, none of what she might have learned from her 'breve viaggio impossibile', could save her from the established role of secondary character, which builds up in anger and pain.

> [...] a living memory that bears no other name than excess of grief. In Sophocles, Electra is in fact the perfect incarnation of this living memory, and when she claims *ou lathei m'orga*, she says not only 'my anger does not escape me' or 'I do not forget my anger' but also 'my anger does not forget me'. It is as if only anger

> gives the self the courage to be entirely given to anger, because for the subject
> anger is uninterrupted presence of self to self.[61]

Electra can only be present in her own tragic existence, determined by this
ferocious mourning for her father, while monumentalising him by devoting her
own self to his death. Rosselli instead might find a way and a place to define her
identity in autonomy, breaking the circle that would want her forever as (only) a
medium to glorify the hero.

> (Elettra! Le tue terribili università! Le esperienze
> del peccato arrotondando il tuo misero stipendio).

The poetic Subject, once again speaking in the first person, distances itself from
Electra (as proven also by the parentheses and the blank space in between verses
anticipating the admonishment). Even though, as remarked on in these last lines,
the permanence in the time of myth has been a terrible — and yet valuable —
experience of identification (*Le tue terribili università!*), this temporary assimilation
does not define the whole identity of the poetic Subject. The Subject does not
only belong to a different time but is a resolving medium for Rosselli's personal
mourning in an abstraction specifically created by herself. Poetry is therefore a
fundamental space for mourning, but most of all is the space-time fundamental for
enacting her own attempt of existing as an author, rather than just as a daughter. In
self-proclaiming adherence first and, later, conscious distance from Electra, Rosselli
is investigating and then removing herself from the symbolic system; by creating
her own space of mourning, in poetry, Rosselli is inevitably shaping a different
system in which autonomy is the ultimate aspiration. In contrast with the first lines,
in which the subject finds itself in the necessity of leaving behind a certain space of
mourning, the power dynamic between Electra, the poetic subject, and poetry —
'lei, io ed essa' — is perfectly balanced.

Tandello is able to discern a pattern of development within the deceptively
'blocked' biographical stance of the lyrical self in Rosselli's *oeuvre*. If the
biographical fiction underpinning the corpus depicts a self always frozen in a
permanent adolescence, the fanciulla of *Variazioni belliche* is nevertheless animated
by a euphoric/disphoric dislocation.[62]

The topic of isolation is a prominent one in Rosselli's poetics: as already
investigated in detail by Carpita,[63] Rosselli defines her poetics as being 'straniera
in patria', dealing with different ways of coping with the traumatic experience of
persecution. In presenting a poetic self in motion, Rosselli is responding to the
forced exile that she personally experienced in life and to the historical trauma of
her century. Rosselli has authority over her choices of movements and those turn
into affirmative actions of the self. She re-establishes, but on her own terms, the
nomadic experience as a subject, and re-appropriates the terms in which one always
feels like a foreigner.[64]

6. Conclusions

As established in this contribution and in the many critical resources that have examined Rosselli's production from both an historical and literary perspective,[65] and as synthesised by Nelson Moe, Rosselli's 'poetry counters the traditional view of lyric poetry as the exclusive precinct for the intimate matters of the heart and soul, separate from the "public" world of politics'.[66]

The experience of loss for Rosselli has inevitably always been a public one, because of the political connotations of the assassination. The long tradition of social justice in her education meant she would never abdicate such a role, and she proudly accepts the investiture of 'daughter of Carlo and Nello'. In contrast from the archetype of Electra, though, which only exists in the story written for her, Rosselli does recognise the possibility of being also the daughter of Carlo and Marion, and to mourn the loss of her parents in a process that is also private and not exemplary. The overlapping of the private and public experience is presented in verses, defining strategically the authority over the narrative of her own self and experience in and through poetry.

As demonstrated by the identification and interaction of the *dramatis personae* of the poem, poetry represents the space in which it is possible to create a unification as much as a distance between the personal self and its symbolic representation. Far from confessional poetry (despite the recalling of biographic events) and not confinable to pure elegy (despite a degree of lament extended throughout the whole book), the temporal and special dimensions of poetry form a positive field of experience in which to remember, discuss, and reinvent oneself. This poem stages the mechanisms through which to address the experience of mourning of Rosselli, and more broadly her inception of private into public and vice versa. The conscious intersection of private and public demonstrates a rhetorical attitude to present a polyvalent poetic self:

> In primo luogo presentandosi altera, sia *altra* che *alterata*, attratta e insieme distratta da un sé che cerca [...] altri sé di cui nutrirsi e da portare, in un certo senso, al patibolo (al suo stesso patibolo?)[67]

> [In the first place presenting itself as aloof, both *other* and *altered*, attracted and at the same time distracted by a self that seeks [...] others to feed on and, in a certain sense, to take to the scaffold (to its own scaffold?)]

Following on from the extensive investigation by Nelson Moe, particularly his observation on the subject with 'desinenza in a' (feminine inflection), I believe that this analysis proves once again that 'we can see that lines like these don't merely reflect a sociological change (the appearance of women writers on the poetry scene, the publication of women poets by major publishing houses) but rather a change of considerable relevance to the discourse, and practice, of Italian poetry'.[68]

However, rather than 'modern lyric' — as referred to by Moe — I argue it is important to acknowledge the shift of categories and codes. Amelia Rosselli establishes a subversion of the normative codes of the lyric tradition in aspiring towards new forms of poetry: what appears as an elegy turns into a self-elegy, since it is Electra who is the focus of the dramatic events represented on the syntactical stage. Deprived of the lament for Agamemnon, the discourse is focused on the presence of a female Subject, which is nonetheless not even Electra but the poetic self. This continuous shifting is part of a long-term staging of the relationships between embodied ghosts and dematerialised subjects: '[p]rodurre figure e narrare storie in poesia come esito di un processo di proliferazione interiore' [To produce figures and to narrate stories in poetry because of a process of internal proliferation].[69]

> Nel caso della poesia di Rosselli la risposta ai traumi privati (l'essere donna in una società patriarcale, la malattia mentale, le difficoltà finanziarie) e collettivi (la guerra, la persecuzione fascista) diventa atto politico nella prassi poetica: l'io poetico dimostra come sia possibile resistere alla violenza e costruire una società non violenta solo ispirandosi all'etica relazionale che si oppone alla logica capitalista patriarcale.[70]

> [In the case of Rosselli's poetry, the response to private traumas (being a woman in a patriarchal society, mental illness, financial difficulties) and collective traumas (war, fascist persecution) becomes a political act in poetic practice: the poetic self demonstrates how it is possible to resist violence and build a non-violent society only by drawing inspiration from the relational ethics that opposes patriarchal capitalist logic.]

The explicit historical context offered by the title of the collection deeply permeates her extensive writing. In poetry, Rosselli researches, refines, and presents new forms of relationality in opposition to the violent power dynamics that defined the twentieth century. Formally, she is not only creating *variazioni* in the lyric genre but also leaning towards a full hybridism of genres. Amelia Rosselli's poetry escapes the established categorisation and generates a mixture of references and modes through which she reinvents forms of poetry to serve the shifting world and its community with a fair narration.

Bibliography

AZARI, EHSAN, *Lacan and the Destiny of Literature* (New York: Bloomsbury, 2011)

BALDACCI, ALESSANDRO, *Amelia Rosselli* (Rome: Laterza, 2007)

BISANTI, TATIANA, *L'opera plurilingue di Amelia Rosselli* (Pisa: Edizioni ETS, 2007)

BLATT, JOEL, 'Carlo Rosselli's Socialism', in *Italian Socialism: Between Politics and History*, ed. by Spencer M. Di Scala (Amherst, MA: The University of Massachusetts Press, 1996), pp. 80–99

BRAIDOTTI, ROSI, *Nomadic Subjects: Embodiment and Sexual Difference in Contemporary Feminist Theory* (New York: Columbia University Press, 1994)

BURKERT, WALTER, *Creation of the Sacred: Tracks of Biology in Early Religions* (Cambridge, MA: Harvard University Press, 1996)

BUTLER, JUDITH, *Precarious Life: The Powers of Mourning and Violence* (London: Verso, 2004)

CAMPI, ENZO, 'Epico, sapido, quasi sadico: per un (auto)ritratto di Amelia Rosselli', in AA. VV., ed. by Enzo Campi, *Il colpo di coda: Amelia Rosselli e la poetica del lutto* (Milan: Marco Saya Edizioni, 2016), pp. 82–102

CAPORALI, MARCO, 'Donne che traducono donne: Amelia Rosselli e Sylvia Plath', in *La furia dei venti contrari*, ed. by Andrea Cortellessa (Florence: Le Lettere, 2007)

CARBOGNIN, FRANCESCO, *Le armoniose dissonanze: 'Spazi metrici' e intertestualità nella poesia di Amelia Rosselli* (Bologna: Gedit Edizioni, 2008)

CARPITA, CHIARA, 'Per una poetica dell'inclinazione: Scrittura del trauma ed etica relazionale nella poesia di Amelia Rosselli', *Carte Italiane*, 11 (2017): 21–42

CAVARERO, ADRIANA, *In Spite of Plato: A Feminist Rewriting of Ancient Philosophy* (London: Routledge, 1995)

DE FELICE, RENZO, *The Jews in Fascist Italy*, trans. by Robert L. Miller (New York: Enigma Books, 2001), p. 79

DE MARCH, SILVIA, *Amelia Rosselli tra poesia e storia* (Naples: L'Ancora del Mediterraneo, 2006)

DICKMANN, IDDO, *The Little Crystalline Seed: The Ontological Significance of Mise en Abyme in Post-Heideggerian Thought* (Albany: State University of New York Press, 2019)

DISTIN, KATE, *Cultural Evolution* (Cambridge: Cambridge University Press, 2011)

DI VITO, LUCA, and MICHELE GIALDRONI, *Lipari 1929: Fuga dal confino* (Rome-Bari: Laterza, 2009)

FRANCE, PETER, *The New Oxford Companion to French Literature* (Oxford: Oxford University Press, 1995)

FREUD, SIGMUND, 'Mourning and Melancholia', in *The Standard Edition of the Complete Psychological Works of Sigmund Freud* (London: Hogarth press, 1957), XIV, pp. 243–58

FUSCO, FLORINDA, *Amelia Rosselli: La scrittura e l'interpretazione* (Palermo: Palumbo, 2008)

LA PENNA, DANIELA, '"Cercatemi e fuoriuscite": Biography, Textuality, and Gender in Recent Criticism on Amelia Rosselli', *Italian Studies*, 65:2 (2010), 278–85

LEFKOWITZ, MARY R., *Heroines and Hysterics* (London: St. Martin's Press, 1981)

LORAUX, NICOLE, *Mothers in Mourning* (Ithaca, NY: Cornell University Press, 1998)

—— *The Divided City: On Memory and Forgetting in Ancient Athens* (New York: Zone Books, 2002)

—— *The Mourning Voice: An Essay on Greek Tragedy* (Ithaca, NY: Cornell University Press, 2002)

LORENZINI, NIVA, *Poesia del Novecento italiano* (Rome: Carocci, 2002)

LORETO, ANTONIO, *I santi padre di Amelia Rosselli* (Milan: Arcipelago Edizioni, 2014)

LOVATT, HELEN, *The Epic Gaze: Vision, Gender and Narrative in Ancient Epic* (Cambridge: Cambridge University Press, 2013)

MALINOWSKI, BRONISLAW, *Myth in Primitive Psychology* (1926) (Redditch: Read Books Ltd, 2014)

MENGALDO, PIER VINCENZO, *Poeti italiani del Novecento* (Milan: Mondadori, 1978)

—— 'Amelia Rosselli', in *Poeti italiani del Novecento*, ed. by Pier V. Mengaldo (Milan: Mondadori, 1978), pp. 993–97

MINORE, RENATO, 'Amelia Rosselli, il dolore in una stanza', *il Messaggero*, 2 February 1984

MOE, NELSON, and AMELIA ROSSELLI, 'At the Margins of Dominion: The Poetry Of Amelia Rosselli', *Italica*, 69:2 (1992), 177–97

MONTEFIORE, JAN, *Feminism and Poetry: Language, Experience, Identity in Women's Writing* (New York: Pandora, 1987)

MOSSALI, MATTIA, '"Condizionata alla morte essa rimava vocabolari tormentosi": declinazioni del lutto nella poesia di Amelia Rosselli e Sylvia Plath', *LEA — Lingue e Letterature d'Oriente e d'Occidente*, 7 (2018), 245–61

NOOTER, SARAH, 'Language, Lamentation, and Power in Sophocles 'Electra', *Classical World* 104:4 (2011), 399–417

O CEALLACHAIN, EANNA, *Twentieth-Century Italian Poetry: A Critical Anthology (1900 to the Neo-Avantgarde)* (Leicester: Troubador Publishing, 2007)

PASOLINI, PIER PAOLO, *Notizia su Amelia Rosselli*, in *La Libellula* (Milan: Studio Editoriale, 1985)

PASSANNANTI, ERMINIA, *Sulla Poesia di Amelia Rosselli* (Salisbury: Brindin Press, 2012)

PELLEGRINI, ERNESTINA, 'Amelia Rosselli', in *Le eccentriche. Scrittrici del Novecento*, ed. by Anna Botta, Monica Farnetti, Giorgio Rimondi, (Mantova: Tre Lune Edizioni, 2003), pp. 137–52

PLUTARCO, *Vita di Solone*, ed. by Mario Manfredini and Luigi Piccirilli (Milan: Fondazione Lorenzo Valla, 1977)

PUGLIESE, STANISLAO G., 'Death in Exile: The Assassination of Carlo Rosselli', *Journal of Contemporary History*, 32:3 (1997), 305–19

RAMAZANI, JAHAN, 'Nationalism, Transnationalism, and the Poetry of Mourning', in *A Transnational Poetic* (Chicago: The University of Chicago Press, 2009)

RE, LUCIA, 'Mythic Revisionism: Women Poets and Philosophers in Italy Today', in *Italian Women Writers from the Renaissance to the Present: Revising the Canon*, ed. by Maria Ornella Marotti (University Park: Pennsylvania State University Press, 1996), pp. 187–233

RE, LUCIA, 'Amelia Rosselli and the Aesthetics of Experimental Music', *Galleria: Rassegna quadrimestrale di cultura*, 48, 1–2, special issue devoted to Amelia Rosselli, ed. by Emanuela Tandello and Daniela Attanasio (January–August 1997), pp. 35–46

RICH, ADRIENNE, 'When We Dead Awaken: Writing as Re-Vision', *College English*, 34:1 (1972), 18–30

ROSSELLI, AMELIA, and JENNIFER SUE SCAPPETTONE, *Locomotrix* (Chicago: University of Chicago Press, 2012)

ROSSELLI, AMELIA and LUCIA RE, PAUL VANGELISTI, *War Variations* (Los Angeles: Otis Books/Seismicity Editions, 2016)

ROSSELLI, AMELIA, *L'opera poetica*, ed. by. Stefano Giovannuzzi, preface by Emanuela Tandello (Milan: Mondadori, 2012)

ROSSELLI, AMELIA, 'Istinto di morte e istinto di piacere in Sylvia Plath', *Nuovi Argomenti*, 67–68 (1980), 175–80

ROSSELLI, CARLO, *Socialisme libéral* (Paris: Librairie Valois, 1930); *Socialismo liberale*, ed. by John Rosselli (Milan: Einaudi, 1979)

SCAPPETTONE, JENNIFER, 'La santità dei santi padri', *Alfabeta*, 2 (2015)

SCHEIN, SETH L., *Female Representations and Interpreting the Odyssey*, in *The Distaff Side: Representing the Female in Homer's Odyssey*, ed. by Beth Cohen (Oxford: Oxford University Press, 1995), pp. 17–27

SERENI, VITTORIO, 'Il silenzio creativo', in *La tentazione della prosa* (Milan: Mondadori, 1998), pp. 67–70

TANDELLO, EMANUELA, *La fanciulla e l'infinito* (Rome: Donzelli, 2007)

TANDELLO, EMANUELA, *An enquiry into Italian post-war experimentalism: the poetry of Amelia Rosselli* (doctoral thesis, University of Oxford, 1989)

TANDELLO, EMANUELA, 'Between Tradition and Transgression: Amelia Rosselli's Petrarch', in *Petrarch in Britain: Interpreters, Imitators, and Translators over 700 years*, ed. by Martin McLaughlin, Laura Panizza, and Peter Hainsworth (British Academy Scholarship Online: 2012) <https://britishacademy.universitypressscholarship.com/view/10.5871/bacad/9780197264133.001.0001/upso-9780197264133> [accessed 22 February 2022]

TESTA, ENRICO, *Dopo la lirica: Poeti italiani 1960–2000* (Turin: Einaudi, 2005)

VENTURINI, MONICA, and SILVIA DE MARCH, *Amelia Rosselli: È vostra la vita che ho perso: Conversazioni e interviste 1963–1995* (Florence: Le Lettere, 2010)

YOKE, CYNTHIA, 'Voice, Silence, & Testimony: Recovering Feminist Voices in Italian Poetry and Autobiography' (Honors Thesis Collection 505, Wellesley College, 2017)

Notes to Chapter 5

1. For a general discussion on women's poetry and the male poetic tradition see Jan Montefiore, *Feminism and Poetry: Language, Experience, Identity in Women's Writing* (New York: Pandora, 1987).

2. Cynthia Yoke, 'Voice, Silence, & Testimony: Recovering Feminist Voices in Italian Poetry and Autobiography' (Honors Thesis Collection 505, Wellesley College, 2017).

3. Emanuela Tandello, *An enquiry into Italian post-war experimentalism: the poetry of Amelia Rosselli* (doctoral thesis, University of Oxford, 1989)

4. 'Ifigenia, *Diario in tre lingue* (1955), Elettra, Cassandra, Antigone, *Variazioni Belliche* [...]. These classical figures of death and mourning coexist alongside other *fanciulle* in Rosselli's poetry, from Leopardi's Sappho (who casts her shadow over Rosselli's poetry from *La libellula* to *Impromptu*) and Silvia (in *Serie ospedaliera*), to Rimbaud's Hortense (in *La libellula*) and Montale's Arletta (more diffusely through *Variazioni belliche* and *Serie ospedaliera*) and Esterina (again, in *La libellula*)'; see Daniela La Penna, '"Cercatemi e fuoriuscite": Biography, Textuality, and Gender in Recent Criticism on Amelia Rosselli', *Italian Studies*, 65:2 (2010), 278–85 (p. 283).

5. Renato Minore, 'Amelia Rosselli, il dolore in una stanza', *il Messaggero*, 2 February 1984.

6. All translations into English are mine, unless otherwise stated.

7. Chiara Carpita, 'Per una poetica dell'inclinazione: Scrittura del trauma ed etica relazionale nella poesia di Amelia Rosselli', *Carte Italiane*, 11 (2017), 21–42 (p. 26).

8. Drawing from Gide, the use of the term *mise en abyme* is here to be intended as critically recollected by France as 'the rivalry between the real world and the representation of it which we make to ourselves. The manner in which the world of the appearances imposes itself upon us, and the manner in which we try to impose on the outside world our own interpretation — this is the drama of our lives'; Peter France, *The New Oxford Companion to French Literature* (Oxford: Oxford University Press, 1995), p. 183. Moreover, as expanded by Dickmann: 'Literary theorists and philosophers alike have associated the mise en abyme with the emblem of the mirror right from the start. The type of mirror which they usually invoke, however, is unique — infinite parallel mirrors ("two mirrors would in fact suffice!") — a device which Deleuze, following Bergson, also terms "dynamic" or "mobile" mirroring. The specular relation prevailing in mise en abyme, writes Ricardou, "is not that of a still mirror, but a dialectical one which elaborates itself, incessantly resettles itself, and which escapes any immobilization." Whilst the static mirror bears a relation of correspondence with the object it reflects, so that one can stably determine any part of the mirror-image to represent a part of the person gazing at the mirror (and that part alone) in the mobile mirror one stands on moving sands. In a mobile mirror where "A reflects B while being reflected by it in continuous mirror effects," the "selves" (and features) of both the reflecting device and the reflected object incessantly change. Mirror A cannot reflect mirror B without being always already a different subject reflecting a different object, it is retroactively transformed into a conjunction such as (mirror A within mirror B), that is, mirror C. The subject and object of the mobile mirror bear not a "coded" identity, to use Deleuze's terminology, but only a "situational" one, deriving from a here and now constellation. This also means that though a difference between the reflected and the reflecting does persist, one cannot stably discern here two respective substances, that is, determine which is the origin and which is the copy. There is no unique, singular, "first time," preceding other instances of repetition temporally or qualitatively: The mise en abyme "does not redouble the unit, as an external reflection might do; in so far as it is an internal mirroring, it can only ever split it in two"'; Iddo Dickmann, *The Little Crystalline Seed* (Albany: State University of New York Press, 2019), p. 14.

9. Letter from the Italian Ambassador to the Ministry of Foreign Affairs in Rome (18 August 1929), Confino politico, b. 883, fasc. personali, Rosselli, Marion, Archivio Centrale dello Stato (ACS), Rome.

10. Carlo Rosselli, *Socialisme libéral* (Paris: Librairie Valois, 1930). The book was only later published in Italy. See Carlo Rosselli, *Socialismo liberale*, ed. by John Rosselli (Milan: Einaudi, 1979).

11. Francesco Fausto Nitti (1899–1974) was an Italian anti-fascist and partisan, and Emilio Lussu (1890–1975) was an anti-fascist politician and writer. Together with Carlo Rosselli, they founded the 'Giustizia e Libertà' movement. See more about their escape in Luca di Vito and Michele Gialdroni, *Lipari 1929: Fuga dal confino* (Rome-Bari: Laterza, 2009).

12. Gaetano Salvemini (1873–1957) was an anti-fascist politician, historian, and journalist.

13. Joel Blatt, 'Carlo Rosselli's Socialism', in *Italian Socialism: Between Politics and History*, ed. by Spencer M. Di Scala (Amherst, MA: The University of Massachusetts Press, 1996), pp. 80–99.

14. Eanna O Ceallachain, *Twentieth-Century Italian Poetry: A Critical Anthology (1900 to the Neo-Avantgarde)* (Leicester: Troubador Publishing, 2007), p. 319.

15. Renzo De Felice, *The Jews in Fascist Italy*, trans. by Robert L. Miller (New York: Enigma Books, 2001), p. 79.

16. 'The Manifesto of Racial Scientists' was published for the first time on 14 July 1938. Signed by 180 scientists and academics, it was published by Telesio Interlandi (1894–1965). Interlandi was an Italian journalist and propagandist and one of the leading advocates of antisemitism in Fascist Italy.

17. She signed her letters to Rocco Scotellaro, 'Marion'. Scotellaro's death in 1953 also had a traumatic impact on Amelia's life. As discussed by Freud, a process of assimilation of the dead is part of a pathological experience of mourning, up to the point of '*identification* of the ego with the abandoned object'. Sigmund Freud, 'Mourning and Melancholia', in *The Standard Edition of the Complete Psychological Works of Sigmund Freud* (London: Hogarth Press, 1957), XIV, pp. 243–58 (p. 249). As for her father's death, which happened when she was too young to mourn in an active sense, the social context repeatedly reactivated the process throughout her life.

18. 'Fu mia madre a farcelo sapere che era stato assassinato e ha chiamato mio fratello minore e me in camera sua. Stava molto male di cuore credo già da molto e ci ha semplicemente chiesto se sapevamo cosa voleva dire la parola "assassinio". E abbiamo risposto di sì. E credo io avevo sette anni e mio fratello Andrea sei. Poi mi ricordo con le vestagliette siamo tornati in camera. Poi non ricordo niente.' Amelia Rosselli, *È vostra la vita che ho perso: Conversazioni e interviste 1963–1995*, ed. by Monica Venturini and Silvia De March (Florence: Le Lettere, 2010), p. 259. ['My mother let us know that he had been murdered, she called my younger brother and me into her room. She had been sick, I think, for a long time already and she simply asked us if we knew what the word "murder" meant. And we said yes. And I think I was seven years old and my brother Andrea was six. Then I remember in our dressing gowns we went back to [our] room. I don't remember anything after that'].

19. For the extended bibliography and critical commentary please refer to: Amelia Rosselli, *L'opera poetica*, ed. by Stefano Giovannuzzi, intro. by Emanuela Tandello (Milan: Mondadori, 2012).

20. This implies a biographical-only tendency of interchangeability of idioms, which does not align with the reasoned cultural declaration of intent of Rosselli's statements on language.

21. See Pier Paolo Pasolini, *Notizia su Amelia Rosselli*, later also published as preface to *La Libellula* (Milan: Studio Editoriale, 1985), and Pier Vincenzo Mengaldo, 'Amelia Rosselli', in *Poeti italiani del Novecento*, ed. by Pier Vincenzo Mengaldo (Milan: Mondadori, 1978), pp. 993–97 (p. 995).

22. See Marco Caporali, 'Donne che traducono donne: Amelia Rosselli e Sylvia Plath', in *La furia dei venti contrari*, ed. by Andrea Cortellessa (Florence: Le Lettere, 2007); Amelia Rosselli, 'Istinto di morte e istinto di piacere in Sylvia Plath', *Nuovi Argomenti*, 67–68 (1980): 175–80 (repr. with amendments in *Una scrittura plurale*, pp. 175–80); Pier Vincenzo Mengaldo, 'Amelia Rosselli', in *Poeti italiani del Novecento* (Milan: Mondadori, 1978); Niva Lorenzini, *Poesia del Novecento italiano* (Rome: Carocci, 2002); Enrico Testa, *Dopo la lirica: Poeti italiani 1960–2000* (Turin: Einaudi, 2005). Standing against such a categorisation is the publication by Antonio Loreto, *I santi padri di Amelia Rosselli* (Milan: Arcipelago Edizioni, 2014) in which, however, as observed by Scappettone: 'Loreto si sforza di ricercare i "padri" — i "santi padri" — di Amelia Rosselli nell'avanguardia a lei misconosciuta, con un argomento polemico: intendendo combattere decenni di letture riduttive basate sulla biografia straordinaria e tragica del poeta (o "poetessa") come se la sua opera nascesse in modo confessionale e immediato dalla morte di un padre singolare, Carlo Rosselli. Il suo motivo è di ricostruire un ambiente più ampio, un contesto plurale, per la composizione e la ricezione di *Variazioni Belliche*; tale lavoro di ricerca, il midollo spinale del saggio, è estremamente pertinente. Ne risulta, però, uno strano squilibrio nell'argomento complessivo che favorisce, nel combattimento sopra nominato, il campo neoavanguardistico, senza sciogliere il binarismo ereditato; la neoavanguardia diventa, per certi aspetti, la vera protagonista del saggio'; Jennifer Scappettone, 'La santità dei santi

padri', *Alfabeta*, 2 (2015) <https://www.alfabeta2.it/tag/amelia-rosselli/page/2/> [accessed 24 February 2020]. ['Loreto strives to seek out the "fathers" — the "holy fathers" — of Amelia Rosselli in the vanguard that she did not recognise, through a polemical argument: intending to fight decades of reductive readings based on the extraordinary and tragic biography of the poet (or "poetess") as if her work was created in a confessional and immediate way from the death of a singular father, Carlo Rosselli. His reason is to reconstruct a wider environment, a plural context, for the composition and reception of *War Variations*; such research work, the backbone of the essay, is extremely pertinent. The result, however, presents a strange imbalance in the overall argument that favours, in the above-mentioned combat, of the neo-avant-garde aspects, without dissolving the inherited binarism; the neo-vanguard becomes, in some respects, the true protagonist of the essay.']

23. See Lucia Re, 'Amelia Rosselli and the Aesthetics of Experimental Music', *Galleria: Rassegna quadrimestrale di cultura*, 48, nos. 1–2, special issue on Amelia Rosselli, ed. by Emanuela Tandello and Daniela Attanasio (Jan. — Aug. 1997): 35–46.

24. See in particular Bronislaw Malinowski, *Myth in Primitive Psychology* (1926) (Redditch: Read Books Ltd, 2014).

25. Walter Burkert, *Creation of the Sacred: Tracks of Biology in Early Religions* (Cambridge, MA: Harvard University Press, 1996), p. 22.

26. Kate Distin, *Cultural Evolution* (Cambridge: Cambridge University Press, 2011), p. 209.

27. Daniela La Penna, '"Cercatemi e fuoriuscite"', commenting on Lucia Re, 'Mythic Revisionism: Women Poets and Philosophers in Italy Today', in *Italian Women Writers from the Renaissance to the Present: Revising the Canon*, ed. by Maria Ornella Marotti (University Park, PA: Pennsylvania State University Press, 1996), pp. 187–233.

28. Adrienne Rich, 'When We Dead Awaken: Writing as Re-Vision', *College English*, 34:1 (1972), 18–30 (p. 18).

29. Mary R. Lefkowitz, *Heroines and Hysterics* (London: St. Martin's Press, 1981), p. 73.

30. Seth L. Schein, *Female Representations, and Interpreting the Odyssey*, in *The Distaff Side: Representing the Female in Homer's Odyssey*, ed. by Beth Cohen (Oxford: Oxford University Press, 1995), pp. 17–27 (p. 18).

31. The truth is that only through the hero's departure, even when the story is not told, might those female characters start seeing their unique development as a specific gendered persona instead of being reduced to a simple function of the male hero. Their individual existence begins in the absence of their counterparts. Adriana Cavarero reveals a new possible reading of Penelope's life, for example, that is no more determined by the confines established by her husband needs for himself but finally develops its own singularity, eradicating the need to find a place in the patriarchal order imposed and building a new personal existence. See in particular Adriana Cavarero, *In Spite of Plato: A Feminist Rewriting of Ancient Philosophy* (London: Routledge, 1995). However, the agency is not gained over the events of the myth but developed as an alternative timeline and space, and therefore differently from the cases of revision investigated by Adrienne Rich and to which, to a certain extent, Rosselli's rewriting applies.

32. Helen Lovatt, *The Epic Gaze: Vision, Gender and Narrative in Ancient Epic* (Cambridge: Cambridge University Press, 2013), p. 224. See in particular the chapter entitled *The Female Gaze* for a recollection of relevant literary examples, starting from Helen and Priam in *Iliad* 3.

33. Ibid., p. 225.

34. Nicole Loraux, *Mothers in Mourning* (Ithaca, NY: Cornell University Press, 1998), p. 9.

35. Ibid.

36. Ibid., p. 15.

37. Ibid.

38. Plutarco, *Vita di Solone*, ed. by Mario Manfredini and Luigi Piccirilli (Milan: Fondazione Lorenzo Valla, 1977)

39. William Shakespeare, *Hamlet* (Act IV, scene 7). My emphasis.

40. Helen Lovatt, *The Epic Gaze*, p. 360.

41. *Variazioni belliche* (1964) is now translated into English in different versions. The difficulties encountered in translating, and in translating Rosselli, become clear since the title itself

already finds in English three *variazioni*: 'Bellicose Variations' (Jennifer Scappettone), 'Martial Variations' (Giuseppe Leporace and Deborah Woodard), and the one also adopted here, 'War Variations' (Lucia Re and Paul Vangelisti).

42. Jahan Ramazani, 'Nationalism, Transnationalism, and the Poetry of Mourning', in *A Transnational Poetic* (Chicago: The University of Chicago Press, 2009), p. 82.

43. Judith Butler, *Precarious Life: The Powers of Mourning and Violence* (London: Verso, 2004), pp. 22–23.

44. Nicole Loraux, *The Mourning Voice: An Essay on Greek Tragedy* (Ithaca, NY: Cornell University Press, 2002), p. 34.

45. Stanislao G. Pugliese, 'Death in Exile: The Assassination of Carlo Rosselli', *Journal of Contemporary History*, 32:3 (1997), 305–19 (p. 311).

46. Judith Butler, *Precarious Life*, p. 23.

47. Mattia Mossali, ' "Condizionata alla morte essa rimava vocabolari tormentosi": declinazioni del lutto nella poesia di Amelia Rosselli e Sylvia Plath', *LEA — Lingue e Letterature d'Oriente e d'Occidente*, 7 (2018), 245–61 (p. 255).

48. It is once again Tandello who investigates and explicates 'the use of archaic and literary myth with the aim of constructing a powerful personal myth' in Rosselli's writing as a main element of convergence for her and Petrarch. It is in this practice 'that the poet of Serie ospedaliera, and the poet of the RVF would appear to find an unexpected alliance', Emanuela Tandello, 'Between Tradition and Transgression: Amelia Rosselli's Petrarch', in *Petrarch in Britain: Interpreters, Imitators, and Translators over 700 years*, ed. by Martin McLaughlin, Laura Panizza, Peter Hainsworth (British Academy Scholarship Online, 2012). For the present investigation, it will not be taken into consideration the parallel with another young female figure confined in the realm of the dead, Eurydice, for which again is recommended to see Emanuela Tandello, 'Between Tradition and Transgression: Amelia Rosselli's Petrarch'.

49. Amelia Rosselli and Jennifer Sue Scappettone, *Locomotrix* (Chicago: University of Chicago Press, 2012), p. 153.

50. Enzo Campi, 'Epico, sapido, quasi sadico: per un (auto)ritratto di Amelia Rosselli', in AA. VV., *Il colpo di coda: Amelia Rosselli e la poetica del lutto*, ed. by Enzo Campi, (Milan: Marco Saya Edizioni, 2016), pp. 82–102 (p. 86).

51. Ernestina Pellegrini, 'Amelia Rosselli', in *Le eccentriche. Scrittrici del Novecento*, ed. by Anna Botta, Monica Farnetti, Giorgio Rimondi (Mantua: Tre Lune Edizioni, 2003), pp. 137–52 (p. 145).

52. Amelia Rosselli, *War Variations*, trans. by Lucia Re and Paul Vangelisti (Los Angeles: Otis Books/Seismicity Editions, 2016).

53. Although reluctant at first to produce an explicative essay to be published with the poems, Rosselli decides to follow Pier Paolo Pasolini's advice and entitles her treatise on metrics *Spazi Metrici*.

54. Emanuela Tandello, *La fanciulla e l'infinito* (Rome: Donzelli, 2007), p. 38.

55. Ibid., p. 35.

56. The term is adopted already by Tandello to describe more in details the concept of sexual difference behind this symbolic immolation in the name of the (dead) father. The concept, for the first time appeared in *Womanliness as Masquerade* (1986 [1929]) by Joan Rivière, develops in Lacan's theory of sexual difference: 'Borrowed from Joan Rivière, Lacan's masquerade is more of a mask used by woman to shield against the castrating power of the phallus. With masquerade, a woman acts out her femininity by accepting phallic desire and paradoxically she sustains her own desire by rejecting it.' Ehsan Azari, *Lacan and the Destiny of Literature* (New York: Bloomsbury, 2011).

57. Loraux, *Mothers in Mourning*, p. 61. My emphasis.

58. Sarah Nooter, 'Language, Lamentation, and Power in Sophocles' Electra', *Classical World*, 104:4 (2011), 399–417 (p. 399).

59. Adriana Cavarero, 'Penelope', *In Spite of Plato*, pp. 11–30.

60. Emanuela Tandello, *La fanciulla e l'infinito*, p. 39.

61. Nicole Loraux, *The Divided City: On Memory and Forgetting in Ancient Athens* (New York: Zone Books, 2002), p. 160.

62. Daniela La Penna, '"Cercatemi e fuoriuscite": biography, textuality, and gender in recent criticism on Amelia Rosselli', p. 284.
63. Chiara Carpita, 'Per una poetica dell'inclinazione'.
64. 'Nomadic' is here adopted having in mind Rosi Braidotti's position on nomadic politics and nomadic subjectivity: Rosi Braidotti, *Nomadic Subjects: Embodiment and Sexual Difference in Contemporary Feminist Theory* (New York: Columbia University Press, 1994).
65. In addition to the books mentioned, see Alessandro Baldacci, *Amelia Rosselli* (Rome: Laterza, 2007); Tatiana Bisanti, *L'opera plurilingue di Amelia Rosselli* (Pisa: Edizioni ETS, 2007); Francesco Carbognin, *Le armoniose dissonanze: 'Spazi metrici' e intertestualità nella poesia di Amelia Rosselli* (Bologna: Gedit Edizioni, 2008); Silvia De March, *Amelia Rosselli tra poesia e storia* (Naples: L'Ancora del Mediterraneo, 2006); Florinda Fusco, *Amelia Rosselli. La scrittura e l'interpretazione* (Palermo: Palumbo, 2008); Erminia Passannanti, *Sulla Poesia di Amelia Rosselli* (Salisbury: Brindin Press, 2012). For an exhaustive critical bibliography see Amelia Rosselli, *L'opera poetica*, ed by. Stefano Giovannuzzi (Milan: Mondadori, 2012).
66. Nelson Moe and Amelia Rosselli, 'At the Margins of Dominion: The Poetry of Amelia Rosselli', *Italica*, 69:2 (1992), 177–97 (p. 180).
67. Enzo Campi, 'Epico, sapido, quasi sadico: per un (auto)ritratto di Amelia Rosselli', p. 87.
68. Nelson Moe and Amelia Rosselli, 'At the Margins of Dominion', p. 187.
69. Vittorio Sereni, 'Il silenzio creativo', in *La tentazione della prosa* (Milan: Mondadori, 1998), pp. 67–70 (p. 69).
70. Chiara Carpita, 'Per una poetica dell'inclinazione', p. 22.

❖

CHAPTER 6

Mourning in Translation:
The Sardinian Poetry of
Antonella Anedda

Adele Bardazzi

1. Introduction

This chapter investigates how mourning works in the poetry of Antonella Anedda. In particular, it examines her self-translated poems in Sardinian Logudorese, which highlight mourning as a process rather than as a static experience.[1] The poetic interplay between Italian and Logudorese gives life to a 'third text' — a plurivocal space of cohabitation of two languages through which new images and meanings emerge. Anedda's process of self-translation enables an exploration of the ways in which self-translation creates a further multilingual poetic space, which echoes a non-linear process of mourning. Moreover, this chapter delineates how ritualisation and formalisation of mourning in her poetry initiates a process of objectification/depersonalisation of one's individual loss and grief. In Anedda's poetry, there is a focus on the tensions between individual and collective mourning; an overcoming of individual grief in a process of de-individualisation, which moves towards a collective voice. This collectivisation of mourning results in a contraction or withdrawal from the individual 'I', which leads to the creation of a plural 'we', or a choral voice. The 'I' inscribes itself in this tension through engagement with Sardinian rituals, specifically those performed by a group of women called 'attitadoras'. In this way, individual mourning is made shareable as it is externalised and objectified through shared codes of mournful language and rites that have been crafted over centuries. Furthermore, in rendering her poems in Sardinian, Anedda offers to the reader more than just a different code of communication; she also presents the new cultural, historical, and oral mourning context of this island. This is brought into dialogue with the context of mainland Italy and its cultural, memorial, and literary traditions.

In the concluding lines of the poem 'Parla lo spavento' [Fright Speaks] (ll. 18–19) from *Dal balcone del corpo* [From the Body's Balcony] (2007), we read 'Raccoglierò dettagli come ossa | Un museo affinché non si disperdano' [I will collect details like bones | A museum so that they do not get dispersed].[2] Details are a fundamental element of Anedda's poetic practice.[3] Many of her poems carefully collect these details — they give voice to fragments of the whole, so as to prevent them from scattering and being lost. This process might seem to echo that which several poems concerning the experience of mourning attempt to do: they gather those details, often memories or objects, that still possess the power to summon the memory and life of the one lost, in an endeavour to preserve them; or, rather, they re-compose a presence that is no longer there. Often, in the process of doing so, both the object and the subject become something else. One example is to be found in the 'mille cianfrusaglie' [thousand trinkets] (*Xenia II*.14, l. 9), among which the most memorable 'infilascarpe' [shoehorn] is nothing more to the eyes of strangers than a 'pezzaccio di latta' [scrap of tin] (*Xenia II*.3 ll. 1, 9). Eugenio Montale (Genoa, 1896–Milan, 1981) evokes this in his *canzoniere in morte* to Mosca.[4] Anedda warns us that it is foolish and self-centred to remain attached to our individual personal grief: 'Soffri solo tu al pensiero che soffrano' [It is only you who suffers at the thought that they are suffering] (l. 21).

> Dalla metà della vita in poi aumentano gli spettri
> o forse sono ombre mosse dall'accanimento della luce
> voci che ancora ruotano su corpi ormai irreali.
> Schiere, dall'infanzia a oggi
> sguardi che non siamo in grado di contare,
> vite appena decifrate dai dettagli.
> Sofferenza, dico. Rispondono: proiezioni.
> Soffri solo tu al pensiero che soffrano.

[From mid-life on, spectres increase | or perhaps they are shadows | moved by the fury of light | voices that still revolve around unreal bodies. | Crowds, from childhood to today | Looks that we cannot count, | lives deciphered just by details. | Suffering, I say. They answer: projections. | It is only you who suffers at the thought that they are suffering.] ('Quello che sappiamo sopportare' [What We Know How to Bear], *Dal balcone del corpo*, ll. 14–21)

Anedda returns to this point in a later poem entitled 'Video' from her collection *Salva con nome* [Save As] (2012). The act of considering the perspectives, desires, and sufferings of the lost other lies at the centre of her eschatological vision.

> Chi se ne è andato non desidera tornare.
> Pensiamo che si strugga per il mondo
> prestandogli la nostra nostalgia.
> L'oleandro che trema, l'abete
> che si sfrangia più latteo nella luna
> e tutta la bellezza incomprensibile
> che ci ostiniamo a raccontare.
>
> Se i morti vedono ci guardano scrutare l'illusione di un muro
> bussare per entrare o chiamare
> come i pazzi che cullano le pietre
> bisbigliando loro: amore.

[Those who are gone do not want to come back. | We think they pine for the world | lending him our nostalgia. | The oleander that trembles, the fir |

that frays milkier in the moon | and all the incomprehensible beauty| that we persist in telling. | If the dead see us they watch us | scrutinise the illusion of a wall | knocking to enter or calling | like | madmen who rock the stones | whispering to them: love.] ('Video, Bill Viola: *Ocean without a shore*, Venezia, Biennale 2007')

In *La vita dei dettagli* [The Life of Details] (2009), Anedda dedicates an essay to the contemporary video artist Bill Viola (b. New York, 1951). She writes something that could well be said of her own poetry too: 'I suoi video transformano la *mimesis* in *phantasia*, parlano di cose eterne: dolore, assenza, perdita, nascita, separazione' [his videos transform *mimesis* into *phantasia*, they speak of eternal things: pain, absence, loss, birth, separation]. She returns to the video installation entitled *An Ocean Without a Shore*, which was the subject of the aforementioned poem. She highlights that in this work 'L'acqua è onnipresente [...] i morti tornano infrangendo una barriera d'acqua' [Water is omnipresent [...] the dead come back by breaking through a water barrier].[5] 'Water is something you cannot hold' — Anne Carson (b. Toronto, 1950) opens her *The Anthropology of Water* (1995) with these words. Anedda has since translated Carson's work into Italian and quotes her in the poetic essay on Viola.[6] Water, like the wind, is an element that keeps returning throughout Anedda's poetry. Water is intimately related to loss and death: 'il nuoto come esercizio di morte. L'acqua è legata allo scorrere via, alla perdita' [swimming as an exercise of death. Water is tied to slipping away, to loss].[7] In *Isolatria: Viaggio nell'arcipelago della Maddalena* [Isolatria: Travel in the Archipelago of La Maddalena] (2013), when referring to her frequent travels on the 'traghetto' [ferry] from the mainland to Sardinia, she writes: 'questa traversata è davvero un viaggio legato a un addio, a un distacco, a un solco che fa percepire, con un misto di esaltazione e smarrimento, *l'andare al largo, l'essere al largo*' [this crossing is really a journey tied to a farewell, a separation, a furrow that makes you perceive, with a mixture of exaltation and bewilderment, what it is to go offshore, to be offshore].[8] The wind too gives rise to a similar feeling: 'Il vento ci dice che siamo instabili, che basta una raffica a scardinarci e non stiamo al centro di nulla' [the wind tells us that we are unstable, that a gust is enough to unhinge us and that we are not the centre of anything].[9] This is what she calls the 'ammaestramento [...] di modestia' [the teaching of modesty] that we owe to the wind.[10]

To return to the poem on Viola's video installation, Anedda points out that 'il dato più sconvolgente dell'installazione [consiste nella] [...] consapevolezza che i sentimenti del mondo appartengono al mondo e non resta che abbandonarli ai vivi. [...] Il video dà realtà al fatto che quei corpi sono intangibili, disperatamente separati da noi' [the most shocking aspect of the installation consists in the awareness that the feelings of the world belong to the world and that we can only leave them to the living. The video gives reality to the fact that those bodies are intangible, desperately separated from us].[11] To undo this separation between the living and the dead would be as foolish as trying to grasp and hold water in our hands: both the dead and water are ultimately ungraspable. What Anedda's poetry portrays is precisely this fluid intangibility — death is 'un'acqua senza approdo' [water without a dock].[12]

Poetry should not teleologically aim to achieve an objective, but should, rather, create something through movements of concentration and contraction; to quote Elizabeth Bishop (Worcester, MA, 1911–Lewis Wharf, MA, 1979), poetry is 'a self-forgetful useless concentration'.[13] Concentration and contraction are two words that are key to understanding the nature of the poetic subject and poetic practice in Anedda, especially in relation to mourning. As she writes: 'Concentrazione dimentica di sé, io che non si espande ma si contrae' [a self-forgetful concentration, an 'I' that does not expand itself, but rather contracts itself].[14] The labour of writing consists precisely in this: 'la contrazione, lo scavo, l'andare sempre più a fondo' [contraction, digging, going always deeper].[15] Rather than possessing a destiny, poetry — like mourning — is a gesture towards a constant cycle of transformation:

> La poesia è destinata a morire? Forse. A trasformarsi? Forse, ma finché ci sarà vita ci sarà sempre chi canta i vinti più dei vincitori, i naufraghi, la tempesta, l'esilio. Esistono poesie capaci non solo di parlare della morte alla morte, alla perdita e ai perduti, ai suicidi, a tutti quelli il cui 'ammanco era nel cuore' come scrive Vittorio Sereni in una delle più belle poesie della raccolta *Gli strumenti umani* del 1965 (*Intervista a un suicida*). [...] L'incomprensione davanti a un corpo senza vita fa scrivere dagli argini, dai margini di quell'assenza.

> [Is poetry destined to die? Perhaps. To transform itself? Perhaps, but as long as there is life there will always be someone who sings about the defeated more than the winners, the castaways, the tempest, the exile. There are poems that are also able to speak of death to death, to loss and to lost ones, to the suicidal, and to all of those whose 'deficit was in the heart' as Vittorio Sereni writes in one of the most beautiful poems in the 1965 collection *The Human Implements* (*Interview with a Suicide*). [...] Our lack of comprehension before a lifeless body leads us to write from the margins, from the edges of that absence.][16]

'[L]'assenza, la trasformazione del corpo in un cadavere, il vuoto, gli oggetti abbandonati, il silenzio tutto ciò che noi vivi chiamiamo morte, non ha mai smesso quietamente, inutilmente, di ossessionarmi' [[The] absence, the transformation of the body into a corpse, the void, the abandoned objects, the silence, all that we call death, has never quietly, uselessly, stopped obsessing me].[17] With these words, the essay on Viola's video installation comes to an end. The word 'inutilmente' catches my attention here. What if the dead we mourn do not actually desire to return to the shore? After all, this is what Anedda suggests in both 'Video' and 'Quello che sappiamo sopportare'. There is something fundamentally foolish and, most importantly, self-absorbed and narcissistic in that obsessive 'ostinazione' [stubbornness] ('Video', l. 7) in recollecting their stories and our attachment to them. As she tells us, this is reminiscent of mad people who lull a lifeless stone and tenderly whisper to it. It is worth highlighting that this is clearly not focused on merely safeguarding the subject's integrity or psychic health (which is often the focal point of psychoanalytic and therapeutic theorisations of mourning), but is, rather, a consideration of the ones who left our shores. Let the dead go; stop holding them back or thinking that they are suffering because of the impossibility of making it back to the land. Simultaneously, in voicing this loss, 'L'assenza apre la gola fino al petto' [absence cuts open the throat down to the chest] ('Anniversario

II' [Anniversary II], *Dal balcone del corpo*, l. 60) — I believe this is the 'art of losing' for Anedda.

The concluding prose poem of *La vita dei dettagli* allows us to better comprehend Anedda's vision: 'Perdere: smettere di possedere, dare oltrepassando [...] Scorrere, non trattenere. Perdersi, depossedere, decrearsi' [*Perdere*: to lose, to no longer possess, to overstep [...] To flow, not to withhold, to retain. To lose oneself, to become dispossessed, to be *de-created*].[18] As in 'One Art' by Bishop, Anedda employs the word 'perdere' [to lose] to encompass mourning too: 'perdita' is the 'lost door keys, the hour badly spent' ('One Art', l. 5), a 'mother's watch' (l. 10) to vaster losses, 'two cities', 'two rivers, a continent', (ll. 13, 14) and, eventually, a 'you' (l. 16).[19] As Anedda's text progresses, we read: 'Ognuna di queste possibilità mi appartiene. Credo di avere imparato quest'arte abbastanza ma mai fino in fondo' [Each of these possibilities pertains to me. I believe I have learnt this art well enough, but never completely]. This short prose piece entitled 'Perdere' [To Lose], which is presented as a dictionary entry on this word, echoing those of another book by Carson, *Nox* (2009), ends with a highly evocative image: 'Perdere perdere. Perdere? è una porta sul vuoto' [To lose, to lose. To lose?: it's a door opening onto nothing]. Significantly, this evokes what we find in another of Anedda's poems: 'un vuoto aperto solo al vento' [a void open only to the wind] (l. 10).

> Vattene dico alla parola
> cosa dubbiosa lasciami
> cancella subito me stessa
> fai che un'altra ti prenda e ti raccolga
> e faccia nulla della mia persona
> la privi come vuole di lamento
> le scavi un vuoto aperto solo al vento

[Go I say the word | doubtful things leave me | do immediately erase myself | let another take you and collect you | someone who makes my person nothing | and deprives it of its mourning at will | and digs in it a void open only to the wind] (The opening 'Coro' in the section 'Mondo' [World], *Dal balcone del corpo*, ll. 4–10)

In this poem, we are again presented with the idea of the 'scavamento' [digging/self-emptying] of the poetic subject, particularly in the lines 'cancella subito me stessa', 'e faccia nulla della mia persona', and 'le scavi un vuoto aperto solo al vento' (ll. 3, 5, 7). This is related to one important aspect of mourning in Anedda's poetry, namely that it is also envisioned as a collective experience and practice, not just an individual one. It concerns us as individual subjects belonging to a community, a group, a chorus. This is one of the reasons why there is a movement away from the individual speaking 'I', towards a collective 'we'. It is also why there are several 'Cori' [Choruses] in her poetry. The first section of *Dal balcone del corpo* is entitled 'Cori' and opens with a quotation by Franz Kafka: 'Solo nel coro può esserci verità' [Only in the Chorus is there truth]. If we understand a chorus as an entity that has a collective voice and lacks any individual identity on the part of its constituents, as in Greek tragedy, we can see how this is also part of a de-individualisation of the poetic subject.[20] This collective poetic voice initiates a movement of the poetic subject's contraction, which I mentioned earlier.

In 'Parla lo spavento', the poetic subject directly addresses the 'Coro', asking how to use words in order to bring some level of consolation.

> Che faccio delle parole, Coro?
> Come le uso per consolare.
> Premendole l'una contro l'altra come mani?
> O come spugne imbevute di aceto?
> Dove metto la mia sete di giustizia e quella di verità
> dove dirigo il mio spavento per non spaventare chi amo?
> Come possiamo dire 'massacro'
> se i numeri ci frastornano e colano nella realtà offuscandola?

[What do I do with words, Chorus? | How to use them to console. | Pressing them against each other like hands? | Or like sponges soaked in vinegar? | Where do I put my thirst for justice and that for truth | where do I direct my fear so as not to frighten those I love? | How can we say 'massacre' | if the numbers dazzle us and drip into reality, blurring it?] ('Parla lo spavento', ll. 5–11)

A desire for justice permeates the whole poem. On this point, Anedda states in an interview: 'La poesia non serve a niente. Non aiuta. Non cura. Ma...salva dall'oblio quelle cose che la Storia azzera. È il 101 rispetto al 100 (azzerante, a cifra tonda) della Storia. La vedo come un'isola. Contro tutti gli elementi. Contro il vento. Ma è essenziale perché, proprio come il vento, ci fa sentire la nostra fragilità, la nostra impermanenza' [Poetry is useless. It does not help. It does not care. But... it saves from oblivion those things that history erases. It is the 101 of the 100 (zeroing, a round figure) of history. I see it as an island. Against all the elements. Against the wind. But it is essential because, just like the wind, it makes us feel our fragility, our impermanence].[21] These words recall a poem from her earlier *Notti di pace occidentale* [Nights of Western Peace] (1999); when referring to those who died in the war, she writes that she is 'vecchia abbastanza da sapere | come la storia le arrotondi a zero' [old enough to know | how history rounds them down to zero] ('XV', ll. 33–34). What history can naturally 'forget' naturally instances of collective loss and mourning, as the word 'massacro' [massacre] (l. 7) implies. In this chapter, however, I do not focus so much on how the individual subject mourns the collective in Anedda's poetry; rather, I am interested in understanding how the collective interrelates with the individual dimension of mourning. As we shall soon observe, this is intimately linked to her 'isola' [island] Sardinia and the local ancestral customs and rituals of mourning that belong to the island.

2. Mourning as a collective practice

Particularly in its first stages, mourning is believed to represent a potentially scattering and self-annihilating experience. To use Benedetto Croce's words, grief for the loss of a loved one might lead us to feel 'rimorso di vivere' [guilty for living] and consequently a desire to 'morire con i nostri morti' [to die with our dead].[22] Since antiquity, we have mourned our dead through ritualised practices that allow us to objectify grief. As Croce puts it: 'con l'esprimere il dolore, nelle varie forme di celebrazione e culto dei morti, si supera lo strazio, rendendolo oggettivo' [by expressing grief, through the various funerary celebrations and rites for our dead, one can overcome the stage of being torn apart by making it objective].[23] Without this process of objectification/externalisation, one remains stuck in a stage of potential laceration. Grief threatens the bereaved, cuts at the subject's psychological and emotional integrity. As Ernesto De Martino's seminal studies on Euro-Mediterranean mourning practices suggest, there is a fundamental *aporia* in ritualised mourning performances. They are meant to voice, in a *spontaneous* way, the grief for the individual loss. They do so, however, by following highly scripted gestures that mimic a supposed spontaneity and authenticity. Why is that? Ritualisation and formalisation of mourning behaviours externalise mourning and thus 'depersonalise' that loss and its grief. These mourning practices can contain the crisis with which grief presents us precisely by objectifying the subject of its scripted lament-performance. In the moment the object of love is lost and externalised, the separation between the living and the dead begins; this is where the supposed psychological and emotional stability of the bereaved is safeguarded. This separation, as Robert Pogue Harrison explains, is at the core of funeral rites and rituals and 'serve[s] to separate the *image* of the deceased from the corpse to which it remains bound up at the moment of demise'.[24]

Anedda often blurs the boundaries between prose and verse. These fluctuations that bring prose and poetry, the delineated and undelineated, close to each other are a characteristic element of her poetry. Anedda is known for presenting texts that seem prosaic in form. But I would contend that even works such as *Geografie* or parts of *Isolatria* can be considered fundamentally poetic in nature.[25] Poetry is not a matter of 'andare a capo' [breaking the line] (as partly proposed by Milo de Angelis in his essay 'Andare a Capo'), but rather of creating and sustaining a rhythm within a metric structure.[26] Or, in Franco Buffoni's words:

> Ho molto tradotto nella mia vita e sono andato sempre più convincendomi che la vera differenza non sia tra prosa e poesia, ma tra una scrittua provista di un proprio ritmo interno e una scrittura che tale ritmo non lo possiede. Lo sosteneva già Beda il Venerabile con la chiarissima distinzione: 'Il ritmo può sussistere di per sé, senza metro; mentre il metro non può sussistere senza ritmo. Il metro è una canto costretto da una certa ragione; il ritmo un canto senza misure razionali.'

> [I have translated extensively throughout my life and I have become more and more convinced that the true the point is not the difference between prose and poetry, but rather between a kind of writing that possesses its own internal rhythm and another kind that does not have any. It was the Venerable Bede who already contended that 'rhythm can exist on its own, without metre; but metre cannot exist without rhythm. Metre is a "song" obliged to a certain kind of reason; rhythm is a song without rational measures'.][27]

As Jamie McKendrick highlights in his introduction to his English translations of Anedda's poetry, Anedda's 'breaking the line/breaking with the line' leads also to a breaking with language, specifically with Italian. This occurs at the moment she starts self-translating her poems from Italian to a new *limba*, the Sardinian Logudorese.[28] Anedda first encountered this 'Limba-matre' [mother-language] and

'Fiza-limba' [daughter-language] (as quoted in the poem 'Limba', *Dal balcone del corpo*, ll. 3, 8) through the family's housemaid Micheledda: '[v]eniva dal Capodisopra, cioè dal Nuorese, e credo di dovere a lei se capisco il logudorese e un po' lo parlo' [she was from Capodisopra, that is from Nuorese, and I believe I owe it to her if I understand and speak a little Logudorese].[29]

In *Dal balcone del corpo*, we can identify another distinctive element of Anedda's poetry, namely the use of the sequence. As McKendrick highlights, this suggests 'an attitude towards the poem as process, as something continuous and continuing rather than conclusive'.[30] These words aptly describe Anedda's practice of writing between Italian and Logudorese, as well as describing the process of mourning. In this poetic collection, however, the sequence differs from all of the previous ones as it is written in Logudorese. 'Limba' is the title of the third section, which opens with a series of eight *Attittos* [Dirges], from the Sardinian verb 'attittare', which means 'compiangere il morto nel piagnisteo' [to pity the dead in wailing].[31] The term might also derive, as Anedda suggests in her notes, from 'attitu' — an onomatopoeic word that means sobbing.[32] The *Attittos* are archaic Sardinian verse laments, traditionally and exclusively performed by a group of women at the graveside. Anedda transposes this to the written space of the page. The *Attittos* powerfully underline Anedda's aim to engage with the ritualistic (and oral) dimension of Sardinian culture and its language, specifically in the context of mourning. The so-called 'attitadora' (which is spelt 'attitatora' in some areas such as Bitti) is a 'prefica', a 'piagnona', a woman who is socially invested with the cultural function of lamenting the dead. Pietro Casu explains that 'benché la Chiesa le abbia tanto combattute in ogni tempo, le prefiche han resistito in certi luoghi di Sardegna fino a tempi recenti. Oggi, almeno nel rito barbaro, sono totalmente scomparse. Durante la notte sarda, le tristi donne coi loro canti selvaggi, nei casi di mala morte, fomentavano nei petti esacerbati la fiamma dell'odio e incitavano alla vendetta' [although the church has fought against them so much in every age, the mourners have resisted in certain parts of Sardinia until recently. Today, at least in the barbarous ritual, they have totally disappeared. During the Sardinian night, the sad women with their wild songs, in cases of violent death, stirred the flame of hatred and incited revenge].[33]

There is not much scholarly work available on the figure of Sardinian 'attitadoras'.[34] Grazia Deledda (Nuoro, 1871–Rome, 1936), though, provides us with one of the most poignant depictions of these figures and their performance in her *La via del male* [The Path to Evil] (1896):

> Nella cucina si svolgeva la *ria*, l'antica scena funebre, resa più caratteristica dal chiaroscuro dell'ambiente. Il focolare era spento, la finestra chiusa [...] Le altre donne sedevano per terra, con le gambe incrociate, tutte avvolte nelle loro pesanti *tuniche* e il viso seminascosto dalle bende nere e gialle di lutto.
>
> Ogni tanto la porta s'apriva [...] Nella cucina le donne si misero a piangere con frenesia: due parenti del morto cominciarono *sos attitidos*, canti funebri improvvisati. Cantavano una per volta, e ad ogni versetto le donne rispondevano con un coro di gemiti, singulti e grida [...] ora che la vedova non era più lì, a tutta la foga della loro inspirazione poetica.
>
> — [...] Maledetto colui che ti ha colpito; maledetto.

— Maledetto: quante gocce di latte ho dato al morto, tante ferite ti trapassino il cuore, assassino!

[...]

— Noi ci strappiamo i capelli, chiedendo vendetta al cielo. Sia maledetto il latte che nutrì il tuo assassino; spuntino rovi sul suo cammino! che la giustizia lo afferri e ne faccia strazio.

— Con sette colpi di pugnale bucarono il tuo cuore come si buca un pezzo di sughero: settanta anni ed altri sette duri la pena di colui che ti ha ucciso a tradimento.[35]

[In the kitchen the *ria* took place, the ancient funeral practice, rendered even more characteristic from the *chiaroscuro* of the surroundings. The hearth was cold, the window shut [...] The other women sat on the floor, their legs crossed, wrapped in their heavy *tunics* with their faces half-hidden by the black and yellow bandages of mourning. Every now and then the door opened [...] In the kitchen the women began to cry in a frenzy: two relatives of the deceased began to sing their *attitidos*, improvised funeral chants. They sang one at a time, and at the end of each line the women answered with a chorus of groans, sobs and cries... now that the widow was no longer there they gave voice to all the force of their poetic inspiration.

— Damned the one who hit you; cursed.

— You, damned: for how many drops of milk I gave the dead, so many wounds pierce your heart, killer!

[...]

— We tear our hair, asking revenge from the sky. Cursed is the milk that fed your murderer; snack brambles in its path! Let justice seize him and agony prevail on him.

— With seven dagger strokes shall your heart be pierced as you pierce a piece of cork: seventy years and another seven shall the pain of the one who killed you treacherously last.]

As both Casu and Deledda highlight, the 'attitatoras' often performed for deaths that were the result of violence and encouraged the family to seek revenge. As Anedda writes in her notes, this supports the view that the term *Attittos* might derive from the Latin word 'adtitiare': in Italian, this would be 'attizzare', which means 'to stir up'. Others, however, challenge the view that revenge is present in the improvised performances of the 'attitadoras'. One such scholar is Francesca Pittalis, who argues that in Bitti, 'la figura della prefica non è mai giustificata [...] dall'esigenza di attizzare l'odio e la vendetta, come spesso si è voluto sostenere [...] il motivo della vendetta, non compare mai' [the figure of the wailer has never been justified [...] by the need to incite hate and revenge, as has often been claimed [...] the motif of revenge never appears].[36] Given the limited scholarship on these figures, it is difficult to dismiss views or align them with each other; rather, we can simply acknowledge the presence of different traditions and customs within Sardinia's communities. Yet there is no doubt that the 'attittos' are improvised and belong to the Sardinian oral and folk tradition. In fact, '[i]l componimento delle prefiche perde valore tutte le volte che l'improvvisatrice insiste nelle forme e negli schemi voluti dalla tradizione' [the wailers' composition loses value every time the improviser insists on traditional forms and patterns].[37] The impact of the performances lies in the 'forza del linguaggio comunicativo popolare' [communicative force of folk language].[38] Regarding the metrical structure of the 'attittos', Pittalis explains that they often consist of 'una serie di versi, per lo più ottona[r]i, rimati o con assonanza, all'interno di strofe più o meno lunghe con la disciplina di *isterritas e torratas*, come nella consuetudine di tutti i testi sardi improvvisati, ed in particolare dei *muttos*' [a series of verses, mostly of eight syllables, rhymed or with assonance, within stanzas of various lengths with the presence of *isterritas* and *torratas*, as in the custom of all improvised Sardinian texts, and in particular of *muttos*].[39]

The figure of the 'attitadora' allows us to 'depersonalise grief and provide a formal articulation of its accents'.[40] What Deledda defines as improvised are actually mourning practices based on highly scripted rituals. By following the specifics of these rituals, the 'attidora' performs her own improvisation in relation to the lamented individual. These practices might appear to betray the individuality and the singularity of the loss they are supposed to mourn. Ritualistic practices are a 'series of [...] normative gestures and mimetic enactments'.[41] They allow mourning to become a shareable experience and lead to the creation of a community of voices — a chorus. It is precisely the impersonal character of de-individualised grief that results in interpersonal participation.

Moreover, one could ask if there is a language at our disposal that can fully voice the uniqueness of one's loss. As Jennifer Rushworth has shown in her *Discourses of Mourning in Dante, Petrarch and Proust*, both Jacques Derrida and Roland Barthes are deeply concerned with this issue, 'the ethics of transmuting [their] unique and uniquely lamented mothers into something literary'.[42] As Rushworth points out, although they express an intention not to make 'literature' out of the loss of their mothers, they cannot write about this loss without recurring to Augustine's account of his mother's death in his *Confessions* (Derrida) or Proust's narrative of his grandmother's death in the *Recherche* (Barthes). This is what Rushworth calls 'mimetic mourning'.[43] As she explains, this echoes what Darian Leader has referred to as 'the principle of *borrowed mourning*' or 'a *dialogue of mournings*', which presents literature as '*a set of instruments to help us to mourn*'.[44] As Rushworth argues, 'Writing about grief means inevitably to participate in a wider [...] discourse that may [betray] the uniqueness of the experience [...], but which can offer its own form of slim comfort.'[45] These Sardinian rituals allow us to overcome what De Martino calls the 'irrelative' grief (the potentially self-destructive threat of mourning); they provide an externalisation of grief by making it objective and shareable through language. But if mourning represents such a threat to our integrity as subjects, why mourn? Why mourn in poetry? I believe the answer lies in the social and emotional 'shareability' that mourning our dead through a collective language, taking care of the disposal of their bodies, entails: it is the 'sealant' that holds us together as a community. This is because, as Harrison tells us, '[t]o be human means above all to bury', continuing: 'Vico suggests as much when he reminds us that "*humanitas* in Latin comes first and properly from humando, burying" (*New Science* § 12). [...] As *Homo sapiens* we are born of our biological parents. As human beings we are born of the dead.'[46]

Logudorese mainly has an oral tradition, particularly in the context of mourning.[47] Writing in Logudorese is an important aspect of the originality of Anedda's poetry. In employing the form of the *Attittos*, Anedda inserts herself into the Sardinian oral and improvised tradition. She enters the non-written and non-literary space of the Logudorese and brings it into dialogue with the space created in her poems. In using this new *limba*, Anedda manages to negotiate and play with the idea of a linguistically 'pure' lyric poetry. Most importantly, this allows her to suggest a kind of homogeneity of its language — an aspect that various Italian poets have challenged during the twentieth century.

These poems in Logudorese, as Anedda herself has suggested on several occasions, are not the result of 'mechanically' translating them from Italian into Sardinian. Instead, they emerge from a cohabitation of two separate worlds, landscapes, and cultures: one on the mainland and one oral culture on the island that has historically been in a subaltern relationship with Italy (see Anedda's poem 'Contro Scaurum' [Against Scaurus], as well as *Dal balcone del corpo*, in which she powerfully touches on this conflicting relationship). This sense of cohabitation is further highlighted by her decision to present each poem in both languages: placing Italian and Logudorese side by side is a practice that she has maintained in all subsequent collections, including her most recent *Historiae* (2018). As Carmelo Princiotta rightly points out, this 'parità tipografica' [typographic parity] is noteworthy, as it is rather rare in Italian poetry in dialect.[48]

As Anedda herself states: 'Molte poesie sono nate in italiano e poi trasportate in sardo. Mi sono accorta passando e traducendo da una lingua all'altra quanto l'una ammaestrasse l'altra e viceversa, per sottrazione' [Many of these poems were born in Italian and subsequently transposed in Sardinian. I noticed how, moving and translating from one language to another, one was guiding/teaching the other and vice versa, by subtraction].[49] But it is interesting to note that Anedda does not always present her practice of self-translation as starting in Italian and moving towards Logudorese. On another occasion, she writes: 'It began after an operation ... I can only say that at a certain time the sounds that rose in my memory were those harsh ones of a prescholastic language, thick with consonants and shorn of adjectives. And I understood my own Italian in the light of those sounds. When I translated these poems from Sardinian into Italian, I saw that one language steered or guided the other and that most likely I had always "translated into Italian from that language".'[50] This ambiguity regarding the language in which she begins and that she subsequently translates further highlights the cohabitation of Italian and Logudorese in Anedda's poetic practice. Her practice of self-translation is a much more fluid, non-linear process in which both languages cohabit and come into being. In a more recent interview, she confirms this process of self-translation and the interweaving of different languages: 'andando e tornando tra l[e] lingue, alcuni testi sono passati dall'italiano al sardo, o viceversa. Mi sono accorta che il sardo è più conciso, così come la traduzione italiana è più lunga. La stessa cosa succede quando si traduce dall'inglese, infatti queste poesie in sardo vengono molto bene in inglese' [going back and forward between languages, some texts moved from Italian to Sardinian, or viceversa. I have noticed how Sardinian is more concise, just as the Italian translation is longer. The same thing happens when one translates from English; these poems in Sardinian can actually be very good in an English translation].[51]

There is another element connecting Anedda's decision to write in this new *limba* and her presentation of the process of mourning: '[q]uesta *limba*, come giustamente viene chiamato un linguaggio che non è un dialetto, è affiorata in un momento in cui il dolore mi sembrava indicibile' [This *limba*, as a language that is not a dialect should be rightly called, emerged at a moment in which pain seemed unspeakable].[52] Until the publication of *Dal balcone del corpo*, Anedda had only written in Italian. Once mourning enters her poetry, she begins her practice of self-translation between Italian and Logudorese — a language she never fully owned and only gradually mastered through translating her own poems. Anedda's mourning presents itself as unspeakable. In her words:

> Tempo fa ho perso a distanza ravvicinata due persone a me molto care. Mi sembrava di non avere più voce: *muda*. Poi, come seguendo un mormorio a bocca chiusa ho scritto otto poesie sulla memoria degli *Attittos*. Nel ritmo di quei singhiozzi che attraversavano i secoli, nelle figure della madre, della sposa, della figlia e della sorella che piangono il morto, ho ritrovato la scrittura.

> [Some time ago I lost, in close succession, two people who were very close to me. It seemed to me that I no longer had a voice: *muda*. Then, as if following a whisper with my mouth closed, I wrote eight poems in memory of the *Attittos*. In the rhythm of those sobs that passed through centuries, in the figures of the mother, the bride, the daughter, and the sister who mourn the dead, I found writing again.][53]

The figures of the 'attitadoras' can voice that grief precisely because it is often not their own personal loss that they are mourning.[54]

> Si ripeteva: canto per chi muore.
> Compongo il dolore con cautela.
> Resto vicino al corpo.
> Aspetto che il grumo si sciolga nella gola
> e il sangue riconosca l'alfabeto.
> È facile quando piangi un estraneo
> non quando il lutto cresce a dismisura
> e poi diventa muto.
> [...]
> Furono le altre anime a circondarla dicendo
> canta e poi riportalo tra i vivi
> dagli altre attese.
> Rabbrividì, cercò una musica, un ritmo,
> ma dal corpo non usciva a fiotti che silenzio.
> La videro muovere le labbra
> nell'aria, senza un suono.
> Basta, dissero: non sai i nostri respiri,
> non sei adatta a noi morti.
> Non sei chi aspettavamo.
> Lui resta con noi.

[She kept repeating herself: I sing for the ones who die.| I compose pain with caution. | I stay close to the body. | I wait for the lump to melt in my throat | and for blood to recognise the alphabet. | It is easy | when you cry for a stranger | but not when mourning grows out of proportion | and then it becomes mute. [...] | The other souls surrounded her and told her | sing and then bring him back to the living | give him other hopes. | She shuddered, searched for music, for a rhythm, | but from the body only streams of silence flowed. | They saw her lips move | in the air, without a sound. | Enough, they said: you don't know our breaths, | you are not suited to us dead. | You are not who we were waiting for. | He stays with us.] ('Eco, che un tempo fu Orfeo' [Echo, Who Was Orpheus Once], *Dal balcone del corpo*, ll. 3–10, 24–34)

For the kind of grief that presents itself as 'indicibile' [unspeakable], 'muto' [silent], when 'L'assenza apre la gola fino al petto' [absence cuts open the throat down to the chest], Anedda turns to the harsher, consonantal acoustics of Logudorese. This is the only *limba* that could voice this loss. As Anedda herself states: 'il movimento era quello di una discesa in quella lingua non bassa ma profonda di cui parla Luigi Meneghello in *Il Tremaio*. I suoni erano aspri, fitti di consonanti e poveri di aggettivi. Mi sono accorta che li avevo sempre cercati anche in italiano' [the movement was that of a descent not into a language that is low, but rather, into one that is profound, as Luigi Meneghello writes in *Il Tremaio*. The sounds were harsh, thick with consonants and sparse in adjectives. I realised that I had always looked for them also in Italian].[55] There is a natural affinity between the sonorous essence of Logudorese, with its 'consonanti-spine' [consonants-thorns], as she calls them in 'Il destino della poesia', and the quality of the emotions that Anedda searches for and finds in and through this language. This is the harshness of a 'metallo interiore' [interior metal] ('Getsemani' [Gethsemane], *Dal balcone del corpo*, l. 3).[56] 'Indicibile' is also the title of another sequence of three short poems in *Dal balcone del corpo*. This 'passione' for consonants, as Anedda calls it, is also linked to an awareness that poetry should go beyond mere harmony. As Anedda states, citing Celan:

> Ancora un appunto di Celan: 'Nessuna poesia dopo Auschwitz (Adorno). Ma qui cosa s'intende per "poesia". La boria di ciò che si sottintende ipoteticamente — speculativamente raccontare o considerare Auschwitz dalla prospettiva degli usignoli o dei tordi'. La sola poesia che non è possibile dopo Auschwitz è quella della sola bellezza, della sola armonia, 'del bel suono capace', scriverà ancora Celan, 'di risuonare piu o meno indisturbato accanto all'orrore'.

> [One more note from Celan: 'No more poetry after Auschwitz (Adorno). But here what is it meant by "poetry". The arrogance of what is hypothetically implied — speculatively narrating or considering Auschwitz from the perspective of nightingales or thrushes.' The only poetry that is not possible after Auschwitz is that of mere beauty, of harmony, of 'beautiful capable sound', Celan will write again, 'to resonate more or less undisturbed alongside the horror'.][57]

Anedda was born in Rome, but her Sardinian lineage goes back generations. The languages she was brought up hearing, apart from Italian, were Logudorese, Catalan from Alghero, and Corsican French mixed with the dialect of the archipelago of La Maddalena, a small island off the north coast of Sardinia. Anedda lives and works in

Rome for most of the year, but frequently returns to La Maddalena. Another island that belongs to this archipelago is of particular importance: the island of S. Stefano. We learn why this is so from a poem in *Il catalogo della gioia* [Catalogue of Joy] (2003):

> questa piccola isola forata sott'acqua dai sommergibili americani,
> dove mio bisnonno piantò viti e agrumi
> costruì stalle e portò dieci vacche dal Continente.

> [this small island riven underwater by U.S. submarines, | where my great-grandfather planted citrus fruits and vines, | built cowsheds and brought ten cows from the mainland.] ('Settembre 2001, Arcipelago della Maddalena, isola di S. Stefano', ll. 1–3)

For this reason, as Anedda points out, her 'limba' is not 'pure' Loguodorese: 'Non si tratta [...] di un loguodorese "puro" ma attraversato da memorie diverse: campidanesi e corse, catalane e galluresi' [It is not [...] a 'pure' Loguodorese, but one interspersed by different memories: Campidanese, Corsican, Catalan, and Gallurese].[58] This makes her linguistic experiments and translations even more interesting and complex. This practice has become increasingly articulated, leading to further linguistic experiments with Italian and Sardinian. Her last poetic collection, *Historiae*, provides us with a linguistic archipelagic pastiche that includes different Sardinian languages. They are set together, much like the islands that form the archipelago of La Maddalena. As such, they form a new whole, a new 'limba':

> Onzi tandu naro una limba mia
> da inbentu in impastu a su passado
> da dongu solamenti in traduzione.

> Ogni tanto uso una lingua mia
> la invento impastandola al passato
> non la consegno se non in traduzione.

> [Sometimes I use a language of my own | I invent it mixing it with the past | and I give it only in translation.] ('Limbas', *Historiae*)[59]

Until now, I have underlined how Anedda's poetry effects a reduction/contraction of the individual poetic subject in order to process the experience of mourning. This opening poem of *Historiae* is interesting because it reminds us that this does not represent an end point. Rather, her evolving exploration highlights a tension between the individual and the collective. The poetic subject's individual voice is extremely present in this poem. It is a *limba* that emerges from the entanglement between past linguistic spaces and her own language, which creates a highly singular language — 'una lingua mia' (l. 1).

It is an 'I' and a *limba* that go through a process of 'smembramento, scomposizione, ricomposizione, fraintendimento' [dismemberment, decomposition, recomposition, misunderstanding].[60] These are words that Anedda uses to discuss translation in her essay 'Il destino della poesia'. Anedda states that it is through translation that poetry can preserve its existence:

> Forse solo nella traduzione il linguaggio compie il suo destino, è costretto a dispiegarsi, a farsi pesare parola dopo parola sulla bilancia del vocabolario. La

sintassi non è più una difesa, i vecchi trucchi non funzionano. All'inizio ci sono parole confuse come di persone che si chiamino da barche lontane. Le prue si accostano, gli equipaggi passano da un ponte all'altro. Viaggeranno verso qualcosa? Non lo sappiamo, ma per non affondare devono buttare la zavorra e per capirsi devono reciprocamente ascoltarsi.

[Perhaps only in translation does language fulfil its destiny, being forced to unfold itself, to be weighed word by word on the balance of vocabulary. The syntax is no longer a defence, the old tricks do not work. At the beginning there are confused words as if from people calling to each other from distant boats. The bows draw near, the crews pass from one bridge to another. Will they travel somewhere? We do not know but in order not to sink they must throw the ballast and to understand each other they must listen to each other.][61]

Anedda continues:

Chi traduce apre il corpo di un testo, più che a fronte, scende al suo interno, parola dopo parola, fino a una resa spesso imperfetta e sempre sotto il segno del fallimento. [...] Chi traduce obbedisce allo stesso compito della poesia: sondare attraverso il linguaggio la 'quieta vulcanica vita', per usare i versi di Emily Dickinson nella traduzione di Rosselli. Osservare il vulcano, lasciare raffreddare la lava, accettare i calchi, i fossili. La poesia sta, come una pietra, o un granello di sabbia sotto cui si può scavare, ma allo stesso tempo si nutre di *amor de lohn*, come precisa ancora Giovanni Giudici.

[Whoever translates opens the body of a text, rather than the front, goes down inside it, word after word, to an often-imperfect surrender and always expects failure. [...] Those who translate obey the same task as that of poetry: probing the 'quiet volcanic life' through language, to use Emily Dickinson's lines in Rosselli's translation. Observe the volcano, let the lava cool down, accept the casts, the fossils. Poetry is like a stone, or a grain of sand under which it is possible to dig, but at the same time it feeds on *amor de lohn*, as Giovanni Giudici points out.][62]

Some words that return in Anedda's reflection on translation are also central in her poetic practice and mourning. Translating is productively failing, 'scavare' [dig], 'ascoltare' [listen], 'smembrare' [dismember], 'restituire' [return]; these are all acts that merge to create a pluri-vocal language of mourning. This conception of poetic practice (mentioned in an unpublished draft of 'Il destino della poesia' she calls a 'terza strada' [third route]) results in the cohabitation of the Italian and Logudorese text, which presents us with a new third possibility.

For Anedda, poetry is *always* translation, a constant movement of losing and rediscovering.

Il mio italiano è comunque di traduzione. È una cosa che rivendico contro chi l'ha usata contro di me, come un insulto perché la poesia è sempre traduzione. [...] Potrei dire che scrivo in una lingua estranea che perdo e ritrovo ogni volta. In un certo senso sono fuori da qualsiasi tradizione; questo se mi ha creato problemi, col tempo mi ha reso libera.

[My Italian is, anyhow, translation. It is something that I claim against those who have used it against me as an insult, because poetry is always translation. [...] I could say that I write in a foreign language that I lose and find again every time. In a sense, I am out of any tradition; this, although it created problems for me, ultimately set me free.][63]

As Italian is already perceived as an *other* language, it is clear that the texts in Logudorese could not be the result of a direct translation from Italian into Sardinian.[64]

In *Poetry & Translation: The Art of the Impossible*, Peter Robinson writes 'you are yourself alive when you translate, though you are translating the results of a past creative moment... Who is translating whom in self-translation?'[65] I believe that this is a key question in the case of Anedda. Self-translation is often presented as an elaboration, a re-writing, of a supposedly 'original' text. This is not necessarily the case in Anedda's poetics, considering how the idea of an 'original' is challenged through her presentation of the language of poetry as always being an act of translation. Nevertheless, her practice of self-translation, while not a mechanical translation from one language to another, can still be seen as a gesture towards a 'different' language and self *in* the moment of mourning when the necessity of finding a language and a self seems even more urgent. Self-translation is thus an extension of the original text, as well as a search for poetic and linguistic novelty (if not self), rather than a direct and faithful reproduction of the original text. In other words, self-translating one's work is an act of re-writing oneself. In this process, a different version of one's poetic voice and self emerges. In this re-writing process, Anedda's self-translating practice is a way of exploring and negotiating her Sardinian identity at a time when the self is undergoing the potentially shattering experience of mourning. Mourning makes the search for a new 'voice' and 'self' even more timely and necessary. Self-translation and mourning are intimately related insofar as both involve a re-enactment of something that has been lost. It is impossible to recover the singularity/originality of the original text/lost beloved; what is created is not a 'faithful' copy, but another authorial 'original' text/object. In other words, they both make 'something else' out of loss; in so doing, they also make a highly individual experience communicable and shareable.

By transposing the oral tradition of Sardinian mourning rites onto the written page, Anedda's *Attittos* reminds us of the fundamental thread that links lyrical poetry and ritual. Giovanni Nencioni helps us to further understand this relationship in his seminal essay 'Antropologia poetica?':

> le forme del codice poetico, le piccole come le grandi — il poema epico e il dramma come il colloquio *in absentia* e la pronominazione ad esso relativa — sono tutte riconducibili a remote forme di comunicazione sociale; e se ciò non è una scoperta, perché molti sono ormai gli studi sul rapporto originario tra le forme poetiche e il rituale magico o religioso, dovrebbe tuttavia essere tenuto più presente di quanto di solito non si faccia.[66]

> [the forms of the poetic code, the minor as well as the major — the epic poem and drama as well as the dialogue *in absentia* and the apostrophic address that relates to it — are all attributable to remote forms of social communication. While this is not a discovery, because there are many studies on the original relationship between poetic forms and magical or religious ritualistic culture, it should nevertheless be kept in mind more than it usually is.]

Nencioni further insists on the connection between poetry and shared structures of communication in the context of mourning. He is indeed interested in the archaic origins of what would later be translated into poetic codes and forms:

> l'evocazione dei morti, prima di divenire un genere poetico, fu un rito arcaico, un atto di effettiva, riconosciuta comunicazione con l'aldilà, che i poeti antichi, Omero come Eschilo, hanno finto nel racconto o nell'azione scenica senza però alterarne il valore; il quale si è in gran parte mutato col ritrarsi dell'antichissimo rito nel codice poetico, ma non tanto da non separare, con un residuo di carica antropologica, il primo nostro colloquio dal secondo, dandogli un suggello di verità che significa conservazione o recupero, a diverso titolo della comunicazione.[67]

> [the evocation of the dead, before becoming a poetic genre, was an archaic rite, an act of effective, recognised communication with the afterlife, which the ancient poets, such as Homer and Aeschylus, have imitated in narrative or in scenic action without altering its value. This has largely changed with the withdrawal of the ancient ritual in the poetic code, but not so much so, as not to separate, with a residue of anthropological charge, our first conversation from the second, giving it a seal of truth that means conservation or recovery, in different ways than communication.]

Moreover, ritualised mourning practices, such as those performed by the 'attitadoras', have another key function: they create a sense of community, a *chorus*. There would be no community without first passing through the process of depersonalisation entailed by ritualised mourning: 'Proprio per il carattere impersonale della presenza stereotipa del pianto viene reso possibile un nesso interpersonale recitato a comando, con scambi e sostituzioni e collaborazioni pianificate e tradizionalizzate che sarebbero del tutto inconcepibili in un regime strettamente individuale di cordoglio' [It is precisely the impersonal character of the stereotypes that makes interpersonal participation in the lament possible, with multiple successive recitals, planned exchanges, substitutions and collaborations, [participation] which would be wholly inconceivable under a strictly personal regime of mourning].[68] As highlighted by De Martino's fieldwork in southern Italy and Sardinia (where lamentation rituals have remained almost unchanged for centuries), the responsibility to perform these mourning ceremonies belongs almost exclusively to women. Why women? Rituals transform biological death into 'human death'. As Harrison argues, this is a kind of birth: '[f]or dying in the full human sense is a kind of birth, while the afterlife — understood phenomenologically and not necessarily religiously or doctrinally — is the new and altered condition the dead are born into (as souls, images, voices, masks, heroes, ancestors, founders, and the like).'[69] This process of 'giving birth' to the dead in the afterlife, and providing them with what Harrison calls an 'active afterlife', forms the basis of ritualised mourning and lamentation practices, that have traditionally belonged to women. As bearers of life, women thus supposedly have a natural connection to our dead — a central responsibility and a unique authority in relation to the dead. They also bear a responsibility towards the living to voice this loss. What is interesting in Anedda's poetry is how the transition from the fleeting space of oral mournful performances by Sardinian women is brought to the tangible written space of mournful poetry.

3. Translation as 'Convivenza': Towards a 'third text'

Barthes writes the following in his *Journal de deuil*:

> Not to suppress mourning (suffering) (the stupid notion that time will do away with such a thing) but to change it, transform it, to shift it from a static stage (stasis, obstruction, recurrences of the same thing) to a fluid state.[70]

I contend that Anedda's poems similarly attempt to evade stasis and enable a fluid state of mourning, particularly in her series of *Attittos*. This is possible because of her conception of poetry as translation, her self-forgetful concentration, and her employment of self-translation and a new *limba*. This is in line with the conception, already mentioned, of the 'sequence' (to which these *Attittos* belong) that frames a poem as a process, rather than a conclusive end point. This can be seen in relation to both her use of self-translation and mourning *as a process*.

> I.
> Tòrrami a fizu tuo
> terra bestia 'e nieddu
> care 'e proya. Mi giamat
> ma tue ses corfu 'e bistrale.
> Eo non podo respondere
> prena de ludu e ispina.

> VII.
> Li kerìa colare un'ispùgnia 'e ferru in su pettus
> lu ferrer a samben che a unu gristos
> po mi lu parrer che torradu vivu

> I.
> Restituiscimi tuo figlio
> terra nero–vestita,
> viso di pioggia. Mi chiama
> ma tu sei colpo di scure.
> Io non posso rispondere
> piena di fango e spina.

> VII.
> Volevo passargli una spugna di ferro sopra il petto
> ferirlo a sangue come un cristo
> per fingerlo risorto.

> [Dirges. I. Give me back your son | earth draped in black | with your face of rain. He calls me | but you're the thud of an axe. | Snared in mud and thorn | I can't call back
>
> VII. I wanted to wash him down with an iron sponge | wound him till he bled like a Christ | to fool myself he would rise again.][71]

What is striking here is the way Logudorese and Italian interrelate and create something new: a 'third text'. This 'third text' goes beyond the individual poems written in Italian and Logudorese; it is the result of their entanglement with one another. This brings the poems into motion and initiates a process of interference; words and meaning fluidly swing back and forth between the two individual poems. I believe that this reflects a vision of mourning as well. Anedda sees mourning as a never-ending, changing process, rather than a static state of grief. In this 'third text', the various 'selves' of the mournful poetic subject can cohabit and develop freely. This third semantic space arises from the way in which words from different languages resonate with each other and initiate a series of linguistic circularities among themselves. It is therefore not only a search for a new *limba* in the face of the unspeakability of loss, but also a language that allows a state of non-linear fluidity. Such fluidity can first be created through the cohabitation of two languages. Let us see how this works in these two 'Attittos'. The word 'ludu' in the concluding line of the first 'Attittu' means 'fango', 'mud'. Logudorese is a Neo-Latin language and, like other languages of this kind, preserves some archaisms. In fact, the Latin word for mud is 'lutum'. Given the overwhelming presence of mourning in this poem, a reader without previous knowledge of Logudorese might first make another connection upon reading the word 'ludu', one that strongly resonates with the Italian word 'lutto', 'mourning'. The Logudorese word for 'mourning' would be 'corruttu'. This is a 'deception' on which I believe the poem plays powerfully. Despite the Latin echoes of the word 'ludu', the poem adds a further layer of meaning to this line and intensifies the grief at the very core of the poem. Similarly, in the first line of the second poem quoted above, the word 'colare' extends the meaning of the line by indirectly engaging with the meaning of the word in Italian. In Italian, 'colare' implies, through an associative chain of thoughts, something involving the presence of blood, something that is bleeding. In the Italian version of the poem, 'colare' is translated as 'passare', a word that does not possess the same painful connotation as 'colare'. 'Passare' in this context simply means 'to wipe something', such as a surface. The Logudorese word 'colare', which literally means 'passare' or 'filtrare' [to filter], extends and amplifies the corporeal meaning of the Italian 'passare' in a poignant way.

Furthermore, with regard to the poem's metre, rhyme patterns, and rhythm, there is a stronger adherence to more traditional rhyme schemes in the Italian poem compared to the one in Sardinian. The Sardinian poem does not follow a regular rhyme pattern or have a regular meter. The opening of the Sardinian poem sets the whole picture into motion. It is a movement, a process, which, much like the process of mourning, cannot be kept in stasis any longer. One also notices that in the Sardinian version of the poem, the sounds that emerge and further intensify the words of the poem are of a harsher quality. As Anedda states in an interview, '[q]uando ho scritto delle poesie in logudorese mi sono resa conto ad esempio, del perché mi piacciano le consonanti. Il sardo è pieno di consonanti, ha anche un suono aspro. È una lingua sintetica, proprio perché appunto è molto vicina al latino' [when I started writing poems in Logudorese I realised, for instance, why I like consonants so much. The Sardinian language is full of consonants; it also has a sharp sound. It is a 'synthetic' language precisely because it is so close to Latin].[72] This search for a sharper, piercing poetic voice is very much in tune with the awareness that her grief in a moment of mourning is unspeakable, 'indicibile' (the title of another poem of mourning in *Dal balcone del corpo*). Another *limba*, another poetic voice, another self is needed to express this quality.

Regarding the different rhythmic patterns of the texts in Logudorese and Italian, it is interesting to note that Logudorese evokes a more archaic, ancestral, and ritualistic rhythm:

> Mi sono chiesta [...] quanto abbia contato nella mia idea di ritmo la sfida di fare poesia con una lingua che traduce da una vera e propria lingua, cioè da quella 'limba' ascoltata nell'infanzia, ritmata sulle *Aninnias* (ninnananne) a anche sugli *Attittos*, cioè sui lamenti funebri delle donne per colui che è stato *attittau* (allattato), o sui *Gosos,* i canti religiosi. Mi sono chiesta quanto la memoria di un ritmo cosi' arcaico, ancora così legato alla ritualità, alla danza, a un canto che ancora oggi si accompagna al battito dei piedi per controllare la giustezza di *sas Cambas*, cioè dei versi, abbia impressionato non solo un modo di scrivere, ma anche un modo di leggere.

> [I wondered [...] how much, in my idea of rhythm, the challenge counted of making poetry with a language that translates from a real and proper language, that is, the 'limba' heard in childhood, which gave its rhythm to the *Aninnias* (lullabies) and even to the *Attittos*, that is, the funeral laments of women for the one who has been *attittau* (breastfed), or the *Gosos*, the religious songs. I wondered how much the memory of such an archaic rhythm, still so tied to rituality, to dance, to a song that still accompanies the beating of feet to check the correctness of *sas Cambas*, that is, the verses, has impressed on me not only a way of writing, but also a way of reading.][73]

In the words of Iris Murdoch, translation '[i]s like opening one's mouth and hearing someone-else's voice emerge'.[74] These words are particularly relevant in the case of Anedda's self-translation of her poetry into Sardinian. For Anedda, self-translation is a key process for finding another poetic voice in a moment in which pain seemed 'indicibile' — unspeakable. It is a way of finding another self and recovering her Sardinian identity. A 'third text' comes into being from the entanglement between the text in Italian and the one in Sardinian: a renewed 'limba' in which the depths of mourning can be voiced. Thus, Anedda's process of self-translation emerges as a particularly interesting practice that allows us to understand how self-translation creates a further multilingual poetic space. This gives rise to new questions and interpretations, as well as challenging ideas about an 'original' text and language. For Anedda, poetry is *always* a translation and the same can be said about the process of mourning, which does not necessarily substitute the lost object of love with the objective of 'moving on', but rather creates something 'new' that, most importantly, can be shared while retaining its individuality.

Bibliography

ADAMO, GIULIANA, 'La poesia di Antonella Anedda tra parola e silenzio', *O.b.l.i.o.: Osservatorio bibliografico della letteratura italiana otto-novecentesca*, 3:11 (2013): 118–23 <http://www.progettoblio.com/files/011.pdf> [accessed 13 June 2019]
ANEDDA, ANTONELLA, *Archipelago*, trans. by Jamie McKendrick (Hexham: Bloodaxe Books, 2014)
—— *Dal balcone del corpo* (Milan: Mondadori, 2007)
—— *Geografie* (Milan: Garzanti, 2021)

—— 'Il destino della poesia', in *Il contributo italiano alla storia del pensiero: Musica e Letteratura*, appendice IX, ed. by Giulio Ferroni (Rome: Istituto della Enciclopedia Italiana, Treccani, 2015), pp. 822–28

—— *Isolatria: Viaggio nell'arcipelago della Maddalena* (Rome: Laterza, 2013)

—— *La luce delle cose: Immagini e parole nella notte* (Milan: Feltrinelli, 2000)

—— *La vita dei dettagli* (Rome: Donzelli editore, 2009)

—— 'Limba: Una nota sull'autotraduzione', in *La soglia sull'altro: I nuovi compiti del traduttore* (Bologna: La Bottega dell'Elefante, 2007), pp. 134–38.

—— 'Otto domande sulla poesia', *Studi duemilleschi*, 2:2 (2002), 17–18

—— 'Una musica diversa', in *Ritmologia: Il ritmo del linguaggio: Poesia e traduzione*, ed. by Franco Buffoni (Milan: Marcos y Marcos, 2002), pp. 325–32

BARTHES, ROLAND, *Mourning Diary*, ed. by Nathalie Léger and trans. by Richard Howard (London: Notting Hill Editions, 2011)

BINETTI, ROBERTO, '"Una zona di tempo / schiuma delle ere": Lirica e storiografia in *Historiae* di Antonella Anedda', *lettere aperte*, 6 (2019), 75–86

BISHOP, ELIZABETH, *Complete Poems, 1927–1979* (New York, Farrar, Straus & Giroux, 1983)

BUFFONI, FRANCO (ed.), *RITMOLOGIA: Il ritmo del linguaggio: Poesia e traduzione* (Milan: Marcos y Marcos, 2002)

CALVIA, GIUSEPPE, 'Usi funebri di Mores', in *Rivista delle tradizioni popolari*, 9 (1894), 949–53

CARSON, ANNE, *The Anthropology of Water*, in *Plainwater* (New York: Knopf, 2004)

—— *Antropologia dell'acqua: Riflessioni sulla natura liquida del linguaggio*, trans. by Antonella Anedda, Elisa Biagini, and Emanuela Tandello (Rome: Donzelli, 2010)

CASU, PIETRO, *Vocabolario sardo logudorese-italiano*, ed. by Giulio Paulis (Nuoro: Ilisso, 2002) <http://vocabolariocasu.isresardegna.it> [accessed 1 September 2019]

CASU, PIETRO MARIA, *Il culto dei sepolcri ed i riti funerari di tutti i popoli* (Cagliari: Timon, 1866)

Choral Mediations in Greek Tragedy, ed. by Renaud Gagné and Marianne Govers Hopman (Cambridge: Cambridge University Press, 2013)

COSTA, ENRICO, *Sassari*, 3 vols (Sassari: Gallizzi, 1992)

CROCCO, CLAUDIA, '"La poesia crea uno spazio, che è un luogo in comune": Intervista ad Antonella Anedda' <https://quattrocentoquattro.com/2011/11/17/la-poesia-crea-uno-spazio-che-e-un-luogo-in-comune-intervista-ad-antonella-anedda> [accessed 1 September 2019]

CROCE, BENEDETTO, *Frammenti di etica* (Bari: Laterza, 1922)

DE ANGELIS, MILO, 'Andare a capo (Autobiografia)', in *Poesia e destino* (Bologna: Cappelli, 1982)

DE MARTINO, ERNESTO, *Morte e pianto rituale: Dal lamento funebre antico al pianto di Maria* (Turin: Bollati Boringhieri, 1975. Reprint, Turin: Bollati Boringhieri, 2000)

DELEDDA, GRAZIA, *La via del male* (Nuoro: Il Maestrale, 2012)

DETTORI, ANTONIETTA, *La Sardegna*, in *I dialetti italiani: Storia, struttura, uso*, ed. by Manilo Cortezza et al. (Turin: UTET, 2002) pp. 897–958

DONATI, RICCARDO, 'Disobbedire all'oblio: Appunti su *La vita dei dettagli*', *Arabeschi* (2015) <http://www.arabeschi.it//uploads/pdf/donati_anedda.pdf> [accessed 23 June 2019]

GIUSTI, FRANCESCO, *Canzonieri in morte: Per un'etica poetica del lutto* (L'Aquila: Textus Edizioni, 2015)

—— 'Parlando la Lingua della Mosca: Gli *Xenia* e la Morte tra Dimensione Domestica e Trauma Epistemologico', *MLN*, 124:1 (2009), 236–53

LEADER, DARIAN, *The New Black: Mourning, Melancholia and Depression* (London: Penguin, 2008)

LINZMEIER, LAURA, *Compendium of the Sassarese Language: A Survey of Genesis, Structure, and Language Awareness* (Munich: Ibykos Verlag, 2019)

McKENDRICK, JAMIE, 'Introduction', in Antonella Anedda, *Archipelago*, trans. by Jamie McKendrick (Hexham: Bloodaxe Books, 2014), pp. 9–14

—— 'A Note on the Translation and Selection', in Antonella Anedda, *Archipelago*, trans. by Jamie McKendrick (Hexham: Bloodaxe Books, 2014), pp. 15–16

MARINELLI, GIOVANNI, ET AL., *La terra: trattato popolare di geografia universale: Regno d'Italia* (Milan: Vallardi, 1883), IV

MAXIA, MAURO, *Studi sardo-corsi: Dialettologia e storia della lingua tra le due isole* (Olbia: Taphros, 2008)

MENEGHELLO, LUIGI, *Il tremaio: Note sull'interazione tra lingua e dialetto nelle scritture letterarie*, with contributions by Cesare Segre, Ernestina Pellegrini, and Giulio Lepschy (Bergamo: Lubrina, 1986), pp. 11–42

MONTALE, EUGENIO, *Satura*, ed. by Riccardo Castellana (Milan: Mondadori, 2009)

MORRA, ELOISA, 'Scomporre quadri, immaginare mondi: Dinamiche figurative e percezione nella poesia di Antonella Anedda', *Italianistica*, 3 (2011), 167–81

MURDOCH, IRIS, *Under the Net* (London: Penguin, 1960)

NENCIONI, GIOVANNI, 'Antropologia poetica?', *Strumenti critici*, 19 (1972), 243–58; now in *Tra grammatica e retorica* (Turin: Einaudi, 1983), pp. 161–75

OTTONELLO, FRANCESCO, 'Una limba tra silenzio e passato: Dialogo con Antonella Anedda', in *Le parole e le cose*, 24 January 2020 <http://www.leparoleelecose.it/?p=37558> [accessed 5 February 2020]

PAU, ANTONIO, 'Usi e costumi funebri in Sardegna', in *Avvenire in Sardegna*, 251 (1887)

PINNA, OFELIA, *Riti funebri in Sardegna* (Sassari: Gallizzi, 1921)

PITTALIS, FRANCESCA, *Rituali di morte e canti di prefiche in Sardegna* (Nuoro: PTM Editrice, 2008)

POGUE HARRISON, ROBERT, *The Dominion of the Dead* (Chicago: Chicago University Press, 2003)

PRINCIOTTA, CARMELO, 'La scuola dei viventi: Il tragico in De Angelis e Anedda', in *I cantieri dell'italianistica: Ricerca, didattica e organizzazione agli inizi del XXI secolo: Atti del XII congresso dell'ADI — Associazione degli Italianisti* (Roma Sapienza, 18–21 September 2013), ed. by Beatrice Alfonzetti, Guido Baldassarri, and Franco Tomasi (Rome: Adi editore, 2014), pp. 1–10

ROBINSON, PETER, *Poetry & Translation: The Art of the Impossible* (Liverpool: Liverpool University Press, 2010)

RUSHWORTH, JENNIFER, *Discourses of Mourning in Dante, Petrarch and Proust* (Oxford: Oxford University Press, 2016)

SANNA, ANTONIO, *Il dialetto di Sassari (e altri saggi)* (Cagliari: Trois, 1975)

SEPE, FRANCO, 'A colloquio con Antonella Anedda', *Italienisch*, 49 (2003): 90–100

TOSCHI, PAOLO, 'Il pianto funebre nella poesia popolare italiana', in *Poesia: Quaderni internazionali*, ed. by Enrico Falqui (Milan: Mondadori, 1947), VII, pp. 11–40

VILLARREAL, IGNACIO, 'Bill Viola Creates Work for Venice Biennale', online art newspaper, ArtDaily.org, 2 May 2007 <http://artdaily.com/indexv5.asp?int_sec=2&int_new=20094> [accessed 3 April 2020]

Notes to Chapter 6

I am grateful for the generous and attentive feedback and corrections received from Emanuela Tandello, Peter Hainsworth, Francesco Giusti, Roberto Binetti, and Maurizio Virdis. All inaccuracies are my own.

1. As this article will discuss, Anedda's poetry in Sardinian is not written in 'pure' Logudorese. Nevertheless, the Sardinian 'limba' with which she engages the most is Logudorese. For this

reason, I will refer to Anedda's highly singular 'limba' as either Sardinian (when it experiments with various Sardinian languages) or Logudorese (when it is closer to the Logudorese language).

2. All translations from English to Italian are mine unless otherwise indicated.

3. Details are at the core of Anedda's *La vita dei dettagli* [The Life of Details] (2009): 'Il corpo è davanti a un quadro. A un tratto un dettaglio ci attira tanto da farci avvicinare. L'intero quadro diventa resto. Il dettaglio è l'isola del quadro. Il quadro scompare. Lo ha inghiottito il buio. Resiste solo il dettaglio che ti ha fatto cenno. Ora è un mondo' [The body is in front of a painting. Suddenly a detail attracts us so much that we draw closer. The whole picture becomes other. The detail is the island of the picture. The picture disappears. The darkness has swallowed it. Only the detail that beckoned you remains. Now it is a world]. Antonella Anedda, *La vita dei dettagli* (Rome: Donzelli editore, 2009), p. 2. On the topic of details in the poetry of Anedda, see Eloisa Morra, 'Scomporre quadri, immaginare mondi: Dinamiche figurative e percezione nella poesia di Antonella Anedda', *Italianistica*, 3 (2011), 167–81; and Riccardo Donati, 'Disobbedire all'oblio: Appunti su *La vita dei dettagli*', *Arabeschi* (2015) <http://www.arabeschi.it//uploads/pdf/donati_anedda.pdf> [accessed 23 June 2019].

4. Eugenio Montale, *Xenia I* and *Xenia II*, from *Satura*, ed. by Riccardo Castellana (Milan: Mondadori, 2009). For an excursus on the 'canzonieri in morte' from Dante to contemporary poets such as Milo De Angelis and Patrizia Valduga, among others, see Francesco Giusti, *Canzonieri in morte: Per un'etica poetica del lutto* (L'Aquila: Textus Edizioni, 2015). On the figure of Mosca, see Francesco Giusti, 'Parlando la Lingua della Mosca: Gli *Xenia* e la Morte tra Dimensione Domestica e Trauma Epistemologico', *MLN*, 124:1 (2009), 236–53.

5. Anedda, *La vita dei dettagli*, p. 127. In Viola's press statement for the Venice Biennale, one reads: 'The video sequence describes the human form as it gradually coalesces from within a dark field and slowly comes into view, moving from obscurity into the light. As the figure approaches, it becomes more solid and tangible until it breaks through an invisible threshold and passes into the physical world. The crossing of the threshold is an intense moment of infinite feeling and acute physical awareness. Poised at that juncture, for a brief instant all beings can touch their true nature, equal parts material and essence. However, once incarnate, these beings must eventually turn away from mortal existence and return to the emptiness from where they came.' As quoted in Ignacio Villarreal 'Bill Viola Creates Work for Venice Biennale', online art newspaper, *ArtDaily.org*, 2 May 2007 <http://artdaily.com/indexv5.asp?int_sec=2&int_new=20094> [accessed 3 April 2020].

6. Anne Carson, *The Anthropology of Water*, in *Plainwater* (New York: Knopf, 2004), p. 117. See also Anne Carson, *Antropologia dell'acqua: Riflessioni sulla natura liquida del linguaggio*, trans. by Antonella Anedda, Elisa Biagini, and Emanuela Tandello (Rome: Donzelli, 2010).

7. Anedda, *La vita dei dettagli*, p. 128.

8. Antonella Anedda, *Isolatria: Viaggio nell'arcipelago della Maddalena* (Rome: Laterza, 2013), p. 6.

9. Ibid., p. 4.

10. Ibid.

11. Anedda, *La vita dei dettagli*, p. 128.

12. Ibid., p. 131.

13. These words are from Elizabeth Bishop's letter to her friend Anne Stevenson in 1964. Anedda quotes this passage in her essay 'Il destino della poesia', in *Il contributo italiano alla storia del pensiero: Musica e Letteratura*, appendice IX, ed. by Giulio Ferroni (Rome: Istituto della Enciclopedia Italiana, Treccani, 2015), pp. 822–28 (p. 824).

14. Ibid.

15. Ibid.

16. Ibid., pp. 824–25.

17. Anedda, *La vita dei dettagli*, p. 131.

18. This translation of 'Perdere' is by Jamie McKendrick and is unpublished.

19. Elizabeth Bishop, *Complete Poems, 1927–1979* (New York: Farrar, Straus & Giroux, 1983).

20. For more information on choruses in Greek tragedies, see *Choral Mediations in Greek Tragedy*, ed. by Renaud Gagné and Marianne Govers Hopman (Cambridge: Cambridge University Press, 2013).

21. As cited by Giuliana Adamo, 'La poesia di Antonella Anedda tra parola e silenzio', *O.b.l.i.o.: Osservatorio bibliografico della letteratura italiana otto-novecentesca*, 3:11 (2013): 118–23 (p. 122) <http://www.progettoblio.com/files/011.pdf> [accessed 13 June 2019].

22. Benedetto Croce, *Frammenti di etica* (Bari: Laterza, 1922), pp. 22–24. Eng. trans. by Robert Pogue Harrison, as cited in *The Dominion of the Dead* (Chicago: Chicago University Press, 2003), p. 55.

23. Ibid., p. 24.

24. Harrison, *The Dominion of the Dead*, p. 147.

25. Antonella Anedda, *Geografie* (Milan: Garzanti, 2021).

26. Milo De Angelis, 'Andare a capo (Autobiografia)', *Poesia e destino* (Bologna: Cappelli, 1982).

27. *RITMOLOGIA: Il ritmo del linguaggio: Poesia e traduzione*, ed. by Franco Buffoni (Milan: Marcos y Marcos, 2002), p. 12.

28. Jamie McKendrick, 'Introduction', in Antonella Anedda, *Archipelago*, trans. by Jamie McKendrick (Hexham: Bloodaxe Books, 2014), pp. 9–14 (p. 12).

29. Anedda, *Isolatria*, pp. 7–8.

30. Jamie McKendrick, 'A Note on the Translation and Selection', in *Archipelago*, pp. 15–16 (p. 15).

31. See Pietro Casu, *Vocabolario sardo logudorese-italiano*, ed. by Giulio Paulis (Nuoro: Ilisso, 2002) <http://vocabolariocasu.isresardegna.it/index.php?key=a&int=0&lemmi=cerca> [accessed 1 September 2019].

32. As quoted in the notes on *Dal balcone del corpo* (Milan: Mondadori, 2007).

33. See Pietro Casu, *Vocabolario sardo logudorese-italiano*.

34. Scholarship is limited and mostly dated. Among works on the subject are the following: Giuseppe Calvia, 'Usi funebri di Mores', in *Rivista Delle Tradizioni Popolari*, 9 (1894), 949–53; Pietro Maria Casu, *Il culto dei sepolcri ed i riti funerari di tutti i popoli* (Cagliari: Timon, 1866); Antonio Pau, 'Usi e costumi funebri in Sardegna', in *Avvenire in Sardegna* 251 (1887); Ofelia Pinna, *Riti funebri in Sardegna* (Sassari: Gallizzi, 1921); Paolo Toschi, 'Il pianto funebre nella poesia popolare italiana', in *Poesia: Quaderni internazionali*, ed. by Enrico Falqui (Milan: Mondadori, 1947), VII, pp. 11–40.

35. Grazia Deledda, *La via del male* (Nuoro: Il Maestrale, 2012), pp. 245, 247–48, 249, 250, 251.

36. Francesca Pittalis, *Rituali di morte e canti di prefiche in Sardegna* (Nuoro: PTM Editrice, 2008), p. 70. Bitti is a relevant place in the context of Anedda's engagement with the figure of the 'attitadora', as she explains in a recent interview: 'Recentemente ho scoperto anche una delle ultime *attitatoras*, Efisina de Grimenta — l'ultima prefica di Bitti (NU) — la cui *poesia in limba* è stata tradotta anche in inglese e molto apprezzata' [Recently I have also discovered one of the last *attitatoras*, Efisina de Grimenta — the last mourner of Bitti (NU) — whose *poesia in limba* has also been translated into English and highly praised]. As quoted in Francesco Ottonello, 'Una limba tra silenzio e passato: Dialogo con Antonella Anedda', in *Le parole e le cose*, 24 January 2020 <http://www.leparoleelecose.it/?p=37558> [accessed 5 February 2020].

37. Ibid., p. 71

38. Ibid., p. 72.

39. Ibid., p. 71.

40. Harrison, *The Dominion of the Dead*, p. 59.

41. Ibid., p. 58.

42. Jennifer Rushworth, *Discourses of Mourning in Dante, Petrarch, and Proust* (Oxford: Oxford University Press, 2016), p. 116.

43. Ibid., pp. 102–04.

44. Darian Leader, *The New Black: Mourning, Melancholia and Depression* (London: Penguin, 2008), pp. 78, 87 (emphases in the original). As cited by Rushworth, *Discourses of Mourning*, p. 104.

45. Rushworth, *Discourses of Mourning*, p. 104.

46. Harrison, *The Dominion of the Dead*, p. xi.

47. Logudorese also has a written tradition. See Laura Linzmeier, *Compendium of the Sassarese Language: A Survey of Genesis, Structure, and Language Awareness* (Munich: Ibykos Verlag, 2019), pp. 149–50. Since the sixteenth century, a relatively small literary tradition has developed. Examples include the Sassarese writer Gerolamo Araolla (Sassari, 1542–Rome, 1615). Other examples include Luca Cubeddu (Pattada, 1748–Oristano, 1828), Gian Maria Pisurzi (Bantine, 1707–Bantine, 1796), and later Paolo Mossa (Bonorva, 1821–Bonorva, 1892). However,

especially in the context of mourning, Logudorese remains an oral language. This is significant in my analysis of Anedda's poetry in Logudorese.

48. Carmelo Princiotta, 'La scuola dei viventi:Il tragico in De Angelis e Anedda', in *I cantieri dell'italianistica: Ricerca, didattica e organizzazione agli inizi del XXI secolo: Atti del XII congresso dell'ADI — Associazione degli Italianisti* (Roma Sapienza, 18–21 September 2013), ed. by Beatrice Alfonzetti, Guido Baldassarri, and Franco Tomasi (Rome: Adi editore, 2014), pp. 1–10 (p. 8).

49. As quoted in the notes on *Dal balcone del corpo*.

50. As quoted in McKendrick, 'Introduction', p. 12.

51. As quoted in Ottonello, 'Una limba tra silenzio e passato. Dialogo con Antonella Anedda'.

52. As quoted in the notes on *Dal balcone del corpo*.

53. Antonella Anedda, 'Limba: Una nota sull'autotraduzione', in *La soglia sull'altro: I nuovi compiti del traduttore* (Bologna: La Bottega dell'Elefante, 2007), pp. 134–38 (p. 137).

54. For this reason, Anedda employs in her 'Attittos' poetic personae like the mother, sister, daughter, and so on.

55. Anedda, 'Limba: Una nota sull'autotradizine', p. 134. Cf. Luigi Meneghello, 'Vorrei far splendere quella sgrammaticata grammatica', in Luigi Meneghello, *Il tremaio: Note sull'interazione tra lingua e dialetto nelle scritture letterarie*, with contributions by Cesare Segre, Ernestina Pellegrini, and Giulio Lepschy (Bergamo: Lubrina, 1986), pp. 11–42 (pp. 40–41). Here Meneghello states: 'Per me il dialetto non è una lingua *bassa* (come qualche volta si sottindende quando si dice che non se ne ha nostalgia), ma una lingua *profonda*, non perché abbia caratteristiche speciali in quanto sistema linguistico, ma perché è stata la lingua delle prime, più vivide fasi della mia vita' [To me dialect is not a *low* language (as is sometimes implied when one says that it is not nostalgically missed), but rather a *profound* language, not because it has special characteristics within a linguistic system, but because it has been the language of the first, most vivid phases of life].

56. Anedda, 'Il destino della poesia', p. 826. As Binetti highlights in his footnote 20, 'ferro' [iron] and more generally 'metalli' [metals] return as an obsessive metaphorical element throughout *Historiae*. The same presence can be found in earlier poetic collections too. See Roberto Binetti, '"Una zona di tempo / schiuma delle ere". Lirica e storiografia in *Historiae* di Antonella Anedda', *lettere aperte*, 6 (2019), 75–86 (p. 86).

57. Antonella Anedda, *Tenebre*, in Antonella Anedda, *La luce delle cose: Immagini e parole nella notte* (Milan: Feltrinelli, 2000), pp. 46–56 (p. 53–54).

58. As quoted in the notes on *Dal balcone del corpo*.

59. 'Onzi tandu' does not mean anything in Sardinian; the 'correct' form should be 'onzi tantu'. The word 'tandu' means 'hence'/'therefore' or 'in that time'. Moreover, both 'dongu' and the third person clitic 'da' (= 'dda') are Campidanese terms and forms, not Logudorese; and the form 'solamenti' does not exist in Sardinian (one would use 'solu'). Anedda uses a language of her own, as she writes in her poem, mixing it with various Sardinian linguistic memories and creating her 'limba'. I am indebted again to Professor Maurizio Virdis for clarifying the presence of different Sardinian nuances in this poem.

60. Anedda, 'Il destino della poesia', p. 822. In this context, it is worth remembering Andrea Zanzotto's 'Prima persona' [First person] from the poetic collection *Vocativo* [Vocative] (1957), which, according to Anedda 'risponde per tutta la modernità' [answers to all modernity]: ' — Io — in tre minuti continui, — io disperso — / e presente' [— I — in three continuous minutes — I dispersed — / and present]. Ibid., p. 827.

61. Ibid., p. 825.

62. Ibid., pp. 825–26.

63. Franco Sepe, 'A colloquio con Antonella Anedda', *Italienisch*, 49 (2003), 90–100 (p. 96).

64. Anedda restates this in another interview: Antonella Anedda, 'Otto domande sulla poesia', *Studi duemilleschi*, 2:2 (2002), 17–18: 17: 'Il mio italiano è "già" una lingua straniera perché le mie origini sono sardo-corse: sono isole, da generazioni. È un italiano letto e ascoltato al suono di un'altra lingua, piu profonda e antica, piu selvaggia' [My Italian is 'already' a foreign language because my origins are Sardinian-Corsican: they have been islands for generations. It is an Italian that is read and listened to, to the sound of another language, deeper and more ancient, wilder].

65. Peter Robinson, *Poetry & Translation. The Art of the Impossible* (Liverpool: Liverpool University Press, 2010), p. 166.

66. Giovanni Nencioni, 'Antropologia poetica?', *Strumenti critici*, 19 (1972), 243–58; now in *Tra grammatica e retorica* (Turin: Einaudi, 1983), pp. 161–75 (174).

67. Ibid., p. 173.

68. Ernesto de Martino, *Morte e pianto rituale: Dal lamento funebre antico al pianto di Maria* (Turin: Bollati Boringhieri, 1975. Reprint, Turin: Bollati Boringhieri, 2000), p. 125. Eng. trans. by Harrison, as quoted in *The Dominion of the Dead*, p. 59.

69. Harrison, *The Dominion of the Dead*, p. 154.

70. Roland Barthes, *Mourning Diary*, ed. by Nathalie Léger and trans. by Richard Howard (London: Notting Hill Editions, 2011), p. 142. As quoted by Rushworth in *Discourses of Mourning*, p. 98.

71. Translation by McKendrick, as published in *Archipelago*.

72. Claudia Crocco, ' "La poesia crea uno spazio, che è un luogo in comune". Intervista ad Antonella Anedda' <https://quattrocentoquattro.com/2011/11/17/la-poesia-crea-uno-spazio-che-e-un-luogo-in-comune-intervista-ad-antonella-anedda> [accessed 1 September 2019]. On the point that Logudorese is a 'lingua sintetica', one should note that this might be because Anedda encounters Logudorese orally; but see footnote 47 for more information on writers who used Logudorese in elaborate ways, at times even making it too verbose. As in the above-mentioned interview, Anedda, on a more recent occasion, restates this idea about this *limba*: 'È come se sentissi l'esigenza di perlustrare un italiano in cui hanno sempre rintoccato altri suoni. Dopo una perdita, quando ho scritto per la prima volta questo sardo che intreccia molte suggestioni e linguaggi, era perché cercavo, sperimentavo qualcosa. Allo stesso tempo mi sono accorta del perché di alcune scelte in italiano: la passione per le consonanti, una certa reticenza nei confronti di suoni troppo armoniosi, la ricerca di un'altra musica, una musica diversa' [It is as if I felt the need to scour an Italian in which other sounds have always struck. After a loss, when I first wrote in this Sardinian language that weaves many suggestions and languages together, it was because I was searching for and experimenting with something. At the same time, I realized the reason behind certain choices in Italian: my passion for consonants, a certain reticence towards too harmonious sounds, the search for another music, a different music]. As quoted in Ottonello, 'Una limba tra silenzio e passato. Dialogo con Antonella Anedda'.

73. Antonella Anedda, 'Una musica diversa', in *Ritmologia: Il ritmo del linguaggio; Poesia e traduzione*, ed. by Franco Buffoni (Milan: Marcos y Marcos, 2002), pp. 325–32 (p. 329).

74. Iris Murdoch, *Under the Net* (London: Penguin, 1960 [1954]), p. 20.

CHAPTER 7

❖

Mourning and Lyric Address in Vivian Lamarque's *Madre d'inverno*

Vilma De Gasperin

1. Apostrophe and the mother

Vivian Lamarque's poetry collection, *Madre d'inverno* [Mother in Winter] (2016), is a tribute to the poet's mother, Rosa, who died on 29 December 2008, at the age of 96. To her, Lamarque previously dedicated the section 'Madri padre figli' [Mothers Fathers Children] in *Una quieta polvere* [Quiet Dust] (1996):[1] 'alla madre che mi ha salvata' [to the mother who saved me], that is, the mother who adopted the poet as a child when her natural mother gave her away.[2] The volume *Poesie 1972–2002* is also dedicated 'a mia madre | per il suo novantesimo compleanno'[3] [to my mother | for her ninetieth birthday]. The first three sections of *Madre d'inverno* — 'Poesie ospedaliere' [Hospital Poems], 'Ritratto con neve' [Portrait with Snow] and 'Compro oro' [We Buy Gold]) — shape mourning for the mother's death. The poems are autonomous, but they also weave a narrative that develops within each section, and the three sections are autonomous cycles which at the same time outline a development within a broader narrative of loss and remembrance across *Madre d'inverno*.[4] Thus each poem needs to be viewed individually but also as part of a whole. Borrowing from Mengaldo's description of Caproni's *Versi livornesi* (the collection from which the epigraphs for 'Ritratto con neve' are taken), the poems in *Madre d'inverno* are 'frammenti o schegge o parti di un insieme narrativamente legato e nello stesso tempo ripetitivo' [fragments or splinters or parts of a whole which is narratively linked and at the same time repetitive].[5]

 Madre d'inverno opens with an epigraph from Rainer Maria Rilke's poem *Requiem*, which introduces the theme of mourning at the outset: 'Ich habe Tote, und ich liess sie hin' [I *have* Dead ones, and I *have* let them go]. Rilke's poem goes on to contrast those 'Tote' who have been let go of, with the lamented *Freundin*, whom he is addressing: 'Nur du, du kehrst zurück'[6] [only you, you return]. Interestingly, in the epigraph Lamarque changes the present tense of *habe* to the imperfect tense: '*avevo* morti e li ho lasciati andare' [I *had/used to have* Dead ones, and I *have* let them go], highlighting the divide between the Dead of the past and the mother, who has recently died. As if to say: I had Dead ones and I let *them* go, but you, *you*, mother, are still here and I am talking to *you* through my poems where you continue to exist as a memory, an image and a voice, ultimately a presence. Poems in *Madre d'inverno* are both a testimony to absence (they are borne *out of* it) and a defiance to absence in so far as they still speak *to* (and not just *of*) the absent one. Indeed, all but three out of 53 poems on Rosa in *Madre d'inverno* address the mother as *you* (as conveyed by personal pronouns, possessive adjectives, and verb morphology) with the exception of the last two poems of 'Poesie ospedaliere' ('Siberia' and 'Scaduta l'epigrafe' [Expired Epigraph]) and the last of 'Ritratto con neve' ('Ritratto con solitudine' [Portrait with Solitude]). The lyric address in the second person creates the illusion of proximity between the speaker and the mother as both the speaker and the addressee share the same lyrical present.

In so doing, the lyric address and the apostrophe defy notions of the 'passing' of the Dead and of the 'working-through' of grief that is inherent or called for in psychoanalytical and anthropological theories of mourning, starting with Freud's seminal essay 'Mourning and Melancholia'.[7] As postulated by Freud, mourning is something to be overcome, for '[t]o tolerate life remains, after all, the first duty of all living beings'.[8] In his short essay 'I trapassati' [The Departed], the philosopher Benedetto Croce crudely suggests that through the work of remembrance such as gathering memories, painting images, composing biographies and eulogies of the deceased, the bereaved in fact begin to forget them, which is deemed a necessary step in order to survive grief:

> Con l'esprimere il dolore, nelle varie forme di celebrazione e culto dei morti, si supera lo strazio, rendendolo oggettivo. Così, cercando che i morti non siano morti, cominciamo a farli effettivamente morire in noi.[9]

> [By expressing our grief, in the different forms of commemoration and cult of the dead, we overcome grief, and in so doing we turn it from subjective to objective. Thus, while we endeavour not to let the Dead die, in fact we begin to let them die within us.]

Similarly, starting from the paradox outlined by Benedetto Croce, the ethnographer Ernesto de Martino writes: 'nella morte della persona cara siamo perentoriamente chiamati a farci procuratori di morte di quella stessa morte'[10] [at the death of a beloved, we are forcefully called upon to cause death to that very death]. He views ancient funeral rituals as a way of transcending mourning by means of making the Dead die within the bereaved,[11] through form and rhythm: 'l'uso di piangere i morti in metro, secondo cadenze, gesti e moduli letterari stabiliti dalla tradizione'[12] [the custom of lamenting the dead in a metre, according to rhythmical patterns, gestures and formulas that are established by tradition]. These theories thus focus on forgetting the Dead in order to transcend grief and consign the Dead to the past.

Conversely, the lyric address and the apostrophe to the Dead hold them in a present time that is shared, albeit imaginatively, between speaker and addressee, as well as readers. As Jonathan Culler writes, 'you' in a poem is 'immediately associated with what might be called the timeless present but is better seen as temporality of lyric articulation or enunciation'. To apostrophise is to locate *you* 'in the time of apostrophe, a special temporality which is the set of all moments at which writing can say "now".[13] The relationship between the past and the present, the time of life and the time after death is thus renegotiated by apostrophe, particularly in poems of mourning. As Culler highlights:

> A temporal problem is posed: something once present has been lost or attenuated; this loss can be narrated but the temporal sequence is irreversible, like time itself. Apostrophes displace this irreversible structure by removing it from linear time and locating it in a discursive time. The temporal movement from A to B, restructured by apostrophe, becomes a reversible alternation between A' and B': a play of presence and absence governed not by time but by poetic ingenuity or power. The clearest example of this structure is the elegy, which replaces an irreversible temporal disjunction, the movement from life to death, with a reversible alternation between mourning and consolation, evocations of absence and presence.[14]

The apostrophe to the Dead thus allows for the absent or dead *you* to be 'iterative and iterable' in 'the lyric present, in the special "now", of lyric articulation', which is quite the opposite of forgetting and transcending.

'For a poem to say *you* is in every sense a complex act.'[15] This does not apply only to poems where *you* is undefined, or an abstract entity, an inanimate object, a natural element, or the reader, but also where *you* is unequivocally another biographical human being.[16] In *Madre d'inverno* poems are addressed to the poet's mother, who is defined by her name and individual story. However, the precise entity of *you* that the poet addresses changes throughout the sections, leading to a repositioning of the lyric *I* in relation to the absent *you*, while determining the spatial and temporal coordinates between *I* and *you*, daughter and mother, poet-speaker and addressee. Therefore, we still need to ask who, where and even what is *you* as it changes across the three different sections. In the opening 'Poesie ospedaliere' *you* lies in the poet's memory and the mother is depicted during her time in hospital towards the end of her life. In 'Ritratto con neve' *you* is no longer an absent memorial figure of the past but a material and visible object in the lyric present, namely, a portrait of the mother as a younger woman, at which the poet gazes. In 'Compro oro' the mother/*you* oscillates between the daughter's memories of past life mostly prior to the illness, and her new state as an absent beloved in the present time. Thus, the ontological status of *you* shifts across the three sections, while *you* transits from memories of the mother as a living human being ('Poesie ospedaliere'), to a painted image on the wall ('Ritratto con neve'), to a figure who no longer inhabits the world of the living ('Compro oro').

Lyric address in Lamarque is not peculiar only to the elegiac poems to the mother. This mode of articulating poetic discourse features extensively, though not exclusively, in poems dealing with abandonment and longing for an absent one. For example, in *Teresino* (1981) the poet addresses a loved man and highlights his absence: 'Il tuo posto vuoto a tavola | parla racconta chiacchiera ride forte'[17] [your empty place at the table | talks tells chats laughs loudly], or 'non sei venuto questa sera all'appuntamento'[18] [tonight you didn't come to meet me as we planned]. *Poesie dando del Lei* (1989) [Poems using formal *You*] is entirely constructed as a second-person lyric address, where the female *I* voices her desire, longing and frustration to the inaccessible psychoanalyst, 'B.M.', to whom this and two other collections are dedicated:[19]

> Basta senza di Lei restare!
> non dico sempre
> ma almeno qualchelungavolta
> mi tenga accanto a sé.[20]

> [No more being without You!
> I don't mean always
> but at least somelongtimes
> keep me by Your side.]

Similarly, the abandonment of the child by the natural mother is depicted via the second-person poetic address in earlier poetry, with the mother as the object of longing:

> Mangiavo dormivo
> facevo la brava-bambina
> per conquistarti 'mammina'.
> Corteggiamento vano
> a nove mesi mi hai presa per mano
> mi hai lasciata a Milano.[21]

> [I used to eat sleep
> be a good girl
> to conquer you 'mammy'.
> Vain courtship
> when I was nine you took me by the hand
> you left me in Milan.]

Hence, Lamarque's poems characteristically employ the lyric address in order to convey longing for an absent figure following separation and abandonment. In *Madre d'inverno* the speaker addresses her mother who has died and, in so doing, she holds on to her in the present.

2. 'Poesie ospedaliere': lyric address and the mother's voice

'Poesie ospedaliere' (15 poems) focusses on the time when the mother is in hospital and ends with the implied allusion to her death. The title of the very first poem takes the form of a dedication to readers and bridges the autobiographical with a universal experience to which readers can relate: 'Per *chi* ha vegliato una notte *una* madre' (p. 11) [For *those who* have sat by the bedside of *a* mother one night], where the universality is conveyed by the pronoun *chi* [those who] and the indefinite article *una*. The poem explicitly calls the reader within its textual boundaries, enacting what Culler calls 'triangulated address', that is 'the pretence to address someone or something else, while actually proffering discourse for an audience'.[22] In this case, the poet speaks *to* the mother *for* readers who have lived a similar experience and can therefore understand it in relation to themselves.[23] As the philosopher Salvatore Natoli writes, 'grief is at once a personal and a cosmic event [...] It is only its universal reverberation — inherent in each individual experience of grief — that enables those suffering to communicate their grief and those looking on, to feel it and recognise it'.[24] The opening poem speaks thus of an experience which is both unique and universal. The mother is depicted in her hospital bed, trying to speak: 'affacciata alla sponda del tuo letto d'ospedale | [...] *stai cercando* di formare la frase' [leaning out of your hospital bed | [...] you *are trying to* utter a sentence]. The present continuous tense (*stai cercando*) captures not a memory of the past, but an ever-present moment crystallised in the temporal boundaries of the poetic utterance. Whereas other poems contribute to building a narrative in the past, this poem, in virtue of the present tense, is set in what Jonathan Culler calls a 'timeless present', or 'a temporality of lyric articulation'.[25] The present tense is abandoned for the rest of the section until the last poem, 'Scaduta l'epigrafe' ('Non *vale* ormai più' (p. 25) [it *is* no longer valid]). Like opening and closing parentheses of present tense/time, the first and the last poems enclose past events within the 'special "now" of lyric articulation'.[26] Within these two poems, lies the descriptive or repetitive nature of the *imperfetto*, the imperfect tense: 'Non eri proprio capace | di morire' [You were really incapable | of dying], 'poi chiudevi gli occhi' [then you would close your eyes] (p. 12), 'tu non trovavi il telecomando' [you would not find the remote control] (p. 13), 'Non ti andava se parlavo | con la vicina di letto' [you did not like it /if I talked to the neighbouring patient], 'eri gelosa' [you were jealous] (p. 14), 'Non volevi mangiare più' [you no longer wanted to eat], 'inghiottivi' [you would swallow] (p. 16) and so on. The *passato prossimo*, expressing a concluded action that is still felt as psychologically close to the speaker,[27] is used by the poetic voice on four occasions to recount a specific event: 'mi hai fatto un sorriso | come un sole' [you gave me a smile | like a sun] (p. 16); 'un giorno | di nascosto | ti abbiamo portato | i bambini' [one day | we secretly | brought you | the children] (p. 20); 'ci siamo addormentate e poi ancora domani tutto da capo risvegliate' [we fell asleep and then again tomorrow we woke up all over again] (p. 21); 'hai avuto anche tu il tuo canto | del cigno' [you, too, had you own | swan song] (p. 22). Instead, the literary *passato remoto*, which nonetheless clashes here, in terms of register, with the colloquial use of the definite article before Christian names typical of Northern Italian ('la Giovanna' [the Giovanna]), is used only in the poem 'Allegretto I' to refer to a third person-subject who lies outside the intimate mother/daughter dyad: 'Quella volta che la Giovanna di Ferruccio ti venne a trovare all'ospedale e ti parlò' (p. 18) [when the Giovanna of Ferruccio came to see you in hospital and spoke to you]. Mourning is rooted in the present tense, and finds solace in the psychological closeness and familiarity of the *passato prossimo*, and in the comforting repetitive or descriptive nature of the *imperfetto*. It does not bear the detachment inflicted by the *passato remoto*.[28]

The first-person *I* is both the subject of the poetic utterance and a poetic *persona* interacting with the mother: 'E io non trovavo l'infermiera' [And I couldn't find the nurse] (p. 13), 'mi dividevo tra te | e le piante' [I would divide my time between you and the houseplants] (p. 15), 'Ti dicevo buona notte' [I would say goodnight to you] (p. 17) and so on. Occasionally the subject merges with the addressee in the unifying plural *noi* [we], as in 'Contramal':[29] 'poi nella quieta stanza ci siamo addormentate e poi ancora domani tutto da capo risvegliate' [then in the quiet room we fell asleep and then again tomorrow we woke up all over again] (p. 21).

From the very beginning of this section, the mother is given a voice which is inscribed within the poem as direct speech. The first poem ends with a question posed by the mother: 'senti che | freddo qui che freddo che fa?' [can you feel how | cold here how cold it is?] ('Per chi ha vegliato una notte una madre', p. 11). In the second poem 'Alitalia' (p.12), three voices intermingle: the mother's voice (which I highlight in italics), the poet-daughter's words to the mother (underlined) and the poet addressing the mother from the lyric present (the remaining text):

Non eri proprio capace
di morire *aiutami mamma*
le dicevi che era morta nel '18'
di spagnola che avevi 6 anni
e tuo padre nel '25 che ne avevi
13, perché di ferite di guerra
si muore non contabilizzati anche
dopo la Guerra, e *aiutami Dante,*
il Biondo marito rapito dagli dèi
a 34 che avevi già aperto
la finestra per volare via anche tu.

Aiutatemi su, poi chiudevi gli occhi
e mi salutavi come fosse per sempre
sei stata una brava figlia, <u>no sei tu</u>
<u>che sei stata una brava madre,</u> *no tu*
<u>no</u> *sì* <u>no</u> congedo gentile, prova
generale del morire.
Ma la mattina dopo con voce squillante
allora con l'Alitalia come va? mi chiedevi,
l'hanno finalmente trovato un accordo?

[You *were* really incapable
of dying *help me mamma*
you would ask her who had died in 1918
of Spanish flu when you were 6
and your father in 1925 when you were
13, because of war wounds
one can die unrecorded even
after the War, and *help me Dante,*
the Blond husband taken by the gods
at 34 and you had already opened
the window to fly away with him.

Do help me, do, then you would close your eyes
and bid me goodbye as if it were forever
you have been a good daughter, <u>no it's you</u>
<u>who has been a good mother,</u> *no you*
<u>no</u> *yes* <u>no,</u> a gentle farewell, a rehearsal
for dying.
But the next morning with a piercing voice

> *so what's happening with Alitalia?* you would ask me,
> have they finally agreed on a deal?]

Let us look at the implications of the mother's own address to the Dead in the first stanza: 'aiutami mamma' [help me mamma], 'aiutami Dante' [help me Dante], 'Aiutatemi su' [Do help me, do]. These lines defy the assumption that it is absurd to speak to the Dead, except in poetry or in ritualised contexts, as suggested by Giovanni Nencioni.[30] Here, Rosa is performing neither a lyric nor a ritual address, but something of a personal and spontaneous nature. A similar instance of Rosa calling her dead husband is also recounted (diegetically, instead of mimetically) in the first and longer version of the poem 'L'albero' (2002) [The tree]: 'padre mio ti chiama sempre la tua bella Rosy sai'[31] [oh father your beautiful Rosy keeps calling you, you know]. Two distinct kinds of address or invocation coexist in this line: the first is performed by the poet addressing her dead father in the second person singular ('padre mio, ti... tua' [oh father, you, your]); the second, which is represented diegetically in 'L'albero' ('*ti chiama* sempre la tua bella Rosy' [your beautiful Rosy *calls you* all the time]) and mimetically in 'Alitalia' ('aiutami Dante' [help me, Dante]), is neither ritualistic, nor lyrical, and by no means absurd: it is common to those who grieve and expresses the need of the bereaved to continue addressing the person they have lost. In the second stanza the mother addresses the poet, her words alternating with the daughter's, without inverted commas to signal the change of speaker: 'sei stata una brava figlia, no sei tu | che sei stata una brava madre, no tu | no sì no' [you have been a good daughter, no it's you | who has been a good mother, no you | no yes no] in a see-saw of affectionate reassurance during the gentle goodbyes that prepare them for the definitive farewell. In the final, unexpected and uplifting turn of the poem, the mother's voice swerves the grief for imminent death into the enquiry about Italian current affairs: 'Ma la mattina dopo con voce squillante | allora con l'Alitalia come va? mi chiedevi, | l'hanno finalmente trovato un accordo?' [But the next morning with a piercing voice | so what's happening with Alitalia? you would ask me, | have they finally agreed on a deal?]. The mother's phrases inscribed in Lamarque's poems allow for a colour of Rosa's character to emerge and bring forth her *persona* to the present time. In the original, however, there are no graphical markers (e.g. inverted commas, italics, etc.) to differentiate between the different voices and dialogic exchanges: the words of the mother, as well as the poet's own words to the mother, have been appropriated and merged within the poet's own lyric.[32]

Rosa's voice takes over entirely in the poem 'Contramal' (p. 21), a continuous flux of questions, exhortations and observations, jumping from one topic to another in a colloquial tone:

> Beata che vedrai i bambini crescere mi piacerebbe
> l'hai poi spedita la lettera non dire sempre c'è tempo
> che non è vero e non ti dimenticare come quella volta
> l'ora legale non essere distratta prendi nota sai che mi
> ha telefonato Paolo gentile no? perché non vi risposa-
> te si può, che bella giacca è della Grazia? ringraziala
> pettinati però e la Minia e la Gianna e la sua mamma?

[Lucky you who will see the children grow I would like it
did you remember to post the letter don't say as usual there's time
as that's not true and don't forget like that time
the Summer time don't be absent-minded make a note of it do you know
Paolo phoned me that was kind of him wasn't it? why don't you get married
again, it's possible, what a nice coat is that Grazia's? do thank her
but do comb your hair and how are Minia and Gianna and her mum?]

The poem continues for twenty-four lines in a mimesis of the mother's spoken words, dealing with everyday enquiries and recommendations, where she appears to be holding fast to her role as a mother admonishing her daughter ('non essere distratta' [don't be absent-minded], 'pettinati però' [but do comb your hair]). Then gradually the mother's words reveal her physical pain: 'ora mi fa un po' male rimani?' [now it hurts a little will you stay?]), 'mi fa male il braccio della flebo' [my arm with the drip-feed hurts]. Within these snippets of conversation on which the reality of physical pain casually encroaches lies a more serious dialogue on death and the afterlife between the mother (here in italics) and the daughter (which I have underlined): 'ora vorrei andare <u>dove vuoi andare</u>, *dai che lo sai già*, <u>starete tutti insieme là</u>, *see non ci credo neanche... troppo bello*' [now I'd like to go, <u>where do you want to go</u>, *come on you already know that*, <u>you'll all be together there</u>, *yeaah I don't even believe it... too wonderful*]. The dialogic nature of these lines results in a changing relationship between the grammatical subject and the *persona* to which it refers, with *tu* being alternatively the mother and the daughter. Mention of *'andare'* [going], *'voi'* [plural you], *'insieme'* [together] and *'là'* [there] speaks of an afterlife where the mother will join those she has been mourning, harking back to the earlier poem 'Alitalia'. The format and vocabulary in these lines is also used in a poem from 'Il giardino dell'aldilà' [The Garden of the Hereafter] in *Poesie per un gatto* (2007) [Poems for a Cat], a series of mini dialogues between the poet and her cat Ignazio who is mourning the death of the cat Zarina:

> — Aspetta di rivederla *là*
> nell'*aldilà* dicono
> che ci risveglieremo *tutti*
> *insieme* chissà.[33]

> [— Just wait to see her *there*
> in the *hereafter* they say
> that we'll wake up *all*
> *together* who knows.]

The verb 'risvegliarsi' [waking up] is the final word in the poem 'Contramal' ('tutto da capo *risvegliate*' [woke up all over again]) and *rivederla* [to see her again] echoes the verb *vedere* [to see] at the beginning of 'Contramal' ('Beata che *vedrai*' [Lucky you who will *see*]. Just as the poet appears to comfort the cat with the promise of a reunion with Zarina in the afterlife (*aldilà*), so does the poet/daughter's *persona* appear to be reassuring the mother in 'Contramal' that 'starete tutti insieme là' [you'll all be together there], where the deictic adverb *là* [there], inscribed in the noun *aldilà*, is a euphemism for death.

Death is a recurring theme in Lamarque's poetry. In particular, the long poem 'Questa quieta polvere' (1986) [This Quiet Dust] is 'un drammatico dialogo con la morte'[34] [a dramatic dialogue with death], where death interweaves with quotations from, for example, Emily Dickinson (e.g. 'poiché non potevo fermarmi per la morte | lei gentilmente si fermò per me' ['Because I could not stop for Death –– | He kindly stopped for me')[35] and Marina Tzvetaeva ('dove si ritira l'amore | avanza la Morte Giardiniera'[36] [where love retreats | Gardener-Death advances]).[37] From her first collection *Teresino*, Lamarque's poetry weaves what Rossana Dedola called a '"corteggiamento" della morte' [wooing of death].[38] The *poemetto* 'L'albero' is imbued with mourning and it addresses the Dead, as in *'morti ma come vi hanno messi?* | *divisi per millennio? per secolo?* | *per causa di decesso?'*[39] [oh Dead, how have you all been sorted? | arranged by millennium? | by century? | by cause of death?]. In 'Poesie ospedaliere' death is no longer a literary construct, but a real event experienced by the poet and the actual moment of death is left unspoken. Death is the unnamed watershed that splits *before* from *after*. As we shall see below with the adverb *dopo* [after] in the third section 'Compro oro', the temporal adverb *prima* in 'Poesie ospedaliere' is used without specifying anaphorically, in the linguistic context, the temporal point of reference which would fulfil its meaning.[40] In 'Marlboro': *'Prima hai avuto anche tu il tuo canto* | *del cigno'* (p. 22) [*Before* you too had your own | swansong]. In the penultimate poem 'Siberia' (p. 24) the adverb *prima* [before] is the pivot around which the poem's meaning is poised:

> Poco prima a casa sentivo
> un gelo una Siberia
> mi ero fatta un tè. Bollente
> mi si era rovesciato sul ventre,
> sulla mano, sullo squillo del telefono
> già in giro per l'aria.

> [Just before at home I felt
> a freeze a Siberia
> I had made myself some tea. Boiling hot
> it had spilt over my lap,
> over my hand, over the phone ring
> already wandering in the air.]

'Poco prima' [just before] leaves an implied and unanswered question: before what? The event is left unspoken but for the first time the mother/you is absent from the linguistic context: she is neither addressed nor mentioned nor referred to by any object associated with her or any pronouns. The entire focus is on the poet's feeling of freezing cold in her own home, which recalls the mother's words in the very first poem set in hospital — 'senti che | freddo qui che freddo che fa?' [can you feel how | cold here how cold it is?] (p. 11) — , thus linking the end with the beginning, and closing the cycle. After the Siberia-like freeze, boiling tea is spilt over the lap, the hand and the phone ring, thus tracing a movement, at the level of imagery, from the literal (lap, hand) to the metonymic (phone ring). The significance of the phone ringing is conveyed not explicitly, but by association. After thirteen poems addressing the mother in hospital, this poem is set at home, and the phone ring, given its place within this section, suggests it is the phone call from the hospital that summons the newly bereaved person. The poem expresses the chilling sensation of death and the poet is seen for the first time entirely alone.

'Siberia' is followed by 'Scaduta l'epigrafe' (p. 25) [Expired Epigraph], which conveys that death has occurred through negative adverbs 'non... ormai più' [no... more alas], evoking the point of rupture between life (with the doctor's reassuring words) and implied death:

> Non vale ormai più, ormai scaduta
> l'epigrafe Szymborska 'per adesso,
> dice il medico, nulla di serio,
> si rivesta'.

> [It is no longer valid, it's expired by now
> the epigraph Szymborska 'for now,
> says the doctor, nothing serious,
> you may get dressed again'.]

The metapoetic 'Scaduta l'epigrafe' alludes to Lamarque's common practice of using epigraphs in her poems and collections, as a way of weaving a wider literary discourse with her own, and 'commenting on the *text*, whose meaning [the epigraph] indirectly specifies or emphasizes'.[41] No longer viable as an epigraph *en exergue*, the lines from Szymborska's 'Vestiario'[42] [Clothes] merge with the poetic fabric of Lamarque's poem in order to avoid acknowledging that illness has ended and death has commenced, or, to quote from Lamarque's poem 'Questa quieta polvere', 'la vita è finita | è incominciata la morte'[43] [life has ended | death has begun].

3. 'Ritratto con neve': the image and the gaze

Speaking of the work of mourning, Valerio Valeri writes:

> una certa continuità dell'oggetto è probabilmente condizione di continuità per il soggetto: l'oggetto perduto deve pertanto persistere in qualche modo, per mezzo di un'immagine, di una reliquia, ecc., o deve essere ricuperato in un nuovo oggetto, che funziona come metafora dell'antico.[44]

> [a certain continuity of the object is probably needed for the continuity of the subject: therefore, the lost object needs to be prolonged in one way or another, via an image, a relic, etc., or it needs to be retrieved in a new object, which will act as a metaphor for the old one.]

The image (an effigy, a portrait or a photo) acts as a metaphor (from Gr. *metapherein*, to transfer), to which the presence of the Dead has been transferred. Similarly, in Roman aristocratic households, it was customary to take a wax mask (*imago*) of the Dead, so that they would live on. As Harrison writes, this ancient custom has evolved into new forms:

> This ancient practice has its modern counterparts. To this day the photograph retains essential links to its ancestral origins in the death mask, if only because it allows a person's likeness to survive his or her demise, to say nothing of the

photograph's similar ceremonial role as ancestral portrait in the family album or domestic interior. In this respect the photograph follows in the footsteps of its immediate predecessor, the painted portrait, itself a modern descendant of the death mask. Whether cast in wax, painted in oil, or exposed on celluloid film, the image is essentially mortuary.[45]

It is highly significant, then, that following the implied reference to death at the end of 'Poesie ospedaliere', in the second section 'Ritratto con neve' the addressee is now a *simulacrum* of the mother. 'Ritratto con neve' ['Portait with Snow'] is a series of twelve poems in which the bereaved poet addresses the painted portrait of her mother. The actual portrait at the heart of this cycle of poems was a gift for Rosa's ninetieth birthday and had been painted by Gioxe De Micheli, to whom the first poem is dedicated ('A Gioxe De Micheli | che ti dipinse' [to Gioxe De Micheli | who painted you], p. 29). The portrait was taken from an old photograph of Rosa as a younger woman in her mid-forties. It is thus the artistic image of a photographic image from forty or fifty years earlier, and therefore it has gone through three different processes of change brought about by time, by celluloid film, and painted oil.[46] Thus *you* in 'Ritratto con neve' is different from *you* in 'Poesie ospedaliere'. Within the enclosed space of the poet's living room a new kind of lyric address takes place between the poet, sitting on the sofa, and the mother's portrait on the opposite wall, with a large window at the side. In the stillness of this domestic stage, everchanging reflections are superimposed on the surface of the painting and testify to the passing of time. The number of poems in this section (twelve) recalls the months of the year, and the sense of time passing is strengthened by imagery marking seasonal change, in a cycle going from geraniums, falling leaves, the snow, the Christmas tree.

Structurally, each poem is related to the whole as the repetition of something different: the painting remains the same but the reflections on it change. It therefore contains an inherent paradox between fixity and mutability. Each poem is entitled 'Ritratto' [Portrait] followed by a further defining feature: in the first poem 'Ritratto rosa' the adjective 'rosa' [rosy] refers, as in Petrarch's pun on 'l'aura–Laura', both to the colour of the geranium and the mother's name, Rosa; 'Ritratto d'inverno' [Winter Portrait] links the poem to the title of the collection, *Madre d'inverno* [Mother in Winter], Winter being the season which defines Rosa as a 'morta d'inverno' [dead in Winter] in 'Ritratto con neve' [Portrait with Snow] (p. 39). In the remaining ten titles, 'Ritratto' is further defined by a noun phrase introduced by the preposition *con* [with]. Each defining feature refers to an object or a circumstance that is mirrored on its glass surface or related to it thematically or intertextually and prompts memories and thoughts in the poet. The poems appear in the following order:

I.   'Ritratto rosa' [Rosy Portrait]
II.   'Ritratto con mare I' [Portrait with Sea I]
III.   'Ritratto con mare II' [Portrait with Sea II]
IV.   'Ritratto con Dante' [Portrait with Dante]
V.   'Ritratto con eleganza' [Portrait with Elegance]
VI.   'Ritratto con vela' [Portrait with Sail]

VII.   'Ritratto con Orazio' [Portrait with Horatio]
VIII.   'Ritratto con baciamano' [Portrait with Hand-kissing]
IX.   'Ritratto d'inverno' [Winter Portrait]
X.   'Ritratto con intermittenza' [Portrait on and off]
XI.   'Ritratto con neve' [Portrait with snow]
XII.   'Ritratto con solitudine' [Portrait with Loneliness]

The repetition of the title with a lexical variation characterises much of Lamarque's poetry that expresses impossible longing, such as in *Il signore d'oro* [The Golden Man] and *Il signore degli spaventati* [The Man of the Frightened Ones].[47] 'Ritratto con neve' thus represents a typical mode of Lamarque's poetic style where repetition coupled with partial variation conveys an attachment and a refusal to let go of the loved object, which is repeatedly at the heart of the poem and at the forefront of the title. It is significant that now that this characteristic formula is employed in the expression of mourning for the mother, it does not relate to memories of her as a living human being but to her fixed transfigured image, so as to conjure up, through repetition, a physical presence that may enable the illusion of the absent one being within reach.

This section begins with two epigraphs by Giorgio Caproni's *Versi livornesi*, the opening lines of 'Sulla strada di Lucca' [On the Road to Lucca]: 'Com'erano alberati | e freschi i suoi pensieri!...' [How lined with trees | and fresh were her thoughts!]; and of 'L'uscita mattutina' [The morning outing]: 'Come scendeva fina | e giovane le scale Annina!...' [How fine | and young was Annina climbing down the stairs!...].[48] The epigraphs, both exclamations, inscribe Lamarque's poetry within the lyric tradition of filial mourning for the mother figure.[49]

The first eleven poems are apostrophes, but *who*, or rather *what* is the poet addressing? *You* has now split into a double: it is the static portrait of the present, highlighted by the present tense and the temporal adverbs *ora* [now] (used 4 times) *oggi* [today] (used 5 times), *non più* [no longer] (used once); and it is the mother of the past, who is remembered and addressed in the *imperfetto*. Let us look at the opening poem, 'Ritratto rosa':

> Ti guardo dal divano
> stai di fronte a me.
> Ma causa riflessi entrano
> a coprirti il viso e l'abito
> a fiori il platano del viale,
> i fiori rosati del balcone. O sei tu
> ora madre alberata quelle foglie,
> tu quel geranio rosa come
> il tuo nome, quel fiore
> che <u>bagnavi</u> da viva
> da severa regina del balcone?

> [I look at you from the sofa
> you are before me.
> But because of reflections, come in
> to cover your face and flower-patterned dress
> the sycamore of the road,

> the rosy flowers of the balcony. Oh are you
> now, tree-lined mother, those leaves,
> you that geranium rosy like
> your name, that flower
> that you <u>used to water</u> when still alive
> you, stern queen of the balcony?]

'Ti guardo' [I look at you]: from the beginning this poem defies absence by affirming a visible presence that can be gazed at. However, the direct object of the address (*ti* [you]) is no longer the mother, as in 'Poesie ospedaliere', but her image, which testifies to the 'presence of her infinite absence'.[50]

The *I/you*, daughter/mother, speaker/addressee dyad is at the heart of a precise spatial setting called into play through deixis: 'ti... dal divano... di fronte a me' [you... from the sofa... before me]. Other objects are placed in relation to this intimate stage: the demonstrative 'quelle foglie' [those leaves] and 'quel geranio' [that geranium] refer anaphorically to 'platano' [sycamore] and 'fiori' [flowers] and at the same time have deictic value, as *those* flowers and leaves that the poet sees from her seat on the sofa. It would seem that all elements in the poem refer to the same physical space, i.e. the poet's living room. In fact, the same word or image is used to refer to two distinct 'referenti del mondo'[51] [referents of the world]: 'del balcone' [of the balcony] in l. 6 is the poet's balcony, whereas 'del balcone' in l. 11 refers to the balcony at the mother's house prior to her illness. Similarly, 'quel geranio' [that geranium] in l. 8 refers to the flower in the poet's balcony as it is reflected on the portrait, whereas the hypernym 'quel fiore | che bagnavi da viva' [that flower | that you used to water when still alive] refers both to the flower watered by the mother at her own home and to the geranium/flower *per se*. The flower is a recurring emblem in Lamarque repeatedly associated with the human transformation after death. In 'L'albero': 'guarda da una morta | è spuntata una margherita allora era | lei quella margherita?'[52] [look from a dead woman | a daisy has sprouted, was she, then, | that daisy?]. And in a poem from *Poesie per un gatto*, the poet replies to the cat who enquires whether the afterlife exists: 'Ma sì vedrai è come una specie | di giardino si diventa tutti erba fiori'[53] [Oh yes, you'll see it's a kind | of garden we all turn into grass flowers]. By asking 'O sei tu | ora madre alberata quelle foglie, | tu quel geranio rosa [...]?' [Oh, are you | now, tree-lined mother, those leaves, | you that geranium rosy...?] the poet inscribes this death within her recurring *topos* of death as metamorphosis. Owing to the effects of reflections superimposed on the portrait's glass surface ('causa riflessi'), *you* is now undergoing a series of changes: 'madre alberata' [tree-lined mother] and, in subsequent poems, she is 'diventata quadro' [turned into a painting] (Ritratto con mare I'), 'mi sembri madre in gabbia' [you look to me an encaged mother] ('Ritratto con Orazio'), 'non sei più madre fiorita' [you're no longer a flowery mother], 'mamma albero di natale' [christmas tree mamma] ('Ritratto d'inverno').

Starting in the timeless present of the poetic utterance, the poem then harks back to memories of the past: 'sei tu [...] quel fiore | che *bagnavi* da viva' [are you [...] that flower | that you *used to water* when still alive]: 'da viva' with the verb in the *imperfetto* implies that in the present she is *morta* [dead], a word that is eschewed and mentioned only once in the penultimate poem in the series, 'Ritratto con neve': 'Tu, protetta dal vetro | del tuo giardino d'inverno | — di morta d'inverno' [You, protected by the glass | of your Winter garden | — of a woman who died in Winter] (p. 39).

'Ritratto rosa' and the following three poems form a sort of sub-section, as they are coherently united by the theme of looking (*guardare*) and each refers to four distinct pictures that interact within the poems: the mother's painting ('Ritratto rosa'), two painted seascapes ('Ritratto con mare I' and 'Ritratto con mare II'), and the enlarged photograph of Rosa's late husband and poet's adoptive father Dante ('Ritratto con Dante'). In this carefully staged setting from which the poet/speaker gazes at the likeness of the Dead, even the two seascapes acquire symbolic value: 'Oggi di fronte a te | ho messo un mare' [Today in front of you | I hung a seascape] ('Ritratto con mare I'); followed by 'Ritratto con mare II':

> E accanto a quello
> ne ho appeso un altro
> ancora una marina
> ma solo un 18x24
> un mare-bambina.

> [And next to it
> I hung another one
> another seascape
> but only a 18x24
> a child-seascape.]

The two seascapes next to each other reproduce a mother-daughter dyad: indeed, by inserting one letter (as in the *enigmistica* [puzzle] game of *zeppa*) in 'mare-bambina' [sea-child] we have 'maDre-bambina' [mother-child]. In 'Ritratto con mare I', there are three distinct gazes: the gaze of the mother and the gaze of the painted splashes of foam captured in the opposite painting look at one another; then there's the poet's gaze which is not returned:

> spruzzi lievi di bianca
> schiuma ti guardano
> che li guardi
> mentre io guardo te
> diventata quadro.

> [light splashes of white
> foam look at you
> looking at them
> while I look at you
> now turned into a painting.]

Similarly, in 'Ritratto con Dante':

> Sappi che sopra il tuo ritratto
> ho appeso il babbo [...]
> anche lui
> vive ora di vita a specchio, riflessa.

> Uno sopra l'altra guardate davanti
> a voi lontano molto molto oltre
> questa me che vi guarda dal divano.
>
> [Just so that you know, above your portrait
> I hung Daddy [...]
> he, too,
> now lives a mirrored life, reflected.
> One above the other you both look ahead
> of you far, far beyond
> this me who is looking at you from the sofa.]

The metonymic 'babbo' [Daddy] for 'ritratto del babbo' [Daddy's portrait] reinforces the identification of the image with the Dead, whose gaze does not meet the poet's eyes: while the poet is gazing at the portraits of her parents, they gaze 'lontano molto molto oltre | questa me che vi guarda dal divano' [far, far beyond | this me who is looking at you from the sofa], thus denying the possibility of any form of mutual encounter. Initially, the grammatical subject of the verb *guardare* ('ti guardo', 'guardo te' [I look at you]) coincides with the subject of the poetic utterance through the use of the first-person. At the end of 'Ritratto con Dante' the poet's voice and the daughter's gaze are separated by the shift from the personal pronoun *io* [I] to the nominalised direct pronoun *me* [me] and subsequently the third person verb ('questa me che vi guarda' [this me who is looking at you]). Thus, the poetic voice has momentarily split from the daughter's *persona* gazing at her mother and appears to look on to the scene as an outsider.

Death is a spatial concept: it is *là* [there] as opposed to *qui* [here] of the poet's utterance: 'Che *là* dove sei, nel diciamo cielo, | si stia in gabbia così?' [I wonder if *there*, where you are, let's call it heaven, | one is in a cage like this?] ('Ritratto con Orazio'). The place adverb *là* [there, over there], short for 'al di là | aldilà' [the hereafter], is used as a euphemism for 'the Dead' in 'tutti gli andati al di là' [all the departed] in 'Ritratto con baciamano' (p. 36) and recurs in other collections, for example, in 'L'albero': 'Morti [...] siete tutti in disordine come stracci | là?'[54] [Oh Dead ... are you all piled randomly like rags | there?]; and in 'Il giardino dell'aldilà': 'Aspetta di rivederla là | nell'aldilà'[55] [Just wait to see her again there | in the afterlife]. In 'Ritratto con Orazio' (p. 35) *là* is rephrased as the more overt image of sky/heaven:

> Che là dove sei, nel diciamo cielo,
> si stia in gabbia così? Un'eternità
> sempre uguale come quando al mare
> sempre solo mare mare per un po'
> bene ma poi... c'è altro c'è altro in cielo
> e in terra Orazio.
>
> [I wonder if there where you are, let's call it heaven,
> one is forever in a cage like this? An eternity
> forever unchanging like when at the seaside
> forever only sea sea for a while
> it's okay but then... there are more things in heaven
> and earth, Horatio.]

The intertextual reference to Hamlet's words 'There are more things in heaven and earth, Horatio, | Than are dreamt of in your philosophy' (I.5, l. 166) points to the unknowability of the afterlife and a possible objection to its everlasting stillness.

Harrison writes that 'dying in the full human sense is a kind of birth, while the afterlife [...] is the new and altered condition the dead are born into (as souls, images, voices, masks, heroes, ancestors, founders, and the like)'.[56] By focussing on the portrait, poems in 'Ritratto con neve' touch upon the need for an image in order to continue to relate to, look at, and address their loved one.

3. 'Compro oro': after death

The first two sections of *Madre d'inverno* are each centred on a specific interior space: the hospital in 'Poesie ospedaliere' and the living room in 'Ritratto con neve'. 'Compro oro' broadens to encompass more varied and exterior spaces such as the We Buy Gold shop, the street and the cemetery. Equally varied are the events recounted in the present (dealing with the paperwork, selling the mother's jewels, emptying and selling her house, opening a posthumous letter) and the memories from Rosa's life. In most poems something in the present time triggers the memory of a specific event or of a certain habitual action in the past, thus affirming the continuity of the past into the present.

In the narrative developed within this section, the sequential nature is sometimes suggested by the poems themselves. 'La predetta' [The aforesaid], which begins 'E, sempre in tema...' [And on the same topic...], picks up on the theme of bureaucracy and paperwork of the previous poem 'Modulo ACI' [ACI Form].[57] Similarly, the two poems that tell of the poet's dream follow one another: in 'Ospedale con elicotteri' [Hospital with helicopters]: 'Ho sognato che tossivi come dal vero' [I dreamt you were coughing as for real]; and in 'L'età' [Age]: 'chiedevo ostinata | nel sogno' [I was asking, stubbornly, | in my dream]). If 'Ritratto con neve' is the repetition of something different, 'Compro oro' can be described, instead, as the sequence of different but closely related tesserae along the uneven path of mourning.

The opening poem of the eponymous section, 'Compro oro' (p. 44), begins with an apology to the mother/*you* for having sold her gold brooch. After the details of the exchange with the shop assistant, which divert from what is personal and painful to that which is commonplace, and the justifications for this decision, the poem ends with a meta-poetic affirmation of the soothing power of poetry:

> Scusa che ho venduto quella tua spilla
> d'oro, quella come un ramo d'oro
> a un Compro Oro [...]
> Disapproveresti, sei la solita
> mi diresti [...]
> tanto la tua spilla —
>
> ce l'ho infilzata nel petto, mi sanguina, però
> ora che l'ho posata qui sulla carta
> un poco meno (sai facciamo così noi poeti).

> [Forgive me for selling that golden brooch
> of yours, the one like a golden branch
> to a We Buy Gold [...]
> You would disapprove, so typical of you,
> you'd say to me [...]
> anyway your brooch
>
> I have got it pierced on my bosom, it bleeds me, yet
> now that I have put it down on paper here,
> a little less (you know, that's what we poets do).]

The object, a golden brooch in the shape of a branch with little rubies recalling the intensity of the mother's love ('colore | del tuo smisurato cuore' [the colour | of your boundless heart]), is charged with symbolic value. Yet it is not by cherishing the material precious object that the poet seeks to keep close to the mother who owned it, but by relinquishing it and transforming it into a metaphor. While the real brooch has been sold and its parts (gold and rubies) are due to be dismantled, a metaphorical brooch is now pierced on the poet's heart: 'ce l'ho infilzata nel petto, mi sanguina' [I have got it pierced on my bosom, it bleeds me]: the intransitive verb *sanguinare* [to bleed] is normally used with an indirect object when the subject is part of a person's body, as in *mi sanguina la ferita/il naso* [my wound/my nose is bleeding], or metaphorically, *mi sanguina il cuore* [my heart is bleeding].[58] As the subject of *to bleed* ('la spilla [...] mi sanguina' [my brooch is bleeding]), the brooch has become part of the poet, in one of the few explicit mentions of her grief. What does the poet do with such grief, symbolised by the brooch? She puts it down on paper, transforms it through poetry, and thus alleviates it: 'ora che l'ho posata sulla carta | un poco meno' [now that I have put it down on paper here, | a little less]. The last line in brackets '(sai facciamo così noi poeti)' [you know, that's what we poets do] is also used *en exergue* to this section: this is a declaration of what poets, and not just the lyric *I*, do with their pain through the transformative power of poetry. There is a hinted apology for what Ramazani calls 'the economic problem of mourning' that wracks modern elegists, 'the guilty thought that they reap aesthetic profit from loss, that death is the fuel of poetic mourning'.[59] The poem 'Manna' (p. 54) suggests that this fuel is willingly given by the deceased as an ongoing expression of her generosity:

> Da casa tua si usciva sempre tutti
> a mani piene. È ancora così, scendo
> le scale carica della tua casa da svuotare
> un grumo di sangue alla volta, nodi
> alla gola, come ti piaceva farti
> saccheggiare.
>
> P.S. e ancora mi dai: poesie su poesie
> mi piovono dal tuo cielo, manna
> di mamma.
>
> [From your house we always came out
> with our hands full. It is still like that, I walk down
> the staircase loaded with your house that needs emptying

a clot of blood at a time, lumps
in my throat, you really loved being
looted.

P. S. and you are still giving to me: poems and poems
appear out of your blue, manna
of mamma.]

The poem affirms continuity between the past and the present, conveyed by the use of tenses and the adverb *ancora* [still] 'si usciva' — 'scendo' [we came out — I walk down], 'ti piaceva farti saccheggiare'– 'ancora mi dai' [you loved being looted — you are still giving me], 'è ancora così' [It is still the same]. Rosa is, in some form, still present. As psychological studies reveal:

> A *sense* of immortality reflects a compelling and universal inner quest for a continuous symbolic relationship between our finite individual lives and what has gone before and what will come after. It is a search for symbolizing continuities, despite the discontinuities of death.[60]

The search for continuities can take various forms. It can be expressed by an action, as with the act of *giving* in the poem above, or by objects. For example, the recurring *topos* of the balcony characterised the mother when she was alive: 'severa regina del balcone' [stern queen of the balcony] ('Ritratto rosa', p. 29); and 'quell'anguria | che incredibile ti era spuntata | sul balcone' [that watermelon that | incredible sprouted up on your balcony] ('Anguria' [Watermelon], p. 67); 'al balcone dalla sua sentinella | non più presidiato' [At the balcony no longer guarded | by its sentinel] ('Bombola d'ossigeno' [Oxygen Bottle], p. 47); 'le sue aghiformi braccia | ti entravano nel balcone' [Its needle-shaped arms | entered your balcony] ('Cedrus atlantica', p. 50). After Rosa's house is left empty and subsequently sold, the balcony image is transferred, via a simile, to the graveyard in 'Fioriera' (p. 51) [Flower Trough]: the grave's flower trough is likened to a balcony and the mother is defined as a ghost, creating continuity in spite of the discontinuity of death:

la fioriera di marmo che sotto
ti sporge come nuovo balcone di una spanna,
fantasma di mamma.

[the marble flower trough that juts out
below you like a new balcony a few inches wide,
ghost-like mamma.]

There is an urge constantly to weave analogy and continuity between the world as it was then and as it is now. The anaphoric or deictic adverb *dopo* [after/afterwards/later] is repeatedly employed to signal, elliptically, the time of the mother's death. For example, in 'Chagall' (p. 58):

E chi cucirà per voi
dopo? [...]
lo sapevi che tu andata
mi si sarebbe scucito
il guardaroba il mondo
[...] ma un bel
mattino, dopo, poco dopo, nella via

sotto casa mia è spuntato un botteghino
[...]
Tranquilla, sappi che ora c'è chi
mette in fila bastimenti e imbastimenti
di punti su punti come da te
a me, da te a noi.

[And who is going to sew for you
afterwards?
[...]
you knew that when you were gone
my wardrobe my world
would get unstitched
[...] but one morning
afterwards, shortly afterwards, in the street
just below my place, a little shop sprung up
[...]
Don't worry, be reassured that now there's someone who
lines up vessels and basting stitches
of stitches upon stitches like from you
to me, from you to us.]

The poem builds on a series of analogies: the literal meaning of the mother's sewing acquires the metaphorical meaning of her holding the daughter's world together ('tu andata | mi si sarebbe scucito | il guardaroba il mondo' [when you were gone | my wardrobe my world | would get unstitched]). The newly opened clothing repairs shop creates some form of compensation or replacement, which in turn serves to affirm the continuity of the bond between the dead and the living, reinforced by the metaphor of stitches ('punti su punti da te | a me, da te a noi' [stitches upon stiches from you | to me, from you to us]). The verb *andare* [to go] used in the participle *andata* [gone] is a euphemism for *dead* (as in 'tutti gli andati al di là' [all the departed] in 'Ritratto con baciamano', p. 36; 'ora vorrei andare' [now I'd like to go] in 'Contramal, p. 21). And just as with the adverb *prima* in 'Poesie ospedaliere', here the temporal adverb *dopo* is used without expressing the anaphorical referent, which is left unspoken: in the mother's words 'chi cucirà per voi | dopo?' [who is going to sew for you | afterwards?] death is viewed prospectively; in the poet's 'dopo, poco dopo' [afterwards, shortly afterwards], it is viewed retrospectively. Similarly, in the poem 'Calligrafia' (p. 48) [Calligraphy]: 'nell'ultima | lettera quella inattesa | con sulla busta scritto | "per dopo"' [in the last | letter the unexpected one | with 'for afterwards' | written on the envelope], death is merely conveyed by the temporal adverb. Such avoidance of the word 'death' is given up in the poem 'Ma non te lo ricordi più?' (p. 65) [But Don't You Remember?]:

Quando si telefona, dopo, nelle loro case
si fa suonare a lungo più a lungo
[...]
P.S. (che poi tu mi diresti
ma cos'hai nella testa a telefonare
non te lo ricordi più che sono morta?)

[When you phone, afterwards, in their homes
you let it ring for longer
[...]
P.S. (you'd actually say to me
but what are you thinking, phoning me
don't you remember that I am dead?)]

According to studies in bereavement, the deliberate disbelief that death has occurred, exemplified here by the act of dialling the mother's number in the now vacated house, can be a way of mitigating the pain.[61] It is in response to such disbelief, that for the first time there is explicit mention of the mother being dead, through words in direct speech that she is imagined saying if she were alive: 'non te lo ricordi più che sono morta?'[don't you remember that I'm dead?]. This poem presents an instance of the use of a hypothetical clause where the protasis is only implied: if you could see me, 'tu mi diresti | ma cos'hai nella testa' [you'd say to me | what are you thinking?]. The pattern of the implied protasis recurs in other poems: if *you* could see me selling your brooch, 'Disapproveresti, sei la solita | mi diresti' [you would disapprove, typical of you | you would say to me] ('Compro oro', p. 43); if you were still alive, 'Con questo sole avresti messo | il cappello di paglia e saremmo andate | al mercato' [on such a sunny day you would have put on | your straw hat and we would have gone | to the market] ('Macramè', p. 46). The conditional clause suggests attachment with the time prior to death, and at the same time it reveals the awareness of absence: you would say this, but you don't because you are dead.

As in 'Poesie ospedaliere', the mother's voice is inscribed in this section, but in different ways. In 'Algasiv' (p. 57) her words are presented as the transcript of her conversation with a nurse:

Che casino questo comodino
diceva l'infermiera, ha ragione
sa mia figlia è fissata con gli
alberi di natale

[What a mess this bed-side table
the nurse would say, you're right
you know my daughter is obsessed with
Christmas trees]

And in 'Scambio di mamme' (p. 68) [Mix-up of mothers]:

All'infermiera della flebo
raccontavi l'equivoco del giudice
fresco di sessant'anni fa, 'pensi che lui
mi aveva guardata con cipiglio severo [...]'

[To the nurse fixing your feed-drip
you used to tell of the Judge's misunderstanding
that just happened sixty years ago, 'fancy that he
had looked at me sternly [...]']

Towards the end of the section, the voice is heard from more uncanny places. In 'La

predetta' (p. 64) [The Aforesaid] she speaks 'da un dove' [from some where]: since
the place adverb *qui* [here] is uttered by the Dead, it actually means *là* [there], that
is, *aldilà* [here–after]:

> [...] l'avvocato oggi ha scritto
> su carta bollata 'la predetta signora Pellegrinelli
> Maria Rosa coniugata Provera' e all'istante:
> "Sono qui! io!", da un dove la tua voce!
> "Maria Rosa io! io! è il nome mio!"
>
> [[...] today the solicitor wrote
> on stamped paper 'the aforesaid Mrs Pellegrinelli
> Maria Rosa married into Provera' and right away:
> 'I'm here! It's me!', from some where your voice!
> 'Maria Rosa it's me! me! it's my name!']

Unlike poems in 'Poesie ospedaliere' where the mother's words are undifferentiated
from the daughter's and appear graphically merged with the poet's own voice, here
both her reported speech (in 'Scambio di mamme') and the imagined words of
a female subject speaking from beyond are marked by inverted commas. In 'Vai
già via?' (p. 66) [Are you going already?], the mother's voice stems from *lì* [there],
the beyond, reinforced by vocabulary specifically associated with death ('lapide'
[gravestone], 'tomba' [tomb], 'fiore' [flower] and 'cimitero' [cemetery]): 'Anche
da lì con voce di lapide mi dici *vai già via?* | Con immediato senso di colpa faccio
subito | marcia indietro' [Also from there in a gravestone-like voice you ask me
are you going already? | With an immediate sense of guilt, I instantly | retreat my
steps]. 'Anche' [also] suggests that the mother's reproach for the daughter's hurry,
too, is a form of continuity with what was before, like the balcony and the clothing
repair shop: 'sempre di fretta | questi figli [...] nemmeno al cimitero camminiamo
piano' [always in a hurry | these children [...] we don't slow down not even at the
cemetery]. Change is thus marked by the prolongation of what was before death.

5. Mourning and a story

In expressing the poet's mourning for her mother, *Madre d'inverno* creates a lyric
space for the mother: as these poems hark back to different points in the past, they
allow for Rosa's own story to emerge: it is the story of an orphaned child, a bereft
widow, an adoptive single mother, grieved by jealousy for the natural mother. The
harshness of her life and the inner strength that sustains her is glimpsed in the poem
'Alla mia mamma dritta come un fuso' [To my mamma as straight as a ramrod]:
'Le spine della vita | l'hanno ferita, ma lei cammina | dritta'[62] [Life's thorns | have
wounded her, but she walks | upright].

   This is Rosa's story as it can be pieced together from the poems in *Madre d'Inverno*.
'Pellegrinelli Maria Rosa coniugata Provera' [P. M. R. Married P.] ('La predetta',
p. 64) was 'nata a Darfo Boario [...] l'uno dieci dodici' [born in Darfo Boario on
the 1/10/1912] ('Modulo ACI', p. 63). At the age of six her mother died, and at the
age of 13 her father died: 'aiutami mamma | le dicevi che era morta nel '18 | di

spagnola che avevi 6 anni | e tuo padre nel '25 che ne avevi | 13' [help me mamma | you would ask her | who had died in 1918 | of Spanish flu when you were 6 | and your father in 1925 when you were 13] ('Alitalia', p. 12). Her husband Dante died at the age of 34: 'aiutami Dante, | il biondo marito rapito dagli dèi | a 34 anni che avevi già aperto | la finestra per volare via anche tu' [help me Dante, | the Blond husband taken by the gods | at 34 and you had already opened | the window to fly away with him] ('Alitalia').[63] Rosa's attempt to thrust herself from the window at the news of her husband's tragic death is further captured in 'Cedrus atlantica': 'il luttuoso giorno in cui ti trattennero, | ti impedirono il disperato salto' [the mournful day when they held you back | they prevented you from that desperate leap] (p. 50). Three years before Dante's death and with no children of their own, Rosa adopted Vivian: 'La A112 era il tuo mai da feto abitato | grembo, guidavi con dentro l'auto | me già grande' [The A112 car was your never-inhabited-by-a foetus | womb, you used to drive the car | with me in it already a toddler] ('A112', p. 52). In 'Scambio di mamme' (p. 68) Rosa tells the 'esterefatta infermiera' [flabbergasted nurse] of the preposterous misunderstanding of the judge who believed her to be the natural mother who was abandoning, rather than adopting, the child:

> Io alta bella vistosa, l'altra
> una santerellina, ci aveva scambiate
> quel somaro, capisce? credeva che
> fosse lei che adottava e io
> IO che abbandonavo!

> [I, tall handsome striking, the other one
> a little saint, he had mixed us up
> that jackass, you see? he thought
> that she was the one adopting and I
> — I! — the one abandoning!]

In 'Vasca da bagno' (p. 56) [Bathtub] the trauma of being abandoned that is felt by the child and healed after many years of psychoanalysis is looked at from the adoptive mother's perspective and reveals the mother's own grief at never being called *mamma*:

> non ti chiamavo mai
> me lo hai detto tu che da bambina
> ti chiamavo solo la domenica mattina
> dalla vasca per lavarmi la schiena
> tu facevi finta di non sentire
> per sentirmi ripetere due volte
> ho finito mamma.

> [I would never call you
> you told me yourself that as a child
> I called you only on Sunday morning
> from the bathtub, to wash my back
> you pretended not to hear
> so that I'd say it twice
> I am ready mamma.]

As her adopted child grows up, Rosa is depicted as enduring permanent jealousy towards the natural mother: 'La madre biologica | la chiamavi sempre l'altra' [The biological mother | you always used to call her], whose death brings her a sense of relief, as of a finally concluded competition in the daughter's affections: 'Quando a 83 anni era mancata | avevi tirato un respiro di sollievo' [When at the age of 83 she died | you heaved a sigh of relief] ('Madre l'altra', p. 73). Even in the afterlife Rosa is imagined asking the persisting question, in the concluding poem of 'Compro oro', 'Specchio mio bello specchio' (p. 69) [Mirror mirror in my hand]: 'quale mamma lei ama di più?' [which mamma does she love the most?]. These poems, while shaping the poetic subject's mourning, reach beyond the autobiographical lyric I to reveal something of the mother from her own perspective: her words, her own story of loss and endurance, and the primacy in her rivalled motherhood.

'Poesie ospedaliere', 'Ritratto con neve' and 'Compro oro' depict different moments of the poet's experience of mourning. By addressing the mother as *you*, Lamarque's poetry perpetuates the mother's presence, even while affirming and mourning her death. The changes in the relationship between *I* and *you* in the poems, and the changes in the entity of *you* — from a remembered living person to a lifeless painting and to the imagined voice speaking from beyond the grave — point not to the passing of the loved mother but, rather, to her being ever more present, though inevitably changed and unable to respond.

Anthropological theories that claim the need to forget the dead, to make them die within us, to perform rituals to bury the Dead so that mourners can go on with their lives, overlook the inner realm, which is more nuanced, melancholy, unpredictable and holds the Dead close, in the present. Lyric that speaks *to* as well as *of* the Dead suggests, instead, how the passing of time is not a moving away from the loved one, and that mourning is not a process of forgetting, but one of cherishing continually, in the present. As Antonio Prete writes in his poem 'Madre': 'Si fa lontano il giorno dell'addio, | ma non divieni una parvenza fioca [...]. La mancanza è sottile trama d'aria, | ma sei qui'.[64]

Bibliography

ALIGHIERI, DANTE, *Vita Nuova*, intro. by Giorgio Petrocchi, ed. by Marcello Ciccuto (Milan: Rizzoli, 1994)

ANEDDA, ANTONELLA, *Historiae* (Turin: Einaudi, 2018)

BLANCHOT, MAURICE, 'The gaze of Orpheus', in *The Gaze of Orpheus and other Literary Essays*, trans. by Lydia Davis (New York: Station Hill Press, 1981), pp. 99–104

CAPRONI, GIORGIO, *L'opera in versi* (Milan: Mondadori, 1999)

CROCE, BENEDETTO, 'I trapassati', in *Frammenti di etica* (Bari: Laterza, 1922), pp. 22–24

CULLER, JONATHAN, *Theory of the Lyric* (Cambridge, MA: Harvard University Press, 2015)

CVETAEVA, MARINA, *Poesie*, trans. and ed. by Pietro A. Zvetermich (Milan: Feltrinelli, 1992)

DE GASPERIN, VILMA, 'Dialogo e intertestualità in "Questa Quieta Polvere" di Vivian Lamarque', in *La Citazione: Atti del XXXI Convegno Interuniversitario (Bressanone/Brixen, 11–13 luglio 2003): Quaderni del Circolo Filologico Linguistico Padovano*, ed. by Gianfelice Peron (Padua: Esedra, 2009), pp. 589–608

De Martino, Ernesto, 'I lamenti funebri e l'esperienza arcaica della morte', in Ernesto de Martino, *Panorami e spedizioni: Le trasmissioni radiofoniche del 1953–54*, ed. by Luigi M. Lombardi Satriano and Letizia Bindi (Turin: Bollati Boringhieri, 2002), pp. 68–75

De Martino, Ernesto, *Morte e pianto rituale: Dal lamento funebre antico al pianto di Maria*, 2nd ed. (Turin: Bollati Boringhieri, 2000)

Dedola, Rossana, 'Dalla poesia innamorata all'elegia dell'albero', in Vivian Lamarque, *Poesie 1972–2002* (Milan: Mondadori, 2002), pp. v–xiv

Dickinson, Emily, *The Complete Poems*, ed. by Thomas H. Johnson (London: Faber and Faber, 1975)

Freud, Sigmund, 'Our attitude towards death', in the *Standard Edition of the Complete Psychological Works of Sigmund Freud*, 24 vols (London: Vintage, 2001), xiv, 289–302

Genette, Gérard, *Paratexts: Threshold of Interpretation* (Cambridge: Cambridge University Press, 1997)

Lamarque, Vivian, *Il signore d'oro* (Milan: Crocetti, 1986)

—— *Il signore degli spaventati* (Forte dei Marmi: Pegaso, 1992)

—— *Poesie dando del Lei* (Milan: Garzanti, 1989)

—— *Poesie per un gatto* (Milan: Mondadori, 2007)

—— *Poesie: 1972–2002* (Milan: Mondadori, 2002)

—— *Teresino* (Milan: Società di Poesia & Guanda, 1981)

—— *Una quieta polvere* (Milan: Mondadori, 1996)

Natoli, Salvatore, *L'esperienza del dolore: Le forme del patire nella cultura occidentale* (Milan: Feltrinelli, 2002)

Nencioni, Giovanni, 'Antrolopologia poetica?', *Strumenti critici*, 19 (1972), 243–58; now in *Tra grammatica e retorica* (Turin: Einaudi, 1983), 161–75

Harrison, Robert Pogue, *The Dominion of the Dead* (Chicago: Chicago University Press, 2003)

Ovid, *Metamorphosis: Books 9–15*, trans. by Frank Justus Miller, rev. by G. P. Goold (Cambridge, MA: Harvard University Press, 1984)

Parkes, Colin Murray, *Bereavement: Studies in Grief in Adult Life* (London: Penguin, 1998)

Petrarca, Francesco, *Canzoniere*, ed. by Marco Santagata (Milan: Mondadori, 2004)

Piemontese, Felice, ed., *Autodizionario degli scrittori italiani* (Milan: Leonardo Editore, 1989)

Prete, Antonio, *Tutto è sempre ora* (Turin: Einaudi, 2019)

Ramazani, Jahan, *Poetry of Mourning: The Modern Elegy from Hardy to Heaney* (Chicago: Chicago University Press, 1994)

Rilke, Rainer Maria, *Requiem e altre poesie*, ed. by Giuliano Donati (Milan: Mondadori, 1992)

Testa, Enrico, 'Sur la corde de la voix' : *Funzioni della deissi nel testo poetico*, in *Linguistica, pragmatica e testo letterario*, ed. by Umberto Rapallo (Genoa: Il Melangolo, 1987), pp. 113–46

Shakespeare, William, *Hamlet* (London: Penguin, 1988)

Szymboroska, Wisława, *La gioia di scrivere: Tutte le poesie (1945–2009)*, ed. by Pietro Marchesani (Milan: Adelphi, 2009 [2013])

Valeri, Valerio, 'Lutto', in *Enciclopedia* (Turin: Einaudi, 1979), pp. 594–604

Vanelli, Laura and Lorenzo Renzi, 'La deissi', in *Grande grammatica di consultazione (III): Tipi di frase, deissi, formazione delle parole*, ed. by Lorenzo Renzi, Giampaolo Salvi and Anna Cardinaletti, 2nd edn (Bologna: Il Mulino, 2001), pp. 261–375

Vincenzo Mengaldo, 'L'uscita mattutina di Caproni', in *La Tradizione del Novecento. Quarta serie* (Turin: Bollati Boringhieri, 2000), pp. 196–238

Waters, William, *Poetry's Touch: On Lyric Address* (Ithaca, NY: Cornell University Press, 2003)

Notes to Chapter 7

1. Vivian Lamarque, 'Madri padri figli', in *Una quieta polvere* (Milan: Mondadori, 1996), pp. 11–41.
2. I am indebted to Vivian Lamarque for her narration of her childhood and family history.
3. Vivian Lamarque, *Poesie: 1972–2002* (Milan: Mondadori, 2002). All translations are mine, unless otherwise stated.
4. In referring to *Madre d'inverno*, I shall henceforth refer to the 52 poems in the first three sections, plus 'Madre l'altra' [Mother, the Other One] which opens the fourth section, a cycle of 8 poems centred on the natural mother.
5. Pier Vincenzo Mengaldo, '*L'uscita mattutina* di Caproni', in *La Tradizione del Novecento; Quarta serie* (Turin: Bollati Boringhieri, 2000), pp. 196–238 (p. 196).
6. Rainer Maria Rilke, *Requiem e altre poesie*, ed. by Giuliano Donati (Milan: Mondadori, 1992), p. 4.
7. Freud distinguishes between mourning that has been accomplished and mourning for someone who is 'psychically prolonged' in the present. Sigmund Freud, 'Mourning and Melancholia', in *The Standard Edition of the Complete Psychological Works of Sigmund Freud*, 24 vols (1914–1916) (London: Vintage, 2001), xiv, pp. 239–58 (p. 245).
8. Sigmund Freud, 'Our attitude towards death', in the *Standard Edition of the Complete Psychological Works of Sigmund Freud*, 24 vols (London: Vintage, 2001), xiv, pp. 289–302 (p. 299).
9. Benedetto Croce, 'I trapassati', in *Frammenti di etica* (Bari: Laterza, 1922), pp. 22–24 (p. 23).
10. Ernesto de Martino, *Morte e pianto rituale: Dal lamento funebre antico al pianto di Maria* (Turin: Bollati Boringhieri, 1975 and 2000), p. 8. On Croce and de Martino, see also 'The voice of grief' in Robert Pogue Harrison, *The Dominion of the Dead* (Chicago: Chicago University Press, 2003), pp. 55–71.
11. Ernesto de Martino, *Morte e pianto rituale*: 'grande tradizione culturale che riconduce il lavoro del cordoglio al "far morire i nostri morti in noi", cioè far passare i morti nel valore, trascendendo con ciò la situazione luttuosa' (pp. 52–53) [great cultural tradition that views mourning as 'making our dead die within us', that is, make them pass symbolically, and thus overcome the state of mourning].
12. Ernesto de Martino, 'I lamenti funebri e l'esperienza arcaica della morte', in Ernesto de Martino, *Panorami e spedizioni: Le trasmissioni radiofoniche del 1953–54*, ed. by Luigi M. Lombardi Satriano and Letizia Bindi (Turin: Bollati Boringhieri, 2002), pp. 68–75 (p. 68).
13. Jonathan Culler, *Theory of the Lyric* (Cambridge, Mass.: Harvard University Press, 2015), p. 226. In his chapter 'Lyric Address', Culler distinguishes between 'Lyric address to Listeners or Readers', 'Addressing Other People', and 'Apostrophe', where 'there is no limit to the range of things that can be addressed by a lyric' (p. 211).
14. Culler, p. 227.
15. William Waters, *Poetry's Touch: On Lyric Address* (Ithaca, NY: Cornell University Press, 2003), p. 12.
16. 'Who is speaking (or writing), to whom, in what context? It is difficult to answer these very basic pragmatic questions with respect to a poem'; Waters, p. 8.
17. *Teresino* (Milan: Società di Poesia & Guanda, 1981), p. 37.
18. Ibid., p. 68.
19. *Il signore d'oro* (Milan: Crocetti, 1986); *Il signore degli spaventati* (Forte dei Marmi: Pegaso, 1992).
20. *Poesie dando del Lei* (Milan: Garzanti, 1989), p. 56.
21. 'Abbandono' [Abandonment], in *Una quieta polvere*, p. 15.
22. Culler, p. 186.
23. Similarly, Dante and Petrarch refer to listeners who can or cannot understand love. Dante: 'che 'ntender no la può chi no la prova' [those who have not felt it cannot understand it], in 'Tanto gentile e tanto onesta pare' (l. 11), in Dante Alighieri, *Vita Nuova*, intro. by Giorgio Petrocchi, ed. by Marcello Ciccuto (Milan: Rizzoli, 1994), p. 200. Similarly, in Petrarch: 'chi per prova intenda amore' [who, having felt it, understands love], from 'Voi ch'ascoltate in rime sparse il suono' (l. 8), Francesco Petrarca, *Canzoniere*, ed. by Marco Santagata (Milan: Mondadori, 2004), p. 5.

24. Salvatore Natoli, *L'esperienza del dolore: Le forme del patire nella cultura occidentale* (Milan: Feltrinelli, 2002): 'il dolore è fatto personale, ma è anche evento cosmico [...]. Solo il riverbero di universale, che è presente in ogni esperienza individuale di dolore, permette a chi soffre di comunicarlo e a chi guarda di presentirlo e di riconoscerlo' [Pain is personal, but it is also a cosmic event [...]. Only the reverberation of the universal, which is present in every individual experience of pain, allows the sufferer to communicate it and the beholder to present and recognise it.] (pp. 8–9).

25. Culler, p. 226.

26. Culler, p. 226.

27. 'Passato prossimo', in Giuseppe Patota, 'Glossario e dubbi linguistici', in Luca Serianni, *Italiano. Sintassi — Grammatica — Dubbi* (Milan: Garzanti, 2005), p. 570.

28. Cf. Patota: 'Il p. remoto indica un'azione che si colloca nel passato ed è priva di legami, obiettivi e psicologici, col presente' [The past historic expresses an action that is in the past and has no ties, either objective or psychological, to the present time]. It is therefore used not only for an action in the distant past but also 'un'azione vicina nel tempo, se la si vuole presentare come un evento compiuto, guardato con distacco' [an action that is close in time, when we want to present it as a concluded event, viewed with detachment], p. 570.

29. Contramal is a painkiller.

30. 'Il vero colloquio *in absentia*, così frequente e così (possiamo dirlo) naturale nella poesia anche moderna, sarebbe assurdo nella realtà quotidiana appunto perché non è un atto di comunicazione previsto dal sistema della lingua parlata, non è un atto costitutivo del rapporto sociale. [...] il parlare ad un assente che non può rispondere sussiste tuttora in situazioni fittizie, cioè non poetiche, ma reali, sociali: quali il congedo rituale od oratorio dal cadavere presente, la lamentazione funebre, quelle iscrizioni sepolcrali in cui si attarda l'uso dell'*alloqui cinerem*, e la preghiera pubblica e privata' [The real address to an absent one, so frequent and, we may say, so natural in poetry both old and modern, would be absurd in daily life precisely because it is not a communicative act that belongs to the system of spoken language, it is not a fundamental act of social intercourse. [...] Speaking to an absent one who cannot reply can persist still today in fictitious contexts (i.e. not in poetry), but real and social, such as in the ritual or oratorial separation from the corpse, in funeral lamentations, tomb inscriptions where we can still find traces of the address to the ashes, and in prayer, both public and silent]. Giovanni Nencioni, 'Antrolopologia poetica?', *Strumenti critici*, 19 (1972), 243–58; now in *Tra grammatica e retorica* (Turin: Einaudi, 1983), 161–75 (pp. 170–71).

31. Lamarque, *Poesie. 1972–2002* (Milan: Mondadori, 2002), p. 220. A shorter version of this poem appears in *Madre d'inverno*, pp. 93–95.

32. See the discussion on giving a voice to the dead in the present volume: Adele Bardazzi, Francesco Giusti, Emanuela Tandello, 'Introduction: Why Mourning in Poetry?'.

33. *Poesie per un gatto* (Milan: Mondadori, 2007), p. 135.

34. 'Vivian Lamarque', in *Autodizionario degli scrittori italiani*, ed. by Felice Piemontese (Milan: Leonardo, 1989), p. 191.

35. Emily Dickinson. *The Complete Poems*, ed. by Thomas H. Johnson (London: Faber and Faber, 1975), p. 712.

36. Marina Cvetaeva, 'Da "Due canzoni"', in *Poesie*, trans. and ed. by Pietro A. Zvetermich (Milan: Feltrinelli, 1992), pp. 94–95 (p. 95).

37. On death and Lamarque's use of quotations, see Vilma De Gasperin, 'Dialogo e intertestualità in "Questa Quieta Polvere" di Vivian Lamarque', in *La Citazione: Atti del XXXI Convegno Interuniversitario (Bressanone/Brixen, 11–13 luglio 2003): Quaderni del Circolo Filologico Linguistico Padovano*, ed. by Gianfelice Peron (Padua: Esedra, 2009), pp. 589–608.

38. Rossana Dedola, 'Dalla poesia innamorata all'elegia dell'albero', in Vivian Lamarque, *Poesie 1972–2002* (Milan: Mondadori, 2002), pp. v–xiv (p. xiv).

39. *Poesie*, p. 217. Italics in the original.

40. '*Prima* e *dopo* sono termini essenzialmente relazionali in quanto richiedono sempre un punto di riferimento temporale rispetto al quale un determinato evento è anteriore o posteriore' [Before and after/afterwards are relational terms in that they always require a temporal point of reference, that is either preceded or followed by an event]. Laura Vanelli and Lorenzo Renzi,

'La deissi', in Lorenzo Renzi, Giampaolo Salvi and Anna Cardinaletti, eds, *Grande grammatica di consultazione (III): Tipi di frase, deissi, formazione delle parole*, 2nd edn (Bologna: Il Mulino, 2001), pp. 261–375 (p. 295).

41. Gérard Genette, *Paratexts: Threshold of Interpretation* (Cambridge: Cambridge University Press, 1997), p. 157.

42. Wisława Szymborska, 'Vestiario', in *La gioia di scrivere: Tutte le poesie (1945–2009)*, ed. by Pietro Marchesani (Milan: Adelphi, 2009 [2013]), p. 427.

43. Lamarque, 'Questa quieta polvere', in *Una quieta polvere*, p. 77.

44. Valerio Valeri, 'Lutto', in *Enciclopedia* (Turin: Einaudi, 1979), pp. 594–604 (596).

45. Robert Pogue Harrison, *The Dominion of the Dead* (Chicago: Chicago University Press, 2003), p. 148. A similar purpose underlies the current practice of distributing a photo of the deceased to relatives and attendants at funerals and having a picture of the deceased outside the church.

46. In the poem 'Machina' [Machine] by Antonella Anedda, the passing of time apparently implies a lack of continued identity: 'Ogni sette anni si rinnovano le cellule: | adesso siamo chi non eravamo' [Every seven years our cells are renewed: | now we are what we were not], *Historiae* (Turin: Einaudi, 2018), p. 22.

47. *Il signore d'oro* (1986) consists of 58 poems entitled 'Il signore...' [The Man...], e.g. 'Il signore mai' [The Never Man], 'Il signore meno' [The Minus Man], 'Il signore del buio' [The Man of Darkness], 'Il signore che partiva' [The Man Who Used to Leave], and twenty poems starting with 'La signora...' [The Lady...]: ('La signora della neve' [The Lady of Snow], 'La signora non gelosa' [The Lady not Jealous], 'La signora dell'ultima volta' [The Lady of the Last Time]). This formula is repeated in *Il signore degli spaventati* (1992), e.g. 'Il signore del luogo lontano' [The man of the distant place], 'La signora della paura' [The Lady of Fear], and so on.

48. From Giorgio Caproni, *L'opera in versi* (Milan: Mondadori, 1999), p. 192; 196.

49. See Ch. 3 in this volume: Francesco Giusti, 'Mourning Over Her Image: The Re-enactment of Lyric Gestures in Giorgio Caproni's "Versi livornesi"'.

50. Maurice Blanchot, 'The gaze of Orpheus', in *The Gaze of Orpheus and other Literary Essays*, trans. by Lydia Davis (New York: Station Hill Press, 1981), pp. 99–104 (100).

51. Enrico Testa, *'Sur la corde de la voix': Funzioni della deissi nel testo poetico* (1986), pp. 113–46 (p. 117).

52. *Una quieta polvere*, p. 226, and *Madre d'inverno*, p. 94.

53. *Poesie per un gatto*, p. 152. Also in the section 'Come i fiori' in *Una quieta polvere* flowers are associated with the afterlife (pp. 121–31).

54. Lamarque, 'L'albero', in *Una quieta polvere*, p. 217; and in *Madre d'inverno*, p. 93.

55. *Poesie per un gatto*, p. 135.

56. Harrison, p. 154.

57. ACI stands for *Automobile Club d'Italia* and deals, among other things, with forms related to the ownership of a car.

58. Italian does not use the possessive adjective with body parts, but the indirect object pronoun identifies whose nose, heart is bleeding, hurting, etc.

59. Jahan Ramazani, *Poetry of Mourning: The Modern Elegy from Hardy to Heaney* (Chicago: Chicago University Press, 1994), p. 6.

60. Lifton, *et al*, cit. in Parkes, p. 79. Italics in the text.

61. Colin Murray Parkes, *Bereavement. Studies in Grief in Adult Life* (London: Penguin, 1998), pp. 65–66. For Ernesto de Martino, such denial, if protracted, would represent pathological mourning: 'la presenza malata cerca di instaurare un comportamento *come se* il morto fosse ancora in vita' [the pathological presence attempts to set up a behaviour *as if* the deceased were still alive]; de Martino, *Morte e pianto rituale*, p. 47.

62. *Poesie*, p. 239.

63. Dante died in a motorcycle crash with a speeding police car in 1950. He features in 'Babbi' [Daddies] (*Una quieta polvere*, p. 18), in 'L'albero' (*Poesie. 1972–2002*, p. 220), 'Ritratto con Dante' and 'Cedrus atlantica' (*Madre d'inverno*, p. 32; 50).

64. Antonio Prete, *Tutto è sempre ora* (Turin: Einaudi, 2019), p. 25.

EPILOGUE:
TOWARDS AN ELEGIAC MODE

❖

Adele Bardazzi, Francesco Giusti, and Emanuela Tandello

The world has changed significantly since Philippe Ariès published *Western Attitudes toward Death* (1974), in which he claimed that, in modern times, public acknowledgement of death had been reduced to personal grief and thus interdicted in European cultures committed to the pursuit of 'collective happiness':

> The interdiction on death suddenly follows upon the heels of a very long period — several centuries — in which death was a public spectacle from which no one would have thought of hiding and which was even sought after at times. The cause of the interdict is at once apparent: the need for happiness — the moral duty and the social obligation to contribute to the collective happiness by avoiding any cause for sadness or boredom, by appearing to be always happy, even if in the depths of despair. By showing the least sign of sadness, one sins against happiness, threatens it, and society then risks losing its *raison d'être*.[1]

This historical process creates a paradoxical situation for the modern individual: on the one hand, there is no longer space for mourning to be processed in a social context and through collective practices, as it used to be in pre-modern societies; on the other hand, the state of mourning following the experience of a personal loss should be shortened and hidden from society. Therefore, modern individuals are asked to process their grief and return to active 'happiness' as soon as possible, but they are not offered any social space in which they could share it with others, thereby facilitating the process. This may hold true for the epoch Ariès is investigating, and both the 'pathological' condition of melancholia and the 'healthy' process of mourning presented by the early Freud may well pertain to an economy of libidinal life that resonates with the collective pursuit of happiness Ariès detects in European modernity.

Yet, in the last decades, mourning seems not only to have regained public space, but also to have acquired political functions. From the AIDS crisis of the 80s and 90s, through the September 11 attacks and environmental protests, to the Black Lives Matter movement, or, in the Italian context, from the 1963 Vajont Dam tragedy to the *anni di piombo*'s terrorist attacks, the exponential consumption of heroin in the 80s and 90s, the war crimes during the Kosovo War, and the more recent migrant crisis in the Mediterranean Sea, public mourning for individual and collective losses has gained or regained centre stage as a political force that serves to affirm one's own right to live a human life and claim recognition of one's existence.

Among the Italian works of poetry that engage with such collective crises, one could mention Paolo Ruffilli's *La gioia e il lutto: Passione e morte per AIDS* (2001), Francesco Targhetta's 'Elegia per Marghera: Il male, c'era' (2015), Matteo Fantuzzi's *La stazione di Bologna* (2017), and Antonella Anedda's *Historiae* (2018), which engages with the migrant crisis.[2] In the face of such tragic events, elegiac poetry seems to offer a public space in which to engage with the events, perhaps compensating for the lack of other spaces; or perhaps, as the essays collected in this volume seem to suggest, writing elegiac poetry is a cultural ritual of the kind that was explored by Ariès and which has disappeared in modern times.

In the aftermath of the AIDS crisis and other episodes of violence, Judith Butler was at the forefront of the revaluation of the political potential of mourning, at least from the publication of her essay 'Violence, Mourning, Politics', which first appeared in *Studies in Gender and Sexuality* (4:1, 2003) and was then included in her influential book *Precarious Life: The Powers of Mourning and Violence*:

> Many people think that grief is privatizing, that it returns us to a solitary situation and is, in that sense, depoliticizing. But I think it furnishes a sense of political community of a complex order, and it does this first of all by bringing to the fore the relational ties that have implications for theorizing fundamental dependency and ethical responsibility. If my fate is not originally or finally separable from yours, then the 'we' is traversed by a relationality that we cannot easily argue against; or, rather, we can argue against it, but we would be denying something fundamental about the social conditions of our very formation.[3]

In mourning, according to Butler, 'we' can acknowledge our vulnerability and apprehend our commonality. Positing vulnerability, exposure to the other, and relationality as the basis of ethics and politics entails a radical shift from an understanding of life as the pursuit of (Freud's) individual pleasure or (Ariès's) collective happiness. What brings us together as human beings — and possibly allows for the extension of such commonality to non-human beings (though Butler is interested only in the human in the above-mentioned essay) — is our constitutive exposure to others and to the violence they can exert on 'us'. Through grief, rather than pleasure, we can come to realise our intrinsic relationality and openness to others. This approach, for Butler, brings to the fore the respective degree of vulnerability experienced by different people and social groups, and the relative grievability of their lives. As Butler writes, 'The question that preoccupies me in the light of recent global violence is, Who counts as human? Whose lives count as lives? And, finally, What *makes for a grievable life*?'[4] More than the general restriction of death and mourning to the private sphere of human life that interested Ariès as a modern development in Western cultures, the pressing question for contemporary politics of mourning in a global dimension is: who has access to a public display of grief and under what conditions?

Poetic renditions of mourning have addressed such changes, and the 'gaping wound' that gives this volume its title, the wound that keeps bleeding and exposing itself to the eyes of others, has acquired a political potential. Elegy as characterised in *The Princeton Handbook of Poetic Terms* — 'usually formal in tone and diction, suggested either by the death of an actual person or by the poet's contemplation of the tragic aspects of life'[5] and where a sense of consolation is found 'in the contemplation of some permanent principle' — is one that has become problematic for elegiac writing in recent decades, especially in the face of forms of collective violence that have afflicted humankind or come to public attention in the twentieth and twenty-first centuries. Jahan Ramazani's claim, made back in 1994, that modern elegy tends to reject consolation, is thus confirmed; indeed, that rejection increasingly becomes the very site of elegy's potential political impact.[6] While elegy could be considered the most traditional of poetic genres, it remains a vital space not only for cultural reflection, transmission, and reinvention, but also for political struggles. For friends or partners, public figures or collective ideas, vulnerable social groups, endangered species or even a dying planet, the elegiac voice has performed a significant function in private and public discourse in recent decades. The politics of memory and mourning, identity formation, online afterlives, negotiations with personal and collective past(s), as well as environmental emergencies and postcolonial urgencies, are more crucial today than ever. Artistic practices, not only in the literary context but also in the visual and performing arts (re-enactment and archival strategies are widespread in contemporary art),[7] appear to be increasingly committed to rethinking our relations with the past. There is a growing effort to do justice to that which is no longer here or to those who are no longer with us, bearing witness to their past existence. The elegiac mode thus becomes a kind of discourse for reckoning with love, grief, and social power that needs to be re-discussed from a transcultural and transtemporal perspective.[8]

The employment of an elegiac mode at a public level and in relation to collective disasters raises other problems, which are not new to the elegy as a poetic genre. As David Kennedy points out,

> In allowing us to participate in a public performance of immeasurable loss that verges on narcissism, spectacular mourning risks losing the dead altogether. William Watkin raises a similar point in the context of 9/11: 'How to count the dead means also how to group them and divide them and separate them off. I feel our culture is currently unaware as to how to do this ethically' (Watkin 2004: 234). Such ethical inability may derive, as Gillian Rose argues in *Mourning Becomes the Law*, from the impasse of postmodernism. It may also derive from an anxiety that speaking of individual, separate deaths is unethical in the face of the uncountable elegiac occasions of the Holocaust, breast cancer and AIDS.[9]

And we could now add many other 'elegiac occasions' to those mentioned by Kennedy, which may help to revise the ethical conundrum of individual versus collective mourning. The use of poetic elegy and other forms of elegiac art in the Black Lives Matter protests, highly visible thanks to their proliferation on the web and social media, made it evident that, while grieving for individual losses, the systemic forces behind those losses must resist individualisation. In their introduction to *Revisiting the Elegy in the Black Lives Matter Era*, the editors of the volume note that '[c]ontemporary elegies carve out a *public* space for black grief, while decidedly resisting the turn toward consolation that often characterises the poetic form' and address the question of individualisation:

Indeed, the elegy has proven to be a vital vehicle for countering white media representations that either ignore black pain or individualize it, eclipsing systemic forms of oppression in the process. Within these works, the 'I' often manifests as an elegiac 'we', and readers are encouraged to become more than passive bystanders. Instead, they are enjoined to participate in the liberation struggle, refusing the enervating forces of state violence, social apathy, and sociocultural amnesia about America's racially unjust past and present.[10]

This elegiac 'we' is predicated upon a shared vulnerability in the face of 'state violence' that resonates with Butler's proposal of a politics of mourning and makes clear that mourning the individual, each single victim of that violence, is not enough if that mourning does not take into account the fact that the conditions of that particular death are also experienced by mourners who are exposed to the same violence.

The essays collected in this volume, which spans from the early nineteenth century of Giacomo Leopardi's 'Coro di morti' to the poetry of Antonella Anedda and Vivian Lamarque in recent years, engage with some of these crucial questions, among many others, questions that currently animate both the production of and the debate on elegy. Poetry, especially when published or otherwise circulated, is a public space and rendering a personal or collective loss in poetry means inscribing it into that public space. Therefore, in the act of writing, mourning subjects are implicitly assuming that their experience is worthy of being shared with others and that poetry, and in particular lyric poetry, is a suitable literary genre in which to share it. At least two possible reasons for this latter choice emerge from the pages of this volume. The first has to do with the problem of bringing together the individual and the collective, as well as the various instantiations of this seeming dichotomy; the second with a peculiar temporality that the lyric seems to enact.

Concerning the first reason, it has emerged several times in the volume that mournful (lyric) poetry tends to dwell on the boundaries between high lyric and vernacular forms, the personal and the political, the local and the national, one's own story and public history, the masculine and the feminine, individual expression and shared language. Amelia Rosselli radically questions several of these dichotomies. Yet other poetic cases investigated in this volume also show how the lyric, which often appears to offer readers a subjective perspective (not necessarily an 'I' or an individuated 'subject') on experience while relying on the shareability of the gesture underlying the poem and of the words used to articulate it,[11] can be particularly apt for exposing and problematising the individual/collective conundrum that lies at the core of mourning: it is *my* mourning, but *everyone* has to mourn at some point; that's the one *I* loved and have lost, but *others* loved and have lost (or love and will lose) someone too. The issue emerges clearly from the analysis of the rhetorical strategy that Jonathan Culler's dubs 'triangulated address' in Lamarque's poems, in which the speaker aims to include in the communication readers who have had a similar experience.[12] The suitability of the lyric seems to be due at least to two particular features of its discourse. There is, on the one hand, its long intertextual memory: lyric poems find ways of acknowledging that this is not the first time someone is mourning someone dear and that this is not the first time that someone is using a certain language to voice their grief. Giorgio Caproni's reuse of Cavalcanti's medieval *ballata* is a clear example of this, but the lyric's long memory can also lead to explicit retrievals of traditional collective practices of mourning, as in the case of Antonella Anedda's *attittos*, which reanimate archaic verse laments. On the other hand, there is the openness of the speaker's position, which each reader is called upon to assume; by uttering the poem in their own present circumstances, readers already find themselves in a shared space: 'While reading, "I" come to inhabit the open position of the poem's speaker making the utterance my own, but at the same time, "I" inscribe myself into a recurrent gesture, into a transindividual medium.'[13] If Leopardi's 'Coro di morti', which opens the volume, questions a historically situated definition of the lyric as bound to an individual subject, it also grasps a choral dimension that may be proper to the lyric in the context of its longer history.[14]

A second feature that seems to make the lyric particularly suitable for mournful writing is its peculiar temporality. In the entry to his *Mourning Diary* of 15 November, Roland Barthes notes that '[t]here is a time when death is an *event*, an ad-venture, and as such mobilizes, interests, activates, tetanizes. And then one day it is no longer an event, it is another *duration*, compressed, insignificant, not narrated, grim, without recourse: true mourning not susceptible to any narrative dialectic'.[15] This non-narrated *duration* resonates with Denise Riley's observations on the atemporality of her mourning for the death of her son. Riley writes that the condition of the mourner, that of being no longer *in* time, 'militates against narrative' and, she adds, 'You can't [...] take the lightest interest in the activity of writing unless you possess some feeling of futurity.'[16] Mourning imposes on the mourner a temporality that is outside of linear, sequential time, deprived of a projection into a possible future. Therefore, for both authors, non-narrative kinds of writing appear to be more suitable to the attempt to articulate this painful condition. For Barthes these are the fragmentary notes of a diary, on which some degree of linearity is imposed by external calendar time more than by inner cause-effect logic. For Riley, it is a meditative essay, which not only reflects on the condition of the writing subject, but also attempts to share what is perceived as a radically personal and unsharcable experience, in a form of writing that contrasts the investigated atemporality with the flow of calendar time. Lyric poetry offers a similar non-narrative temporality, which, in turn, following Barthes's suggestion, might not be unrelated to the intense interest in photographs, portraits, and imaginary scenes seen in Guido Gozzano, Vivian Lamarque, and Caproni respectively.

The temporality of the lyric, in fact, seems to accord better with the temporality of mourning. Culler's view of the lyric offers a plausible reason for this accordance:

> The fundamental characteristic of lyric, I am arguing, is not the description and interpretation of a past event but the iterative and iterable performance of an event in the lyric present, in the special 'now,' of lyric articulation. The bold wager of poetic apostrophe is that the lyric can displace a time of narrative, of past events reported, and place us in the continuing present of apostrophic address, the 'now' in which, for readers, a poetic event can repeatedly occur. Fiction is about what happened next; lyric is about what happens now.[17]

In this temporality, there is no projection of a solid continuous subject into the future, nor is there the restoration of a previous self after the mourning process. One's openness to others can begin with the undoing of one's self, and of one's narrative, in mourning. As Butler writes,

> What grief displays, in contrast, is the thrall in which our relations with others hold us, in ways that we cannot always recount or explain, in ways that often interrupt the self-conscious account of ourselves we might try to provide, in ways that challenge the very notion of ourselves as autonomous and in control. I might try to tell a story here about what I am feeling, but it would have to be a story in which the very 'I' who seeks to tell the story is stopped in the midst of the telling; the very 'I' is called into question by its relation to the Other, a relation that does not precisely reduce me to speechlessness, but does nevertheless clutter my speech with signs of its undoing. I tell a story about the relations I choose, only to expose, somewhere along the way, the way I am gripped and undone by these very relations. My narrative falters, as it must. Let's face it. We're undone by each other. And if we're not, we're missing something.[18]

Yet, what happens to mourning when 'our relationships' are forcibly put on hold? The global pandemic we have been experiencing since the spring of 2020 may be changing (again) the contours of elegy as it changes the contours of death. The social practices that surround the process of dying and death have been interdicted, this time not because of the 'need for happiness' detected by Ariès, but rather on health grounds: to contain the spread of the virus and to protect ourselves from possible contagion. According to Giorgio Agamben, in his highly controversial interventions on the management of the pandemic, especially in Italy, the denial of funeral rites for sanitary reasons is a most serious crossing of 'la soglia che separa l'umanità dalla barbarie' [the threshold between humanity and barbarism].[19] This is not the place to delve into the philosophical positions taken by Agamben in his critique, but the remark quoted is crucial to understanding the role of poetry and the elegiac mode in a variety of media under these extreme circumstances, in which it is not only the victims of the disease that are being mourned, but also the very possibility of mourning, given the 'social distance' imposed on our bodies as potential spreaders of the virus.

Mariangela Gualtieri's poem 'Nove marzo duemilaventi'[20] was first published in the online magazine *Doppiozero* on the titular date, which marked the beginning of the first lockdown in Italy. The poem was then shared on many other websites and webpages. It is not technically an elegy, but it raises some issues worth considering by way of conclusion. Addressed as a response to a 'you', it begins by evoking a lost collective opportunity for social change:

> Questo ti voglio dire
> ci dovevamo fermare.
> Lo sapevamo. Lo sentivamo tutti
> ch'era troppo furioso
> il nostro fare. Stare dentro le cose.
> Tutti fuori di noi.
> Agitare ogni ora — farla fruttare. (ll. 1–7)

[I'm telling you this | we needed to stop. | We knew. We all felt it | that it
was too furious, | our frenzy. Being inside of things. | Outside of our selves.
| Squeeze every hour — make it yield.]

In following this unconscious desire, the human species, the poem suggests, might
have opened the way for the virus. Now we are all locked in our houses, but there
are seeds of positive developments in this 'strange time' (ll. 28–36). The potential
change is predicated upon mutual help at the level of the species, rather than that
of particular individuals. Human beings have always known this, but the current
circumstances (should) allow them to realise that they share a common fate on this
planet. Exposure to a collective risk might raise awareness of our commonality.
From a quasi-Leopardian perspective (the Leopardi of 'La Ginestra', of course), the
virus (and the measures taken to contain its spreading) reveals the power of a living
and thinking Earth and the power of the universal law that governs everything,
including the existence of human beings. In this context, the death caused by the
virus may be intended to restore some balance and measure in the human species.
The poem does not question the governmental management of the pandemic,
instead crediting an 'imposing' but impersonal 'voice' with the prohibition of
physical proximity and displays of affection that human beings, as mischievous
children, deserved. As the ending of the poem reiterates, the current deprivations
can give rise to a better future:

> A quella stretta
> di un palmo col palmo di qualcuno
> a quel semplice atto che ci è interdetto ora —
> noi torneremo con una comprensione dilatata.
> Saremo qui, più attenti credo. Più delicata
> la nostra mano starà dentro il fare della vita.
> Adesso lo sappiamo quanto è triste
> stare lontani un metro. (ll. 69–76)

[To that grasp of a palm | in another person's palm | to that simple act that we
are now forbidden — | we will return with expanded awareness. | We'll be
here, more attentive, I think. Our hand | will be more delicate in the doing of
life. | Now that we know how sad it is | to stand one meter apart.]

The consolatory mode of Gualtieri's poem relies on an optimistic projection into
a future of restored possibilities of human contact and, more importantly, an
enhanced understanding of our society and our role in the life of this planet (an
optimism that was not entirely alien to the intellectual debate during the first phase
of the pandemic). Thus, it is based on a traditionally elegiac idea: there is something
to be learned in experiences of hardship and suffering, and such learning can unite
human beings and possibly bring about an improvement in their shared life.

The role of Nature, the responsibility of human behaviour, and the anxiety
of isolation and loneliness return in the poems collected in *Dal sottovuoto: Poesie
assetate d'aria* [From the Vacuum: Poems Thirsting for Air],[21] an anthology of poetic
responses to the pandemic edited by Matteo Bianchi and published as early as April
2020, but some of the poems exhibit a much less optimistic tone and are more

rooted in the disquieting uncertainty of the present. In the present, as Maurizio Cucchi observes, it is not clear if the plague is the virus or 'l'infinita, spaventata chiacchiera' [the endless, worried chat] (p. 38, l. 16) in which we are all engaged. 'La paura' [Fear], dated 1 March 2020, is the title of Franco Arminio's contribution to the volume, in which, in the misery of this 'tragico inverno' [tragic winter] (p. 61, l. 2), 'Penso a chi numera più volte la sua febbre. | Penso a chi muore senza testimoni | del suo ultimo respiro' [I think of those who measure their fever several times. | I think of those who die with no one witnessing their last breath] (ll. 8–10). A parallel is established between the (possibly infected) living taking their own temperature and the diseased deprived of the care of their loved ones at the moment of passing away. The lack of funeral rites returns in a poem by Franco Buffoni (p. 99). While looking for the news on the contagion in Gallarate (the town where the poet was born, located in one of the areas in northern Italy most afflicted by the disease in 2020), the 'I' finds a newspaper report with photographs taken from Mars. From that extraterrestrial perspective, the Earth looks like a 'pallino chiaro' [light dot] with 'le fidejussioni i rogiti i contratti | Le zone rosse ed arancioni | Le bare bianche senza estreme unzioni' [sureties deeds contracts | red and orange zones | white coffins with no last rites] (ll. 14–16). What for Agamben is an unprecedented infringement of the human seems to become just one of the many social rituals with which humans keep themselves busy, almost equated with sureties, deeds, and contracts; but the poem may be establishing an implicit and tragically ironic link with the legal nature of the denial of last rites, as well as the division of the country into red and orange zones. Beyond direct political intervention to challenge those impositions and their legitimacy, the question that arises with respect to mourning and the elegiac mode is whether the living and their poetry can do anything to compensate for depriving those who died of Covid-19 during the lockdown of practices of care and funeral rites. Franca Mancinelli alludes to this in her contribution to the volume: 'per ogni morto porterai una luce | nel buio del corpo | e dei suoi firmamenti' [for each dead you will bring a light | in the darkness of the body | and its firmaments] (p. 72). In these lines, Mancinelli seems to reframe the old closing trope of the consolatory or compensatory elegy — the dead or their soul finds their eternal abode among the stars — by making the internal firmament of the physical body of the 'you', possibly every 'you', a personal responsibility and by entrusting the 'you' with the task of taking care of a light for *each* of the dead — a task that is as necessary as it is impossible when mourning the victims of systemic violence and collective disasters.

Bibliography

AGAMBEN, GIORGIO, 'Una domanda', in *Una voce*, 13 April 2020 <https://www.quodlibet.it/giorgio-agamben-una-domanda>

—— *Where Are We Now? The Epidemic as Politics*, trans. by Valeria Dani (London: Eris, 2021)

ANEDDA, ANTONELLA, *Historiae* (Turin: Einaudi, 2018)

ARIÈS, PHILIPPE, *Western Attitudes toward Death: From the Middle Ages to the Present*, trans. by Patricia M. Ranum (Baltimore: Johns Hopkins University Press, 1974)

AUSTIN, TIFFANY, et al. (eds), *Revisiting the Elegy in the Black Lives Matter Era* (New York: Routledge, 2020)

BALDACCI, CRISTINA, *Archivi impossibili: Un'ossessione dell'arte contemporanea* (Milan: Johan & Levi, 2016)

BARTHES, ROLAND, *Journal de deuil: 26 octobre 1977–15 septembre 1979*, ed. by Nathalie Léger (Paris: Seuil, 2009)

—— *Mourning Diary*, ed. by Nathalie Léger, trans. by Richard Howard (London: Notting Hill Editions, 2011)

BIANCHI, MATTEO (ed.), *Dal sottovuoto: Poesie assetate d'aria* (Fanna, PN: Samuele Editore, 2020)

BUTLER, JUDITH, *Precarious Life: The Powers of Mourning and Violence* (London: Verso, 2004)

CULLER, JONATHAN, *Theory of the Lyric* (Cambridge, MA: Harvard University Press, 2015)

FANTUZZI, MATTEO, *La stazione di Bologna* (Milan: Feltrinelli, 2017)

FOGLE, STEPHEN F., 'Elegy', in *The Princeton Handbook of Poetic Terms*, ed. by Alex Preminger, O. B. Hardison Jr, and Frank J. Warnke (Princeton: Princeton University Press, 1986), pp. 62–63

GIUSTI, FRANCESCO, 'Transcontextual Gestures: A Lyric Approach to the World of Literature', in *The Work of World Literature*, ed. by Francesco Giusti and Benjamin Lewis Robinson (Berlin: ICI Berlin Press, 2021), pp. 75–103

GUALTIERI, MARIANGELA, 'Nove marzo doemilaventi', *Doppiozero*, 9 March 2020 <https://www.doppiozero.com/materiali/nove-marzo-duemilaventi> [accessed 24 October 2021]; trans. by Lucy Rand and Clarissa Botsford on the English version of the website <https://en.doppiozero.com/content/march-ninth-twenty-twenty>

JOHNSON, W. R., *The Idea of Lyric: Lyric Modes in Ancient and Modern Poetry* (Berkeley: University of California Press, 1982)

KENNEDY, DAVID, *Elegy* (Abingdon: Routledge, 2007)

RAMAZANI, JAHAN, *Poetry of Mourning: The Modern Elegy from Hardy to Heaney* (Chicago: Chicago University Press, 1994)

—— *A Transnational Poetics* (Chicago: University of Chicago Press, 2009)

RILEY, DENISE, *Time Lived, Without its Flow. Introduced by Max Porter* (London: Picador, 2019)

RUFFILLI, PAOLO, *La gioia e il lutto: Passione e morte per AIDS* (Venice: Marsilio, 2001)

TARGHETTA, FRANCESCO, 'Elegia per Marghera: Il male, c'era', *La Lettura*, no. 197, *Corriere della Sera*, 6 September 2015

Notes to the Epilogue

1. Philippe Ariès, *Western Attitudes toward Death: From the Middle Ages to the Present*, trans. by Patricia M. Ranum (Baltimore: Johns Hopkins University Press, 1974), pp. 93–94.

2. Paolo Ruffilli, *La gioia e il lutto: Passione e morte per AIDS* (Venice: Marsilio, 2001); Francesco Targhetta, 'Elegia per Marghera: Il male, c'era', *La Lettura*, no. 197, *Corriere della Sera*, 6 September 2015; Matteo Fantuzzi, *La stazione di Bologna* (Milan: Feltrinelli, 2017); Antonella Anedda, *Historiae* (Turin: Einaudi, 2018).

3. Judith Butler, *Precarious Life: The Powers of Mourning and Violence* (London: Verso, 2004), pp. 22–23.

4. Butler, *Precarious Life*, p. 20 (italicised in the original).

5. Stephen F. Fogle, 'Elegy', in *The Princeton Handbook of Poetic Terms*, ed. by Alex Preminger, O. B. Hardison Jr, and Frank J. Warnke (Princeton: Princeton University Press, 1986), pp. 62–63 (62).

6. Jahan Ramazani, *Poetry of Mourning: The Modern Elegy from Hardy to Heaney* (Chicago: Chicago University Press, 1994).

7. See Cristina Baldacci, *Archivi impossibili: Un'ossessione dell'arte contemporanea* (Milan: Johan & Levi, 2016).

8. See Jahan Ramazani, *A Transnational Poetics* (Chicago: University of Chicago Press, 2009), pp. 71–93.

9. David Kennedy, *Elegy* (Abingdon: Routledge, 2007), p. 142.

10. *Revisiting the Elegy in the Black Lives Matter Era*, ed. by Tiffany Austin and others (New York: Routledge, 2020), pp. 9–26 (p. 14).

11. For mourning as a lyric 'gesture' whose shareability allows for the formation of a community, see Francesco Giusti, 'Transcontextual Gestures: A Lyric Approach to the World of Literature', in *The Work of World Literature*, ed. by Francesco Giusti and Benjamin Lewis Robinson (Berlin: ICI Berlin Press, 2021), pp. 75–103.

12. Jonathan Culler, *Theory of the Lyric* (Cambridge, MA: Harvard University Press, 2015), p. 186.

13. Giusti, 'Transcontextual Gestures', p. 99.

14. Chorality is crucial to the definition of lyric in W. R. Johnson, *The Idea of Lyric: Lyric Modes in Ancient and Modern Poetry* (Berkeley: University of California Press, 1982).

15. Roland Barthes, *Journal de deuil: 26 octobre 1977–15 septembre 1979*, ed. by Nathalie Léger (Paris: Seuil, 2009); *Mourning Diary*, ed. by Nathalie Léger, trans. by Richard Howard (London: Notting Hill Editions, 2011), p. 50.

16. Denise Riley, *Time Lived, Without its Flow.*, intro. by Max Porter (London: Picador, 2019), p. 16.

17. Culler, *Theory of the Lyric*, p. 226.

18. Butler, *Precarious Life*, p. 23.

19. Giorgio Agamben, 'Una domanda', in *Una voce*, 13 April 2020 <https://www.quodlibet.it/giorgio-agamben-una-domanda>; an English translation can be found in Giorgio Agamben, *Where Are We Now? The Epidemic as Politics*, trans. by Valeria Dani (London: Eris, 2021). Agamben's interventions were first published in his column *Una voce* on the website of the Italian publisher Quodlibet and then widely translated and disseminated, igniting an animated (and sometimes fierce) debate in Italy and internationally.

20. Mariangela Gualtieri, 'Nove marzo doemilaventi', *Doppiozero*, 9 March 2020 <https://www.doppiozero.com/materiali/nove-marzo-duemilaventi> [accessed 24 October 2021]; trans. by Lucy Rand and Clarissa Botsford on the English version of the website <https://en.doppiozero.com/content/march-ninth-twenty-twenty>.

21. *Dal sottovuoto. Poesie assetate d'aria*, ed. by Matteo Bianchi (Fanna, PN: Samuele Editore, 2020). Translations are ours.

INDEX

❖